Healthcare Informatics

Improving Efficiency through Technology,
Analytics, and Management

Healthcare Informatics

Improving Efficiency through Technology, Analytics, and Management

Stephan P. Kudyba

New Jersey Institute of Technology, Newark, USA

Foreword by Dr. David Blumenthal

CRC Press
Taylor & Francis Group
Boca Raton   London   New York

CRC Press is an imprint of the
Taylor & Francis Group, an **informa** business
AN AUERBACH BOOK

CRC Press
Taylor & Francis Group
6000 Broken Sound Parkway NW, Suite 300
Boca Raton, FL 33487-2742

© 2016 by Taylor & Francis Group, LLC
CRC Press is an imprint of Taylor & Francis Group, an Informa business

No claim to original U.S. Government works

Printed on acid-free paper
Version Date: 20160223

International Standard Book Number-13: 978-1-4987-4635-9 (Hardback)

Visit the Taylor & Francis Web site at
http://www.taylorandfrancis.com

and the CRC Press Web site at
http://www.crcpress.com

To my family, for their support and patience
to see me through these projects!

To the contributors of this work, sincere gratitude for sharing their
expertise to enlighten the marketplace of a truly dynamic industry

Contents

CONTENTS

Foreword

Professor Kudyba's new book, *Health Informatics: Improving Efficiency through Technology, Analytics, and Management*, provides a thorough and comprehensive review of the state of healthcare information technology and its application at present. The book also makes clear, however, that many complex issues remain to be addressed if we are to realize the full potential of digitizing health information. Some of these issues involve completing the rapid, but bumpy, journey toward the installation of technologies that translate health information into electronic form. Other issues concern the development of processes for harvesting that digitized information for analysis. Still other challenges involve learning how to draw valid inferences from the oceans of new information that soon will be sweeping over health professionals.

Beyond these technical and analytic questions loom more abstract but equally important issues. One concerns the implications of the health information revolution for managers of healthcare enterprises. As the data available to managers increase exponentially, their ability to make sense and use of those data will become fundamental to their jobs, as will their ability to participate in the design of information systems that will improve the functioning of health systems. In other words, IT management will no longer be the specialized—and isolated—domain of the "IT people." It will be as core to the success of mainstream managers as financial and human resource skills.

Another consequence of the health information revolution will be a raft of new regulatory and business requirements that healthcare leaders and managers will have to deal with effectively. At some point, we will develop the political will and economic rationale to exchange health information in the service of patients' needs. The U.S. Congress is already mobilizing to overcome the social, cultural, and economic barriers to effective information exchange. Welcome as this flow of information will be for patients and clinicians, it will prompt private and public scrutiny of how privacy and security of health information are ensured both at rest and in motion.

Still another area that will draw increased scrutiny is how to facilitate patients' access to their digitized health information. At the current time, meaningful use requires that eligible professionals and healthcare institutions make electronic records available online to patients. It will not be long, however, before patients seek help in making sense of these data. If healthcare providers are unable to meet this need with consumer-friendly interpretive services, then it seems likely that the private sector will rush to fill the gap with information management services that empower patients to make better personal use of their healthcare data. An entirely new consumer-facing analytic and decision-support industry seems likely to emerge. Protecting consumers from the misuse of that information by unscrupulous entities will give rise to consumer protection regulation. And dealing with newly empowered consumers will challenge clinicians and healthcare institutions in ways that are difficult to predict at the current time.

Some of these pending challenges are admittedly speculative. This book prepares readers for the health IT issues that are already on their plates. Those challenges are no less important to the fact that additional mountains will likely need to be climbed in our rapidly evolving, IT-enabled healthcare sector.

Dr. David Blumenthal
President and CEO of the Commonwealth Fund

Dr. Blumenthal became president and CEO of the Commonwealth Fund, a national healthcare philanthropy based in New York City, in January 2013. Previously, he served as Chief Health Information and Innovation Officer at Partners Health System in Boston, Massachusetts, and was Samuel O. Thier Professor of Medicine and Professor of Health Care Policy at Massachusetts General Hospital/ Harvard Medical School. As a renowned health services researcher and national authority on health IT adoption, he has authored more than 250 scholarly publications, including the seminal studies on the adoption and use of health information technology in the United States.

Author

Stephan P. Kudyba, MBA, PhD, is a faculty member in the School of Management at New Jersey Institute of Technology (NJIT), where he teaches graduate courses addressing the utilization of information technologies, business intelligence, and information and knowledge management to enhance organizational efficiency and innovation. He has published numerous books, journal articles, and magazine articles on strategic utilization of data, information, and technologies to enhance organizational and macro productivity. Interviews with Dr. Kudyba have been featured in prominent magazines, and he speaks at university symposiums, academic conferences, and corporate events. He has more than 20 years of private sector experience in the United States and Europe, having held management and executive positions at prominent companies, and he maintains relations with organizations across industry sectors. Dr. Kudyba earned an MBA from Lehigh University and a PhD in economics with a focus on the information economy from Rensselaer Polytechnic Institute.

Contributors

Billie Anderson
Ferris State
Big Rapids, Michigan

John Azzolini
Truven Health Analytics
Ann Arbor, Michigan

Deborah Ballou
Tennessee Technological
    University
Cookeville, Tennessee

Peter Basch
MedStar Health
Washington, DC

Mary Beattie
Health First
Rockledge, Florida

Jason Burke
SAS Institute
Cary, North Carolina

Paul Conlon
Trinity Health
Novi, Michigan

Cali M. Davis
University of Alabama
Tuscaloosa, Alabama

J. Michael Hardin
University of Alabama
Tuscaloosa, Alabama

D. Arlo Jennings
Mission Health Systems (retired)
Asheville, North Carolina

James F. Keel, III
Mission Health Systems
Asheville, North Carolina

Rajiv Kohli
William and Mary College
Williamsburg, Virginia

Stephan P. Kudyba
New Jersey Institute of
    Technology
Newark, New Jersey

David Lubliner
New Jersey Institute of
    Technology
Newark, New Jersey

Ann McKibbon
McMaster University
Hamilton, Ontario, Canada

Tom Miner
Trinity Health
Novi, Michigan

Terry Moore
Hackensack University
    Medical Center
Hackensack, New Jersey

Thad Perry
Tennessee Technological
    University
Cookeville, Tennessee

Frank Piontek
Trinity Health
South Bend, Indiana

Mark Rader
AristaCare Health Services
South Plainfield, New Jersey

Wullianallur Raghupathi
Fordham University
New York, New York

Christi Rushnell
Health First
Rockledge, Florida

Larry Sellers
Mercy Medical Center
Sioux City, Iowa

Richard Temple
Deborah Heart and Lung
    Center
Browns Mills, New Jersey

Michael H. Zaroukian
Michigan State University/
    Sparrow Health System
Lansing, Michigan

1

An Introduction to the U.S. Healthcare Industry, Information Technology, and Informatics

STEPHAN P. KUDYBA AND RICHARD TEMPLE

Contents

Healthcare is probably one of the most complex business models in American industry given the uniqueness of the marketplace in which it operates. It is perhaps the only industry in which the consumer does not necessarily pay for the service he or she receives, but rather third parties (in this case, insurance companies) negotiate arrangements with service providers to determine payment rates and types of service that are to be paid on the consumer's behalf. The nature of the services required corresponds to a variety of ailments that are attributed to vast numbers of patients—factors that add to the mix of issues to manage. Complexities for healthcare organizations are heightened when considering the numerous data exchanges that are involved with services provided to patients. Data exchanges can be plagued by a myriad of formats, captured and stored in a variety of repositories. These exchanges introduce further complexities in the form of "vocabularies," or, in other words, the coding languages that are required to identify types of services that vary considerably from payor to payor, state to state, and service type to service type. Also, data in general come from a multitude of different "niche" systems and are presented in many different ways (e.g., text reports, spreadsheets, HL7 messages, ANSI X12 formats) and need to be integrated and presented to a caregiver or analyst in a consistent and coherent manner. It is the combination of all of these factors that begins to describe the underpinnings of the spectrum of healthcare informatics.

Data provide the building blocks to information and constitute a vital resource to administrators, practitioners, and decision makers in healthcare organizations. The process of transforming data into information is a daunting task, and given the complexities described in the preceding paragraph, the task is particularly challenging in this unique industry. This challenge must be managed, as healthcare is one segment of American industry in which incorrect decisions or errors can cost lives or put innocent people in significant danger. The need to understand which patterns of treatment for a variety of different conditions will produce the best outcomes is profound. Adding to the challenge are the financial burdens healthcare providers are experiencing, as reimbursements are being cut and more and more conditions are being mandated in order to pay for services rendered. Healthcare organizations invariably lose money on certain classes of patients, and it is critical to understand where those areas are and how to address them.

The Affordable Care Act (ACA) has transformed the face of healthcare delivery in profound ways on many levels. It is rapidly changing the very manner through which providers are reimbursed by emphasizing "value-based reimbursement," which in government-speak means that providers will be directly rewarded financially for demonstrating excellent care and may be penalized financially for care that does not meet the quality standards laid out by the Centers for Medicare and Medicaid Services (CMS). A number of different areas are monitored by CMS for adherence to these standards, but the concept of reducing "patient readmissions" has received particular attention. This concept is a fundamental change from the fee-for-service model that healthcare providers have been accustomed to for decades and requires a capability to measure easily outcomes that, up until very recently, was difficult if not impossible to do. Accountable Care Organizations (ACOs) and Patient-Centered Medical Homes (PCMHs) are also new models of care emphasizing collaboration across multiple providers, quality management, and incentives for cost efficiencies. These models fall under the rubric of a new concept that is being adopted by providers to accommodate new payor reimbursement models that are coming to the forefront: the concept of "Population Health Management," or finding ways to keep people well, as opposed to just interacting with them when they are sick. Capturing the myriad of data points required to report properly on relevant metrics has become one of the primary challenges facing the healthcare industry today.

Information Technology, Informatics, and Healthcare Productivity: A Historical Perspective

One way to better manage the complex nature of the healthcare industry is through the incorporation of information technologies. Web platforms, data storage, analytic software, telecom and wireless communications systems, and so forth can help provide critical information and speed of information dissemination to those who require it, when they require it.

During the mid-1990s, organizations across industry sectors retooled their information technology infrastructures in response to dramatic innovations in storage, processing, analytics, and bandwidth (see Table 1.1). The enhanced capabilities facilitated by these technologies offered organizations opportunities to increase productivity in a variety of ways. Factors such as the dissemination of critical information to decision makers regarding process performance; the ability to communicate within organizations, across industry sectors, and

Table 1.1   Growth in Investment in Information Technologies

YEAR	INVESTMENT IN INFORMATION TECHNOLOGY AS A PROPORTION OF INDUSTRIAL EQUIPMENT AND SOFTWARE (%)
1980	30.7
1990	41.1
1999	47.2

Source: Economic Report of the President 2001, Table B-18, p. 296.

on the global spectrum; and simplifying procedures, to name a few, enabled organizations to manage available resources better in providing a good or service to the ultimate consumer.

The significant investment in information technologies was initially questioned by many as to the payoff or gains from these dollar outlays for hardware, software, telecom platforms, and so on. This debate sparked a myriad of research from the academic and private sector arenas to investigate the potential gains to IT. Resulting studies illustrated positive returns on investment in information technologies by firms operating across industry sectors.[1-3] On a macroeconomic perspective, U.S. productivity grew dramatically from levels achieved over the previous decade (see Figure 1.1).

This jump in productivity enabled the U.S. economy to grow at a robust pace without experiencing a noteworthy acceleration in price inflation as gains in efficiency helped reduce costs throughout the economic system (see Figure 1.2). These productivity gains have been

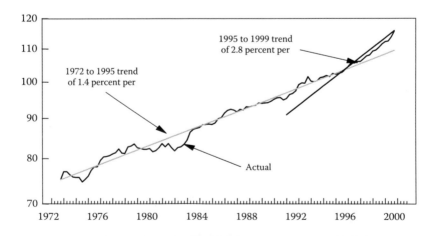

Figure 1.1   The trend rate of nonfarm productivity growth accelerated (Index 1992 = 100, log). (From the U.S. Department of Labor, Bureau of Labor.)

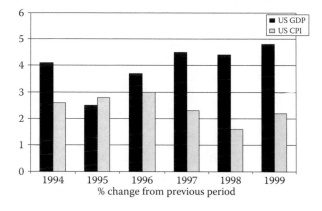

Figure 1.2 U.S. Gross Domestic Product vs. Consumer Price Index. (U.S. GDP data: U.S. Commerce Department Bureau of Economic Analysis. U.S. CPI: U.S. Department of Labor, Bureau of Labor Statistics.)

maintained into current times as companies continue to invest in and apply information technologies in a variety of process-enhancing ways.

Historically, healthcare has been somewhat of a laggard in terms of investing in technology. The fragmented nature of the industry and the abundance of different coding systems and taxonomies are often cited as reasons for the lag in technological implementations, along with the persistence of traditional paper-based procedural modes of operations. The structure of the industry involving numerous individual hospitals and health-related entities created a dichotomous environment that involved diverse naming procedures and formatting standards of critical data resources and breakdowns in the ability to share them. Paper-based methods of operations (e.g., charting by physicians and nurses) limited the creation of vital data resources that describe critical treatment activities of patients.

These factors reduced gains in efficiency that otherwise could be achieved based on network effects of information sharing. In other words, the lack of data resources and the existence of disparate data resources involving diverse naming conventions existing in a variety of storage devices corresponding to separate providers of health services (e.g., hospitals, clinics, private practices) deter the ability of healthcare organizations to create robust information resources from available data. With only pieces of the puzzle (e.g., data existing in isolated systems, information in paper-based form) healthcare providers were limited in the amount of information available to them when attempting to enhance their knowledge regarding service effectiveness and efficiency.

To clarify this point further we need to turn to the evolution of the Internet. Forms of the Internet were actually in existence well before the information boom of the 1990s (e.g., the government ARPANET was in existence in the 1970s). However, the true gains in efficiency resulting from utilization of the Internet for consumers and businesses alike were not achieved until network effects took hold. In other words, the network of users who had access to the Internet needed to reach critical mass.[4] As more and more consumers and businesses had access to the Internet, the more it became a viable mechanism to communicate and conduct commerce. In comparison, as data resources in the healthcare industry become more standardized and integrated within health organizations and across systems of corresponding service providers, the ability to extract information from and generate knowledge regarding better allocating resources to enhance process efficiencies in financial, clinical, and administrative activities should increase dramatically. The result should be fewer wasted resources, enhanced process performance, and a lower cost operating environment.[5]

The past few years have spurred another boom in healthcare information technology investment. The development and incorporation of wireless devices, sensors, apps, and continued advancement of computer processing and storage capabilities have underpinned this second wave of the information pulse. This time the healthcare sector was on board and kept pace with investments and applications in other industries. The Health Information Technology for Economic and Clinical Health (HITECH) Act, which was part of the ARRA (aka "the Stimulus Package") provided billions of federal dollars in economic incentives to providers who could demonstrate "meaningful use" of healthcare information technology. That was the "carrot"; the "stick" was that those incentives would cease and financial *penalties* would begin in 2015 for those providers who could not attest to "meaningful use." The HITECH program was extremely successful in getting hospitals and physicians to invest in Electronic Health Record (EHR) technology, but there are different schools of thought as to whether physicians, in particular, have found EHRs to have made their lives easier. Nonetheless, the need to demonstrate "meaningful use" and the need to capture a multitude of quality metrics has indisputably moved the industry forward. Now, with EHRs in place, there is a valid data source (albeit with many challenges) that can provide the measurements required.

The Internet has made it possible for providers to share patient clinical data across multiple sites of care in near real time, which brings us that much closer to allowing a provider to see a patient's *entire* medical history when he or she is in the exam room. No, we are not there yet, for many of the reasons that you will learn about, but the potential is there and in some regions, very successful Health Information Exchanges (HIEs) are getting close to achieving this laudable goal.

Given recent consolidation of individual providers into systems of providers (e.g., healthcare systems), advancements in hardware, software, telecom, wireless and Internet-based technologies, the ability of treatment- and diagnosis-based technologies to help enhance data capture, the creation of digital data resources from paper-based procedures, and enhanced data input and communication of information, healthcare providers are on the cusp of experiencing increased operational efficiencies that will enable them to manage their cost structure while providing the best care possible to patients. The incorporation of billing and financial related technologies, decision support systems, and data management and analytic capabilities enable healthcare providers to enhance their ability to identify misallocations of resources and increase the effectiveness and speed of processes from administrative and financial to clinical activities.

Enhanced efficiencies made possible by investment in information technologies could result in significant cost savings to healthcare providers. These gains are critical in addressing the ongoing growth in healthcare expenditures in the United States, which now account for roughly 17% of gross domestic product (GDP). Some recent studies have depicted significant returns on the investment in information technologies, with reduction in expenditures ranging from $100 to $450 billion over the coming years.[6,7] Investment in technologies that seek to promote a more automated delivery system through workflow and medical records systems, evidence-based decision support systems, integration of information between healthcare providers, and streamlining the current claim-based transactions billing system to an all-electronic payment at point of service system can yield substantial savings to healthcare providers and the ultimate consumer/patient.[8]

Productivity, Efficiency, and the Uniqueness of Healthcare

Despite the fact that the healthcare industry possesses characteristics unique from those of other sectors (e.g., doctor–patient relationships and the ultimate objective of providing the best quality of care to patients that can override established business profit optimization goals) healthcare still entails procedures and processes that can be made more efficient.

Technologies can help providers discover more effective treatment tactics that may reduce ineffective, redundant, and unnecessary tests and procedures that inconvenience patients and providers and increase costs. The rapid scaling of business intelligence systems, through tools such as Hadoop and others, allow for previously unimaginable amounts of data to be analyzed quickly. New tools such as IBM's Watson computer (the robot that won on *Jeopardy!*) can parse huge amounts of patient data against a massive database of best practices and offer diagnostic advice to physicians in real time. The application of Watson in healthcare is in its early stages but the possibilities for it are limited only by the imagination.

These technologies can reduce bottlenecks in administrative processes, alleviating waiting times for patients and directing them to the most appropriate areas to address their problems. They can minimize complexities in billing activities that can result in overbilling recipients. Technologies can help enhance preemptive treatment to mitigate illnesses from developing into fully developed chronic diseases.

Management of Healthcare Processes

Management and economic concepts can play a key role in enhancing efficiencies in the industry given the methodologies that address the allocation of the correct resources to the demand for those resources. Accomplishing this helps preserve the essence of healthcare organizations and those individuals involved in providing treatment for patients. With the aid of accurate and timely information and the ability to communicate and apply that information, physicians, nurses, technicians, and administrators can improve the process of caring for those in need in a more efficient, less costly manner. Techniques and methodologies that create, disseminate, and analyze data comprise the realm of informatics. Two basic definitions of informatics are provided to clarify what is meant by this concept.

> **Informatics** are the sciences concerned with gathering, manipulating, storing, retrieving, and classifying recorded information. (*Source*: wordnetweb.princeton.edu/perl/webwn)

> **Health informatics or medical informatics** is the intersection of information science, computer science, and healthcare. It deals with the resources, devices, and methods required to optimize the acquisition, storage, retrieval, and use of information in health and biomedicine. Health informatics tools include not only computers but also clinical guidelines, formal medical terminologies, and information and communication systems. (*Source*: Wikipedia)

Effective Informatics through Management Theory

Pure investment in information technologies is not the final solution to enabling providers to operate more productively, however. Applications in management theory are essential to ensure effective implementation and utilization of these technologies to best leverage their capabilities to increase labor and process productivity. Management theory that must be considered includes strategic management, management information systems, project management, knowledge management and organizational behavioral, quantitative techniques, and decision support theory, to name a few. These management concepts focus on the acquisition of technologies that provide the correct functionality to facilitate a particular process and proper implementation of the technology to ensure its proper utilization (this includes creating a receptive culture within the organization by users to adopt the platform as an essential tool to enhance their daily routines). Theoretical concepts also address analysis, communication, and best utilization of the results and outputs of systems that are employed.

Project and Knowledge Management

Project management addresses methods that support successful implementations of information technologies. It addresses the incorporation of correct tactics to acquire the most appropriate technology platform to facilitate an organizational need in the most seamless way possible. For example, when a healthcare provider wants to implement a new database system that facilitates the conversion of paper-based routines into digital assets for clinical and treatment activities, the organization must consider which technology best offers the most feasible functionality corresponding to the operational structure of the organization. This includes the cost of the technology, scalability, ability to integrate with existing systems both within the organization and with other systems at area provider sites, as well as user friendliness. Once the technology is chosen, factors to promote the most seamless integration into the work environment must be considered. This includes timing schedules, training for users, and eventual complete roll out to the workforce. Knowledge management theory overlaps project management to some extent when considering the implementation stages of new technologies. It addresses the additional critical factors of ensuring the systems adoption by users with the ultimate goal that it becomes a key component in the everyday activities of its users and stakeholders. Knowledge management also addresses those factors that support leveraging the output produced by users working with systems and the dissemination and collaboration of corresponding information among individuals connected to processes and procedures. In other works, knowledge management theory promotes the active utilization of information and creation of knowledge within an organization, concepts that drive best practices and innovation.[9,10]

Other management-related concepts also must be considered in attempting to best leverage information technologies and these involve such strategic initiatives as Lean/Six Sigma, Total Quality Management, Supply Chain Management, and Workflow Optimization and advanced analytics such as data mining to not only analyze past data patterns, but also to offer a platform for *predictive analytics* that can identify high-risk patients and offer appropriate treatment for them. The process of treating a patient incorporates a network of activities that are complementary and interdependent in nature, where breakdowns in aspects of one operational entity can cause disruptions to the overall process of patient care. The patient treatment process can include diagnosis, prescription of medications, radiology and lab tests, administration of treatment procedures, monitoring of results and outcomes, and so forth. These activities include input from numerous personnel in corresponding operational departments in the healthcare organization. Workflow analytic methodologies must be considered to understand better the efficiencies of the entire treatment process. The overall process can be compared to managing a supply chain or supply network of activities that are complementary and interdependent, with the ultimate objective of achieving the best allocation of available resources to provide the best care to corresponding patients. These management methodologies can be augmented with the incorporation of statistical and quantitative-based analytics such as the Six Sigma approach.

Six Sigma and Data Mining

Six Sigma is an analytic method that leverages available data resources and incorporates statistical applications and visual capabilities to monitor process variance and efficiencies. By analyzing data resources corresponding to various operational processes with the utilization of statistical techniques, analysts can better determine which types of practices result in unacceptable variances in performance metrics.[11] Lean Six Sigma is a strategic initiative that complements the variance identification focus of Six Sigma and seeks to eliminate non-value-add processes or activities in an organization that can add to waste. Value stream mapping is often used to enhance throughput of processes.

For example, a Lean Six Sigma approach could be implemented in a radiology setting. Are there bottlenecks or unnecessary steps that can be improved on in the network of activities in the radiology department that produce high time delay variances in getting x-ray results back to an attending physician?

More robust and sophisticated techniques to analyze data involve the utilization of quantitative methods to process data and statistical testing to determine patterns and trends that may exist in particular service activities. Traditional regression methods and data mining methodologies enable analysts to better identify recurring trends in the various activities of healthcare services. Resulting models can determine whether particular treatment procedures result in enhanced health outcomes according to patient populations, whether particular procedural activities result in unacceptable outcomes measures, and so on. These types of analyses are becoming increasingly important as "patient experience" feedback directly from clients is now a parameter for the new concept of "value-based reimbursement." A significant percentage of the potential payment adjustment for a provider is predicated on feedback patients share, so being able to directly address likely patient "dis-satisfiers" head-on is very important now.

Business Intelligence and Decision Support Systems

Other methods of data analysis that can help increase the knowledge of healthcare practitioners involve the more simple creation and presentations of reports and graphics through Online Analytic Processing and dashboards. The advantage is these methods focus on presenting data in a timely and understandable manner, enabling decision makers to view these analytic platforms quickly to identify factors impacting operational performances.

These various data driven software technologies and initiatives comprise the realm of decision support systems and business intelligence. The functionalities of the components including report generation, trend and pattern detection, and quantitative and statistical based analytics complemented with graphical interfaces provide users/decision makers in various functional areas of healthcare organizations with timely, actionable information to enhance strategizing. Informatics to improve efficiencies include optimizing resource allocations corresponding to a variety of activities and procedures. The utilization of decision support systems and business intelligence that leverage essential data resources can ultimately help reduce lag times in patients waiting for treatment, adjust treatment procedures to enhance outcomes, reduce inefficiencies in billing, reduce lag times in lab and radiology exam completion and reporting times, and so forth. The ultimate result is better management of healthcare operations and costs and care effectiveness and quality outcomes for patients.

Four Areas of Focus for Healthcare Efficiencies

With all of the turbulence present in the healthcare landscape, it comes as little wonder that healthcare organizations are embracing the potential of leveraging information technologies and informatics and their ability to enhance efficiencies. Informatics applications and capabilities within the healthcare spectrum can be categorized into four different discrete areas:

- Financial (tracking activity-based costing, ensuring that services rendered are properly billed and compensated and that expenses stay within acceptable budgetary parameters). With CMS and other insurers monitoring cost-per-patient and adjusting reimbursement based on this, the financial component is especially important.
- Clinical compliance (ensuring that the appropriate procedures are applied to the right patient at the right time, making sure that staffing patterns and other reportable parameters are within acceptable mandated bounds, and alerting as quickly as possible when they are not). An interesting note is that, with the new reimbursement models that are coming to the fore, for the first time, clinical quality will play a direct role in a significant percentage of a provider's reimbursement. So, in essence, the financial team is directly accountable for clinical excellence and the clinical team is directly accountable for financial excellence.
- Quality improvement (analyzing clinical data to see which treatment protocols provide the best outcomes in an economically sustainable way).
- Patient satisfaction/marketing (what aspects of a patient's stay were problematic—how are those measured, identified, and remedied for the future).

The following section takes a quick look at each of these areas to give a broader sense of just how informatics can be so important in managing the critical factors that healthcare leadership needs to understand better to manage their respective organizations properly.

Financial Activities

Hospitals and many other healthcare providers have undergone a drastic transformation during the last 15 to 20 years. This transformation is characterized by the change in environment as is evidenced by organizations, who saw their role almost as benevolent charities whose mission it was to provide care to all without particular regard to reimbursement (the guiding assumption was "if you bill it, they will pay"), to rough-and-tumble competitive businesses who needed to track all aspects of financial performance to satisfy their boards, shareholders, and other organizational stakeholders. Over this period of time, large public companies or organizations have invested significant sums and acquired many healthcare organizations with the expectation of receiving an aggressive return on their investments. Also during this time, regulations on healthcare payors were loosened, which helped spark the managed care (HMO) and "capitated payment" (fixed monthly payment to providers not directly tied to specific visits) movements. As more players entered the healthcare space with specific bottom-line interests, reimbursement schemas became increasingly more complex; more entities needed to be measured (e.g., are we getting more in monthly capitated payments than we are paying out in actual patient encounters?). With all this going on, one can only imagine how critical it became to understand in great detail what one's reimbursement and cost foundation was, where timeliness and accuracy of information describing these activities was critical to determine potential trends over time. Modeling capabilities needed to be generated to analyze corresponding data and alert mechanisms needed to be incorporated to highlight what key indicators breached certain predetermined levels. Again, the Affordable Care Act has introduced a whole new dynamic for the finance teams at healthcare institutions through its emphasis on quality and requirements that key indicators are measured on an ongoing basis.

In 2015, diagnosis coding migrated from the ICD-9 system, which has been in use for decades, to the ICD-10 system. The change here is profound: the ICD-9 coding set had about 14,000 different diagnosis codes; the ICD-10 coding set has about 69,000 codes with much more granular detail. Payment contracts that pay a certain amount for particular conditions need to be reevaluated using new codes and providers need to have sophisticated modeling tools in place to assess the financial impact of mapping from one ICD-9 code to a potential multitude of ICD-10 codes.

Computerized financial systems have existed in healthcare for decades. Their ability to generate data- and report-driven balance sheets, profit-and-loss statements, and other relevant accounting reports lend themselves to an acute need for informatics. For instance, many hospitals, especially not-for-profit systems, finance growth and other capital initiatives through the use of fixed income securities (e.g., bonds), many of which may be guaranteed by a governmental or quasi-governmental authority. Conditions are attached to many of these securities stipulating that if certain key financial indicators breach agreed-on values, sanctions may be invoked that may include deeming these bonds as in "technical default." This can have far-reaching implications for organizations in terms of ongoing financial viability, future access to credit, and changes in administrative personnel or board membership in impacted organizations. It is critical for an organization to be able to, at the very least, access vital information that would indicate whether variances in financial metrics exceeded preestablished thresholds of acceptance, and also to know *in advance* that trends among various other key indicators may be leading the organization to this precipice.

There are also financial metrics that are unique to healthcare that speak to how efficiently the organization is being run and, indirectly, what the quality of care is likely to be based on important factors such as staffing patterns. Some of those metrics that are typically tracked include "full-time equivalents (FTEs) per occupied bed" (e.g., is the organization staffing its units commensurate with the patient volume on those units?), "net revenue" versus "net cash collected" (is the organization getting properly reimbursed for what it thinks it is rightfully owed for the services it renders?), and productive hours and agency hours (e.g., is the organization having to rely on expensive and less predictable "agency" nursing to fulfill its regulated staffing requirements?), to name a few.

With the advent of managed care and capitated contracts with payors, a whole new realm of tracking becomes critical. These types of contracts have become increasingly more complicated over the years, and it can be a challenge for an organization to have an accurate sense of the correct monetary allocation for particular types of services. Issues such as which services may not be reimbursable, which services may qualify as "outliers," and under what circumstances "extraordinary" services would entitle the organization to reimbursement over and above the agreed-on base rate from the payor may need to be considered. "Contract management systems" surfaced during the 1990s to address this new paradigm and have, over the years, become a much more important part of a healthcare organization's informatics toolkit. Combining information from contract management systems such as gauging receipts for particular services by particular payors with financial decision support systems becomes "strategic" for healthcare providers. Tracking both revenue as a whole and costs per different types of services (e.g., activity-based costing) and disseminating profitability information of different aspects of managed care contracts to decision makers provide the strategic information to implementing more effective initiatives.

Compliance Issues

The next area in which informatics could yield significant efficiencies involves the realm of clinical compliance. There are important regulations that can impact an institution's accreditation status if procedures are not strictly adhered to. Organizations such as the Joint Commission or the Department of Health have very stringent and detailed regulations as to the exact protocols that need to be followed under different care circumstances. Also, governmental entities are reporting on websites accessible to the public the different levels of compliance of organizations corresponding to adherence to protocol standards. This can translate into lost revenue, lost market share, or diminished stature for those who underperform their competitors by registering subpar results of relevant indicators. For instance, at a relatively basic level, any patient who enters a facility exhibiting signs of respiratory problems is supposed to be given smoking-cessation counseling. Another example is that any patient presenting at a hospital with signs of a cardiac "event" is to be given an aspirin right away. These are basic care guidelines that are universally recognized as being important in ensuring that a patient has a desired health outcome. The challenge, however, arises when considering how an entity can capture this type of data and disseminate reports that indicate whether rules are complied with or not. With this information, organizations can take strategic initiatives to mitigate any undesirable performance variances.

There are also important factors to consider regarding time and allocation of resources to minimize the risk of complications to certain classes of patients. There is a particular focus on limiting readmissions: hospitals with unsatisfactorily high rates of readmissions will face a significant reduction in their overall reimbursement. Deviations from quality outcomes for different types of conditions, most of them cardiac in nature, will also result in penalties from a value-based purchasing perspective.

Regulatory mandates govern areas such as medication reconciliation and pain assessments as well, where once again, informatics enables organizations to better identify breakdowns in processes and procedures that cause subpar performance results so appropriate steps can be taken to adjust resources allocations such as staffing to mitigate negative outcomes. When addressing the issue of optimizing staffing resources within the organization, a number of complicated factors need to be considered. These include the notion of "acuity tracking," or matching the severity of the conditions in a particular hospital unit with staffing allocations. Also, because staffing schedules tend to be projected a number of weeks into the future, census trends need to be analyzed. Factors such as day of week or time of year (e.g., winter months involving snow and ice could result in increased injuries and demand for healthcare services) must be considered. Proper staffing in light of these various factors can contribute to improved and more comprehensive care, which in turn will contribute to better outcomes, fewer complications, fewer medical errors, and so forth. However, as noted, because staffing decisions are based on best estimates of what may happen in the future, it becomes all the more important to have the best data available to ideally model what these needs will be. Informatics can synthesize data from a myriad of different systems, such as electronic medical records, financial systems, or even external Web-based systems that can provide information on factors outside of the hospital walls such as temperature, or perhaps the severity of the flu season in the area, and can enhance the understanding of potential demand for staffing resources.

The migration from ICD-9 coding to ICD-10 coding comes with a host of compliance challenges for healthcare providers. Medicare, Medicaid, and other third-party payors are auditing claims more than ever to ensure that the level of care being reimbursed for is consistent with the coding and documentation found on the claim. The newness and specificity of ICD-10 codes will have a major impact on providers as they scramble to ensure that they are appropriately documenting the legitimate level of care being provided to patients.

Quality Improvement in Clinical and Operational Activities

Another area that is rapidly maturing in the healthcare provider arena involves the growing utilization of devices that can interface directly with an EHR system and, ultimately, an informatics system. Ventilators, "smart" pumps, IVs, vital sign tracking monitors, and other devices like these can "talk" to electronic medical records and populate data directly into an EHR. Some EHRs, facilitated by information technologies, offer a capability to page a clinician or otherwise provide a real-time alert if a certain clinical value is outside of accepted medical bounds. These technologies also add to existing data elements to enhance the overall data resources for more advanced analytics.

Statistically based analytics such as correlations can help providers identify the best possible order sets to use for a given condition (in conjunction with evidence-based medicine protocols). Informatics incorporating statistical correlations and causation can identify that individuals who receive a certain type of specialized therapy can have much shorter lengths of stay and lower rates of readmission than those who do not. Analytics can also allow for comparing different clinical regimens to factors such as patient satisfaction survey scores. They can identify whether certain high-priced medications or medical devices may provide a less desirable outcome than lower-priced medications and can identify which doctors have a predisposition to order those medications or devices. Looking at physician comparisons, informatics will enable hospitals and other organizations to compare physician ordering patterns with desired outcomes such as reduced length of stay, lower readmissions, fewer complications or comorbidities, and revenue generation metrics. This provides a key level of accountability for all involved in the interdisciplinary plan of care of a patient to ensure that the right people are doing the right things at the right time.

Many factors affiliated with clinical compliance apply to our third area of focus, quality improvement programs. At the end of the day, all healthcare providers certainly strive to provide the highest quality of care possible at all times. However, attempting to define what constitutes quality can be elusive. Recently, regulatory agencies and payors have offered their own parameters as to what constitutes quality care. So-called "pay for performance" programs and "never event" prohibitions have helped crystallize much of what providers need to measure to demonstrate to appropriate agencies or payors that they are adopting the correct procedures for their patients. Many of the new programs being rolled out to providers are truly "pay for performance" programs that specify that there will be either incentives or penalties based on a providers' demonstrated compliance with a certain set of quality protocols. If the provider complies effectively, incentive payments are provided. If not, differing levels of reduction of payment come into play. "Never events" are significant medical errors that can cause grave patient harm, and Medicare, and other payors, have made it a policy that they will not reimburse providers for costs incurred from provider events that should "never" happen; hence the name. Not only does "pay-for-performance" and "never event" tracking impact the long-term financial viability of healthcare organizations, but these types of statistics now are also among those that typically are compiled by governmental agencies, benchmarked, and posted on websites, where consumers (potential customers) can view them and compare them with those of a provider's competitors.

Other indicators that are being tracked and reported via the web include hospital-acquired infection rates, readmissions, and indicators such as average waits to see a doctor in an Emergency Department. It becomes imperative that healthcare organizations develop the wherewithal to track these types of metrics accurately and in ways that allow for interceding proactively to address procedural issues to manage negative outcomes in the pipeline. "Benchmarking," or comparing an organization against its peers and against what is considered to be "acceptable" performance is becoming increasingly common and increasingly visible to larger sections of the public. For a provider, knowing where its performance *should* be early in the process allows for more aggressive programs to be designed and deployed to ensure that the organization is applying the most optimal procedures.

The concept of quality improvement can also be articulated in a somewhat different, but extremely important, way as well. Though, as noted previously, there are a multitude of clinical metrics that often can and should be shared both internally and externally, quality improvement can also be construed as using data to improve business processes in general and enforce accountability for appropriate and acceptable performance. Informatics can be used, for instance, to compare the length of time it takes physicians in an emergency room to see a patient. This can be a significant motivating factor to enhance performance by comparing individuals to their peers. In general, informatics enables healthcare providers to aggregate and analyze data in constructive and actionable ways, the results of which are continuous improvement in various procedures throughout the organization.

Customer Relationship Management in Healthcare

Our final aspect of healthcare operations that can benefit immensely from informatics is the realm of "patient satisfaction." As noted earlier, healthcare institutions increasingly have to view themselves more and more as businesses, and part of maintaining a viable business is producing positive experiences for your "customers." In the healthcare industry customers can take on a number of forms, ranging from patients, patients' families, to doctors. Providing an exceptional experience for customers remains a significant goal for healthcare organizations as it promotes repeat visits from individuals in need of services. Happy customers also provide good word-of-mouth recommendations of their experiences that help rein in new customers, which maintains positive demand and, hopefully, increased revenue. And while the concept of "happy customers" is certainly important from a marketing perspective, the fact that patient satisfaction scores are significant factors in value-based reimbursement now means that unhappy patients can adversely affect a provider's bottom line. Though much of this is intuitive, certainly, what is not so intuitive is how a healthcare institution gauges satisfaction rates of its customers.

Measuring patient satisfaction in a healthcare setting can take on multiple forms, but the prevalent metric comes from surveys that are sent to patients that, when tallied, generate an Hospital Consumer Assessment of Healthcare Providers and Systems (HCAHPS) score. Not only are these scores important from a bottom-line perspective, but they are also publicly published so patients/consumers can directly compare one hospital's score to another's. These surveys offer patients the opportunity to add comments to their response, where proactive healthcare organizations can build systems to route these comments automatically to the appropriate decision makers in the organization and track the timeliness of issue resolution. Medicare regulations spell out a formal procedure for what are called "grievances," which have mandates attached to them about how facilities need to address them. Clearly tracking these to ensure the responses to these grievances stay within the bounds of the regulations is most important for the organization to avoid falling out of CMS compliance parameters, which may lead to financial or other, perhaps more severe, sanctions.

Another type of patient satisfaction interaction can be performed via surveys that are administered directly to the patient while he or she remains in the facility. These surveys allow for an organization to receive more timely feedback of issues as they are occurring and take steps to address them and, if necessary, initiate a formal service recovery procedure for particular types of unfortunate customer service situations. The general process for how this type of survey works involves interviewing patients (assuming their condition allows the interview) at certain time intervals and asking them questions regarding issues such as their perception of the food they received, demeanor of nurses, and so forth. Responses can be entered into a database and tracked and trended over time through the utilization of informatics methods that can also drilldown to identify if particular areas are problematic. Furthermore, certain types of responses and comments can be routed automatically to key individuals and processes can be built to track the timeliness and completeness of responses to these issues. The main advantage of this type of survey is the rapid-response capability it offers. The organization can find out right away if something is wrong and react and correspond directly with the individual to ensure that the remedy to the problem was effective. This can transform a dissatisfied customer into a satisfied one.

More and more, informatics can and does provide value in a multitude of different care settings and in a number of different operational processes. Organizations invariably will derive significant benefits from having a mechanism to generate an accurate read of data on all fronts and the ability to turn that data into actionable information. This information enhances the knowledge of service providers who can implement appropriate strategic initiatives to enhance efficiencies throughout the organization.

Closing Comments on the Ever Important Issue of Data Privacy

A critical element that needs to be maintained, preserved, and perhaps strengthened refers to the privacy safeguards of healthcare-related data of individuals. The integration of data resources from various healthcare providers and databases no doubt enhances efficiencies from analytics capabilities and information generation. As the process of developing more robust data resources enhances efficiencies, it also introduces the requirement for well-defined and strictly enforced standards to protect the privacy rights of individuals regarding health-related data. New privacy policies (mentioned in the text that follows) need to be designed to address any changes that transpire within the realm of data access and exchanges in the evolving healthcare system. The U.S. Department of Health and Human Services issued a privacy rule to implement the requirement for the Health Insurance Portability and Accountably Act of 1996 (HIPAA) which addresses the use and disclosure of individuals' health information. A major goal of the Privacy rule is to ensure that individuals' health information is properly protected while allowing the flow of health information needed to provide and promote high-quality healthcare and to protect the public's health and well-being. The rule strikes a balance that permits important uses of information, while protecting the privacy of people who seek care and healing.[12] New initiatives are currently addressing privacy requirements in this evolving data intensive environment. The American Recovery and Reinvestment Act of 2009 (ARRA) incorporates improvements to existing law, covered entities, business associates, and other entities that will soon be subject to more rigorous standards when it comes to protected health information.[13] As data resources become more comprehensive, so too should policies that safeguard individual privacy rights.

References

1. Lehr W, Lichtenberg F. 1998. Computer use and productivity growth in US federal government agencies, 1987–1992. *J Indust Econ*, pp. 257–79, June.
2. Brynjolfsson E, Hitt L. 2000. Beyond computation: Information technology, organizational transformation, and business performance. *J Econ Perspect* 14(4):23–48.

3. Kudyba S, Diwan R. 2002. Increasing returns to information technology. *Inf Syst Res*, pp. 104–11, March.
4. Shaprio C, Varian H. 1998. *Information rules: A strategic guide to the network economy*. Cambridge, MA: Harvard Business Press.
5. Kudyba S, Diwan R. 2002. *Information technology, corporate productivity and the new economy*. Westport, CT: Greenwood.
6. Kayyali B, Knott D, Van Kuiken S. 2013. The big-data revolution in US health care: Accelerating value and innovation. McKinsey & Co. Available at: http://www.mckinsey.com/insights/health_systems_and _services/the_big-data_revolution_in_us_health_care.
7. Digital health solutions expected to save U.S. healthcare system more than $100 billion over next four years, Accenture finds. June 4, 2015. Available at: https://newsroom.accenture.com/news/digital-health -solutions-expected-to-save-us - healthcare-system-more-than-100-billion -over-next-four-years-accenture-finds.htm.
8. Patterson N. 2009. The ABCs of systemic healthcare reform: A plan for driving $500 billion in annual savings out of the US healthcare system. Cerner Corporation: Healthcare Industry Brief. Available at: http:// www.cerner.com/ABCs.
9. Davenport T, Prusak L. 2000. *Working knowledge*. Cambridge, MA: Harvard Business Press.
10. Davenport T, Harris J, DeLong D, Jacobson A. 2001. Data to knowledge to results: Building and analytic capability. *Calif Manage Rev* 43(2): 117–38.
11. Pande P, Neuman R, Cavanagh R. 2000. *The Six Sigma way: How GE, Motorola, and other top companies are honing their performance*. New York: McGraw-Hill.
12. U.S. Department of Health Human Services (Summary of the HIPPA Privacy Rule). Available at: http://www.hhs.gov/ocr/privacy/hipaa /understanding/summary/privacysummary.pdf.
13. The American Recovery and Reinvestment Act of 2009. Available at: http://frwebgate.access.gpo.gov/cgi-bin/getdoc.cgi?dbname=111_cong _bills&docid=f:h1enr.pdf.

2

ELECTRONIC HEALTH INFORMATION, HEALTHCARE SYSTEM INTEROPERABILITY, MOBILE HEALTH, AND THE FORMATION OF A COMMUNITY OF HEALTH AND WELLNESS

STEPHAN P. KUDYBA, THAD PERRY, AND DEBORAH BALLOU

Contents

Healthcare reform is not new. As a nation we have been experimenting with different types of care delivery models, reimbursement methods, and the design of treatments and procedures to align with best outcomes for decades. The seeds of our current national healthcare transformation were planted in the 1970s when the medical community recognized that improving healthcare across the entire population required a primary accountable source for the healthcare of individuals.[1] This resulted in the concepts of primary care providers, healthcare homes, managed care, and community-oriented care, to name a few. These concepts are well known in theory but little understood in practice. It is clear, though, that the systems in which these concepts must operate are exceptionally complex and extremely resistant to change.

The Patient Protection and Affordable Care Act (PPACA) was signed into law on March 23, 2010. However, two Acts passed before PPACA, (1) the Health Insurance Portability and Accountability Act (HIPAA) in 1996 and (2) the Health Information Technology for Economic and Clinical Health Act (HITECH) in 2009, led to significant changes in the healthcare industry regarding patient information and electronic health records (EHRs). The HIPAA Privacy Rule protects an individual's confidential health records from misuse and, after nearly 10 years, is generally understood throughout the healthcare community.[2] While providing federal protection of individually identifiable health information, HIPAA also provides a framework to allow covered entities and business associates to disclose health information necessary for patient care coordination and other beneficial purposes. More recently, the HITECH Act was enacted to promote *meaningful use* of EHRs. According to the Act, there are three components of meaningful use: (1) use of a certified EHR in a meaningful way, (2) electronic exchange of health information to improve quality of healthcare, and (3) use of certified EHR technology to submit clinical quality and other measures. Organizations that achieved meaningful use by 2014 were eligible for incentive payments, while those that failed to reach those standards by 2015 would be penalized.[3] Providers must demonstrate that they have complied with the meaningful use requirements to receive incentives. With these recent regulations imposed on healthcare information privacy and meaningful use, there is a greater need for methods and processes that leverage the use of data and health information technology (HIT) to document compliance and produce benefits for healthcare providers.

Currently, the Affordable Care Act is one of the most discussed and debated issues in the United States.[4] This debate is vitally important because it affects every man, woman, and child both today and tomorrow. Major drivers for healthcare reform are (1) the increasingly poor health of our citizens and (2) the fragmented and mismanaged provider community.

Unhealthy patients may be:

- Difficult to diagnose
- Expensive to treat
- Unproductive at work

- Unmotivated to take care of themselves
- Unintentionally affecting the economy through poor health choices and suboptimal care
- Inadvertently affecting future generations by creating a culture of illness

Healthcare providers are often:

- Burdened with administrative and bureaucratic paperwork
- Unable to easily coordinate between primary care providers and specialists
- Pressed to see more patients or provide more services with less time and support
- Pressured to increase revenue and salaries year over year
- Unable to obtain patient information in a timely, cost-effective way
- Confused about how they will be "graded" on the quality of care given to their patients

Adding to this complexity, hospitals, health plans, third-party administrators, and self-insured employer groups are facing an increasingly competitive market landscape demanding price transparency, program safeguards, disease management, health and wellness programs, and a more expansive provider network. These known challenges as well as new challenges that are developing nearly every day as we gain more experience with the Affordable Care Act create innumerable opportunities for healthcare informatics groups to:

- Analyze stakeholder behaviors and experiences
- Define the challenges
- Research the issues
- Refine the problems
- Develop the solutions
- Track the outcomes

Finally, providers must now make the difficult shift away from volume-based healthcare toward value-based healthcare because of recent changes in the healthcare industry.[5] Beginning in 2012, the Centers for Medicare and Medicaid Services (CMS) made changes to provider reimbursement policy by advocating alternative payment models like those used by Medicare Shared Savings Program Accountable Care Organizations (MSSP ACO).[6,7] Providers who participate in these programs are held accountable for both the quality and cost of care and are rewarded for value, improving health outcomes, and reducing costs. The goal is to have 30% of Medicare payments tied to these models by the year 2016, increasing to 50% of payments by the year 2018. This new payment system has already produced a significant increase in quality and reduction in spending with a Medicare savings of $417 million.[8]

Despite these challenges, changes in the healthcare landscape have also produced many opportunities. The increasing use of EHRs and other health information technologies (HITs) provides opportunities to leverage health data to develop and implement community-based health and wellness initiatives. One of the most promising of these initiatives is the formation of Health Information Exchanges (HIEs) that are designed to collect, store, and share data that can be used to develop actionable information for healthcare and social service providers as well as to empower consumers to improve their own health and wellness. To achieve these goals HIEs must assimilate disparate sources of data into information technology solutions that interface with a variety of systems used by healthcare providers, social service agencies, and consumers. One method of HIE provision involves the creation of a single-source information platform to which multiple providers and community organizations contribute and from which those same organizations extract more comprehensive patient and/or client information than each could individually acquire. In this chapter we examine the use of electronic health data and information technology to support accountable care. In other words, accountable care that is reinforced by health information exchanges, data integration, and interoperable systems to support a community of health.

Role of Electronic Health Data and Information Systems

Amazingly, electronic healthcare data in the United States exceeded 150 exabytes (one exabyte equals one billion gigabytes) in 2011 and was predicted to increase annually at a rate of 1.2 to 2.4 exabytes. The use of electronic healthcare data has the potential to lower costs and increase the quality of healthcare by substantially improving the ability to make informed decisions. The benefits to healthcare of electronic data–supported decision making include early detection of diseases, population health management, fraud and abuse detection, and more accurate clinical predictions and financial forecasts. By applying analytics to these data, providers can detect diseases and chronic conditions sooner, thereby increasing the effectiveness and efficiency of patient treatment. For example, Premier, a healthcare alliance network, has estimated that insights provided by electronic healthcare data have resulted in approximately 29,000 lives saved and $7 million in reduced spending, demonstrating that data accessibility can be crucial to providing quality care to patients.[9]

Managing population health through the integration of multiple, disparate data sources is essential to delivering a more complete view of the patient to providers. As illustrated in Figure 2.1, the sources

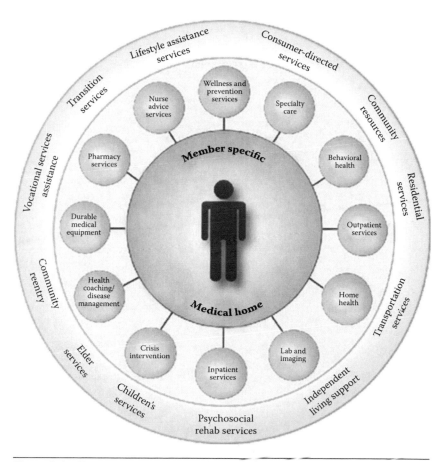

Figure 2.1   The complexity of electronic data integration in healthcare.

of information available for a single member within a medical home (i.e., an accountable care scenario) range from primary and specialty care to behavioral health and nurse advice services. In turn, each type of service benefits from the availability of far more complete information regarding a particular member's situation that is derived from the contributions of all service types.

The use of HIEs plays a major role in supporting this data-driven comprehensive portrait of individual patients. HIEs are networks that facilitate the integration and sharing of relevant patient-level health information between patients and their providers. For example, the purpose of an HIE is to manage all of the electronic data collected and stored by a patient's many care providers such as (1) medical providers, (2) healthcare facility providers, (3) clinic and health center providers, (4) transportation and durable medical equipment providers, and (5) social service and behavioral health providers. This creates a data environment that supports the exchange of health information that providers can use to provide the best possible care based on the most current health-related information about the patient. When used appropriately, HIEs can improve the quality, cost, effectiveness, and efficiency of healthcare.

In particular, as healthcare transitions from volume-based to value-based delivery, hospitals and providers will increasingly depend on HIEs to make this transition. HIEs are critical to the success of value-based healthcare because they:

- Create a foundation for data integration and interoperability
- Provide more efficient physician referral processes
- Enable providers to obtain a more complete understanding of their patients
- Enable broader provider networks
- Support the business transformation of health systems[10]

Value-based healthcare would have difficulty succeeding without a standardized, interoperable HIE that uses the latest HIT, analytics, management solutions, and reporting capabilities.

Although there are a variety of methods for sharing, storing, and retrieving patient data, we advocate a data integration model that relies on a single, interoperable platform that supports the information systems required to acquire, integrate, and store the different data types that are necessary to build a complete health profile for an individual.

The Role of Advanced and Predictive Data Analytics

Advanced data analytics provide risk-bearing healthcare organizations actionable information designed to help key stakeholders better understand the populations they serve by delivering *understandable, consistent information* to all levels of an organization. Analytics are generated by incorporating multiple data sources, such as healthcare claims data, electronic health records, survey and assessment data, as well as others. This ensures data-driven, reliable care—the hallmark of successful and sustainable healthcare programs. Some of the most common complaints against population health analytic solutions are that:

- They provide too much data which overwhelms the user.
- Data and results are not presented in a user-friendly format to the typical physician and his/her staff.
- Data and results are not easily actionable, especially at the patient level.

Consequently, a strong analytics platform should include the following features: (1) identification of the risks and risk drivers for the managed population/s; (2) creation of actionable intelligence for better decision making; (3) simplification of the complexity of managing at-risk populations by means of understandable, consistent information; (4) use of best-practice clinical documentation; (5) correct assignment of an individual patient's healthcare risk; and (6) evaluation of the medical necessity of available healthcare services.

As illustrated in the preceding text, there is a strong link between care management, clinical outcomes, and business performance (Figure 2.2). It is well known that 20% of an ACO's members will generate at least 80% of healthcare costs in a given year.[11] The formula for program success is the ability to identify which members will be among the high cost 20% of members during the next 12 months in the absence of appropriate care management and intervention. Improved predictive accuracy involves going well beyond standard

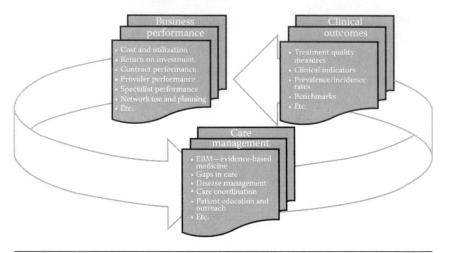

Figure 2.2   Linkage of care management, clinical outcomes, and business performance.

episodic, grouper-based analysis (e.g., Episode Treatment Groups) or utilization-based models (e.g., Diagnostic Cost Groups). The key to better patient identification and targeting is a better understanding of how psychosocial factors *along with* clinical indicators influence the behaviors that result in either good or bad health outcomes. In its simplest form, the ability to incorporate life circumstances data (e.g., living below the poverty level), lifestyle demographic data (e.g., divorced and living alone), personal behavioral data (e.g., depression and stress) with cost, utilization, and clinical data result in a highly accurate approach to patient targeting and resource allocation. This approach provides *actionable* information—information providers and caregivers know how to use to help their patients.

Establishing a Data-Driven Community of Health

There are significant community health challenges in many areas of the United States, especially rural regions. According to the Health Resources and Services Administration division of the U.S. Department of Health and Human Services, 19.3% of the population was rural as of the last Census.[12] Eighty-two percent of rural counties are classified as Medically Underserved Areas, with only 9% of physicians practicing in these areas. To make matters worse, rural areas depend on primary care physicians, but only around 2% of medical students plan to specialize in primary care.[13] Clearly, these workforce shortages cannot be resolved quickly, underscoring the need to increase the efficiency and effectiveness of healthcare services in these economically distressed, rural communities.

Rural healthcare challenges also result from a number of population characteristics, including financial factors and the employment status of citizens in these areas. The number of self-employed workers in rural areas has increased by 240% since 1969. With lower rates of employer-sponsored insurance, rural citizens have significantly higher rates of un-insurance as well as under-insurance, around 70% higher than in urban areas.[14] To meet these challenges rural healthcare providers (e.g., hospitals, clinics, and practices) are developing Accountable Care Organizations (ACOs), Patient-Centered Medical Homes (PCMHs), and community-based health and wellness initiatives. To improve the healthcare in a rural community, these providers must find ways to increase community engagement/awareness, develop and implement population-based health strategies, and work with nontraditional partners such as churches, community centers, and schools.

Given the difficulty delivering optimal healthcare in a rural setting, the importance of secure, interoperable health information technology and tools to support providers and caregivers is paramount. The goal is to create an environment where health information is available to all care providing organizations, thereby supporting rural citizens in establishing and sustaining a community of health. However, one of the major obstacles to realizing this goal is the current lack of integration of data from the various provider types essential to the formation of a community of health. Examples of common provider types in rural communities are small hospitals, primary care provider groups, Federally Qualified Health Clinics (FQHCs), health departments, nursing homes, assisted living facilities, emergency medical services, behavioral health providers, and social service agencies. Providing the foundation and framework for the sharing of health information crucial to the health and wellness of the region requires open-source, interoperable health IT tools. These tools can be used to implement or to support and extend existing health information exchange solutions in a scalable, replicable, and transferable way.

As shown in Figure 2.3, to support the data integration and systems interoperability needed in a rural setting we advocate an IT infrastructure consisting of a centralized data repository with integration

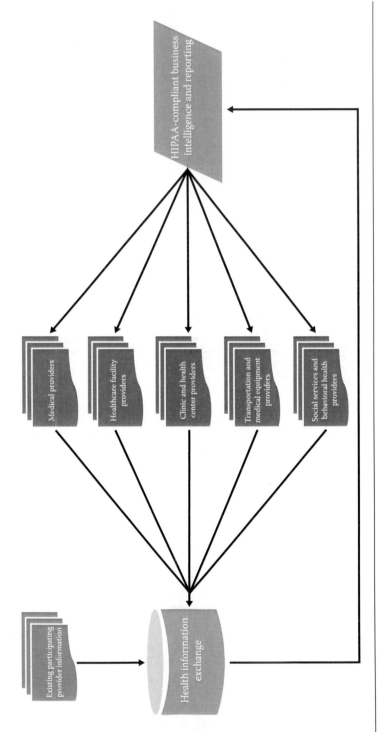

Figure 2.3 Information flow in a general health information exchange framework.

tools designed to execute automated ETL (extract/transform/load) functions with data (e.g., medical claims, electronic medical/health records, behavioral health claims, and social service agencies) from multiple sources. After the data are moved from their sources they are remodeled to fit a standardized framework necessary for analysis and reporting. Secure, HIPAA compliant, database servers store the data. A business intelligence and reporting system is used to present users with summary financial and clinical reports via a web interface. The system is designed to provide improved patient/client information, leading to health improvements as well as cost efficiencies, such as closing referral gaps.[15]

Mobile Health in the Pipeline

Another area that is quickly evolving in the healthcare arena that shows great promise in not only addressing the issue mentioned in the preceding text (e.g., rural health) but for the entire industry, is wireless mobile health technologies. Advancements in wireless capabilities; data storage, processing, and communication; and software applications (apps) have enabled individuals of all walks to communicate and tap into information through mobile devices such as smartphones and tablets.

Mobile devices, enabling texting, emails, access to the web, and use of apps, provide the platform to information access, retrieval, and communication in near real time. Industries of all types have tapped into this electronic highway for marketing, supply chain, customer service, sales, customer relationship management, production, workflow, and so forth. This second wave of the information economy has transformed global commerce.[16] The communication evolution not only has transformed traditional operations of business, but with the vast adoption of mobile devices, social media has impacted behavioral attributes of society as well.

Healthcare has not ignored this second wave of the information economy as the impact of technologies currently deployed in healthcare and the prospects of technologies in the pipeline are impressive. Wireless medical sensors have been deployed to monitor and help track chronic conditions such as diabetes. These devices monitor patients' vital signs (glucose levels, blood pressure, etc.); alerting systems help enhance patient adherence to medications; and portals provide preventative care and care maintenance information. Communication devices such as Fitbit® provide health consciousness consumers with information on calories burned, intensity of physical activity such as walking, and sleep quality. However, the true potential of these initial applications have not nearly been achieved. Issues such as data quality and consistency (e.g., the reliability of data feeds from sensors placed on the body and how metrics are reported), privacy/security, analytics, and network effects must evolve to create a more robust mobile health environment.

Some individuals remain skeptical of the presence of a full-blown mobile health platform given issues just mentioned. However, one must keep in mind the recent evolution of the e-based world that now exists. In the "old days" dating back about a decade ago, it was hard to imagine a phone that could search the web, provide voice based applications, take quality photos, record streaming video, optimize travel activities, and enhance purchase activities to name a few. Nor could many envision the societal adoption of social media and its corresponding functionality and impacts on consumption, marketing, politics, news, and so forth. Just a few years can bring about dramatic change to the world we live in, given the rate of technological innovation.

This time healthcare does not look to be far behind.[17] Some of the promise of mobile health functionality made possible by the development of apps, wireless communication, smartphones, and mobile sensing devices have already been achieved. Today, the utilization of mobile health has been more for providing information and education to patients regarding self-care, treatment, and prescriptions through available web information resources and messaging. However, the future should shift more toward improving communication between patients and their care professionals regarding health status and treatment; improving awareness through self-monitoring; and facilitating social support and knowledge exchange between patients, peers, and providers.[18] Some devices that are in use so far either in actual commercial applications (e.g., glucometers) or in pilot testing include devices that monitor patient information (weight, glucose levels and other vital signs) which can be connected to care providers which provide analytics, which is beneficial for treatment of important chronic ailments such as diabetes and CHF.[19] These devices provide a data feed to care providers that can combine current data with existing medical records on EHRs, and with the incorporation of analytics including visual capabilities, provide an information source to portals that are accessed by mobile devices and enable patients and care providers to interact and exchange messages. Figure 2.4 provides a simplistic but important illustration of the mobile process. Other examples of applications in the pipeline include decision support devices that cover heart and vascular conditions for cardiac patients and workflow apps that enhance scheduling times for patients seeking care at the emergency room (ER). By communicating patient data such as symptoms and accessing workflow activities at an ER (e.g., patient volume, staff) more accurate expected ER service time can be arranged. With the emergence of accountable care organizations, the demand for mobile health intensifies, as the ACO platform involves the use of patient care coordinators who need to communicate with patients in a non-physical remote fashion to manage cases.[20]

Growing demand for mobile service from all areas of healthcare, in conjunction with major organizations providing supportive technologies (e.g., Google Fit, Apple HealthKit, AT&T ForHealth)

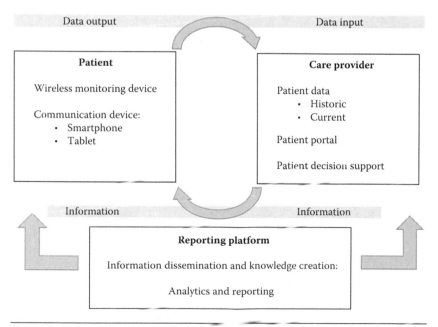

Figure 2.4 Simple but important illustration of mobile health process.

along with government funding to maintain a stable development environment, and the widespread and growing adoption of mobile devices by individuals on a global spectrum, have spurred the supply of technological innovation to eventually create a robust platform for mobile health. The barriers of such a platform such as data quality, consistency, and security; integration between technological components; quality and reliability of reporting capabilities and behavioral issues such as individual adoption of devices, must be overcome. The results could be far reaching with potential cost savings resulting from a reduction in physical meetings and examinations between provider and patient; reduction in readmit rates due to more effective, ongoing care management; reduction in the number of developed cases of chronic diseases; more timely treatment at the episode level; enhanced workflow optimization by providers, and the list goes on.

For further details on the evolution of wireless devices in healthcare, see Chapter 9.

Conclusions

Coordination of care refers to "the integration of care in consultation with patients, their families, and caregivers across all of the patients' conditions, needs, clinicians and settings."[21] To create a community of health and wellness, one of the foremost challenges is how to coordinate the care of individuals across many different provider types, hospitals and other in-patient facilities, government agencies, and social service organizations, as well as other organizations that serve the population. HIEs provide a framework for data integration and interoperability. However, HIEs do not ensure coordination of care unless all healthcare constituents are aware of and actively use the systems.

While the use of EHRs provides a framework to collect, organize, and store healthcare data, significant issues remain that must be resolved to create actionable information at the individual patient level. Many provider groups have difficulty recruiting employees with the appropriate information technology training required to keep these systems operable to meet both the current and future needs of their organizations.[22] Furthermore, once EHRs are operational, the lack of standardization among different EHR software solutions makes it difficult or impossible for multiple sites to efficiently share information, thus falling short of the need for usability, portability, and ease of communication between all constituents.

The inability to coordinate care may also exacerbate another chronic problem faced by healthcare providers. Providers spend an inordinate amount of time and money attempting to effectively treat noncompliant patients, who come into the office suffering from acute or chronic conditions, only to return repeatedly for the same issues. Noncompliance with treatment is often framed as a patients' resistance or inability to care for themselves once they are no longer under the direct supervision of their providers. Newer perspectives in healthcare focus on the importance of patient-centered care, and, ultimately, the engagement of patients, to improve the ability of individuals to actively participate in healthcare along with their care providers. Research shows that encouraging patients to be active consumers of healthcare results in increased engagement and greater responsibility for their own health and wellness. To lessen the occurrence of noncompliance and increase patient engagement with their healthcare it is essential for all types of care providers to share information with each other and with the patient to track and provide support for patient adherence to medical advice.[23]

HIEs facilitated by data integration and interoperable systems are necessary to support a sustainable community of health. Giving providers a more complete, whole health, picture of their patients reduces redundancy, improves efficiency, and builds patient confidence and engagement, all of which can contribute to cost reductions across the continuum of care. By integrating multiple sources of data, such as behavioral and physical health providers, along with information about the life circumstances that affect patients' healthcare behaviors, improvements for individual patients will result in better health of the community. Ultimately, electronic health information and healthcare system interoperability will contribute to building a learning health system by providing timely and actionable information that allows each stakeholder to continuously improve his or her care and contribute to the usefulness of the system as a whole. Better informed decisions will result, reducing the duplication of services, improving patient education, decreasing chronic health conditions, and, finally, decreasing the cost of care.

Acknowledgment

The authors would like to thank contributions from Tennessee Tech University graduate students Zach Budesa and Shannon Cook.

References

1. Fox PD, Kongstvedt PR. 2007. An overview of managed care. In *The essentials of managed health care* (pp. 3–18). Sudbury, MA: Jones & Bartlett.
2. http://www.hhs.gov/ocr/privacy/.
3. http://www.healthit.gov/providers-professionals/meaningful-use -definition-objectives.
4. http://www.hhs.gov/healthcare/rights/.
5. Miller HD. 2009. From volume to value: Better ways to pay for health care. *Health Affairs*, 28(5), 1418–28.
6. https://www.cms.gov/Medicare/Medicare-Fee-for-Service-Payment /sharedsavingsprogram/index.html?redirect=/sharedsavingsprogram/.
7. Gold J. 2015. Accountable Care Organizations, Explained. Kaiser Health News. Available at: http://khn.org/news/aco-accountable-care -organization-faq/, September 14.
8. http://www.hhs.gov/news/press/2015pres/01/20150126a.html.
9. Raghupathi W, Raghupathi V. 2014. Big data analytics in healthcare: Promise and potential. *Health Inf Sci Syst* 2(3), doi:10.1186/2047-2501-2-3.
10. McNickle M. 2012. 5 reasons HIEs are critical to the success of ACOs. *Healthcare IT News* August 7, 2012.
11. Robertson T, Lofgren R. 2015. Where population health misses the mark: Breaking the 80/20 rule. *Acad Med* 90(3):277–78.
12. http://www.hrsa.gov/ruralhealth/policy/definition_of_rural.html.
13. Bailey JM. 2009. The top 10 rural issues for health care reform. Lyons, Nebraska: Center for Rural Affairs, March.
14. Ziller EC, Coburn AF, Yousefian AE. 2006. Out-of-pocket health spending and the rural underinsured. *Health Aff* 25(6):1688–99.
15. Ham N. 2014. Closing the gap on tarnsitions of care. Becker's Hospital Review. Available at: http://www.beckershospitalreview.com/quality /closing-the-gap-on-transitions-of-care.html, Oct.
16. Kudyba S. 2014. *Big data mining and analytics: Components of strategic decisions*. Boca Raton, FL: Taylor & Francis.
17. What is healthcare informatics? Available at: https://www.youtube.com /watch?v=pzS—PaGC9o.
18. McKesson (Editorial Staff), 2015. Major shift coming in the use of mobile health technologies. Available at: http://www.mckesson.com/blog /changing-trends-in-mobile-health-technology/.

19. Steakley L. 2016. Harnessing mobile health technologies to transform human health. *Stanford Medicine*. Available at: http://scopeblog.stanford.edu/2015/03/16/harnessing-mobile-health-technologies-to-transform-human-health/.
20. Conn J. 2014. Going mobile: Providers deploy apps and devices to engage patients and cut costs. *Modern Health*. Available at: http://www.modernhealthcare.com/article/20141129/MAGAZINE/311299980.
21. O'Malley AS, Grossman JM, Cohen GR, Kemper NM, Pham HH. 2010. Are electronic medical records helpful for care coordination? Experiences of physician practices. *J Gen Intern Med* 25(3):177–85.
22. Walker J, Pan E, Johnston D, Adler-Milstein J, Bates DW, Middleton B. 2005. The value of health care information exchange and interoperability. *Health Aff* (Millwood), Jan–Jun; Suppl Web Exclusives: W5-10-W5-18.
23. Vermeire E, Hearnshaw H, Van Royen P, Denekens J. 2001. Patient adherence to treatment: Three decades of research. A comprehensive review. *J Clin Pharm Ther* 26(5):331–42.

3

QUALITY TIME IN HEALTHCARE

Meaningful Use of Health Information Technology and the Journey to Paying for Value

MICHAEL H. ZAROUKIAN
AND PETER BASCH

Contents

To foster healthcare quality and satisfaction, the time health professionals and patients spend interacting with each other should be quality time—important, informative, productive, meaningful, and interpersonally connected. High-quality care is supported when providers, patients, and family members can interact in a mutually convenient and productive manner, with the right information available at

43

the right time and in the right format to effectively and efficiently support the best possible health and care decisions and actions. Recent advances in health information technology (IT) and electronic health record (EHR) adoption and use have helped address our historical overreliance on paper-based care processes and clinical information flows that contribute to the enormous waste and waiting in the current U.S. healthcare delivery system, taking time, energy, and resources away from activities that can improve the value of healthcare. However, clinical information systems that are poorly designed, inadequately implemented, not meaningfully used, or not optimized to transform care also represent barriers to clinical quality and workforce productivity goals. In this chapter, two practicing physicians and clinical informatics leaders share their experiences with leading organizational change, healthcare process redesign, EHR implementation, and information management improvement strategies, as well as their experiences in the first five years of the Meaningful Use (MU) incentive program, to provide a perspective and recommendations for providers and organizations seeking to use health information technology (HIT) to achieve national goals for meaningful use and to be successful as payment policy transitions from traditional fee-for-service medicine to payment for quality and value.

Introduction: The State of Our Current Healthcare System

When it comes to delivering healthcare in the United States today, the fable *Our Iceberg Is Melting*[1] is a fitting metaphor for the disastrous health and economic consequences our country and people will ultimately face if leaders fail to act quickly enough to transform care in a manner that dramatically improves quality and value. In the iceberg fable, noted change leadership expert John Kotter and colleagues illustrate the plight of a colony of penguins coming to the sudden, if not unanimous, realization that their iceberg—the basic foundation of their lives on which they all depend—was at great risk of collapse. Despite the implacable nay-saying of a vocal penguin in the leadership group that argued that change was both unnecessary and dangerous, the influential majority of penguin leaders soon recognized that the survival, health, and happiness of the colony they serve and protect required quickly achieving a shared sense that the status quo was unacceptable and that effective action was urgently needed. The leaders also realized they must come together as a guiding coalition, create a shared vision of a better future, communicate it widely and repeatedly, remove barriers to effective action, gain visible and meaningful short-term successes, reinforce and build on each success, and anchor the improvements in the culture. Finally, the authors provide a framework strategy for survival and success that builds on Kotter's previous work[2] and is relevant to transforming quality in healthcare organizations of any size, from solo physician practices to large healthcare delivery networks.

Along the way, the iceberg fable provides abundant examples of the challenges we in healthcare face in seeing system problems clearly, changing longstanding habits, overcoming barriers to organizational culture change, engaging stakeholders, and consistently aligning our behaviors toward a shared vision of improved quality and value. Indeed, although this chapter focuses on how HIT can be used as a powerful tool to support quality at the point of care, such efforts will fall far short of their full potential unless they are paired with a reformed payment policy that rewards thoughtful health information management and quality outcomes.[3]

In his compelling novel *Why Hospitals Should Fly*,[4] John Nance took many of the important lessons described in John Kotter's work to the next level, as well as adding several of his own from the aviation industry to show just how important cultural change is to our ability to make the transformational changes needed to improve healthcare quality and safety. This compelling book is necessarily a fiction because it describes a hospital (St. Michael's Memorial) that does not yet exist, one that has gotten everything working right and everyone working together with an intense focus on patient safety, service quality, interpersonal collegiality, barrier-free communication, and support for front-line caregivers. However, St. Michael's seems both real and possible because it represents a combination of best practices and effective leadership that can be found in other industries as well as in real-world healthcare settings today. St. Michael's chose to harvest the lessons learned and best practices developed in aviation and leading healthcare institutions and put them to work to dramatically improve safety, collegiality, communication, workforce vitality, process standardization, information technology support, and other elements of organizational care transformation. St. Michael's and the professionals who work there provided a clear and detailed view of how an ideal healthcare environment would look and feel to those giving and receiving care. Like the novel's protagonist, Dr. Will Jenkins, readers of *Why Hospitals Should Fly*[4] may initially be discouraged at the gap between what is possible and what exists in our healthcare delivery system today. However, they can also find comfort and inspiration in the many examples of strategies St. Michael's leaders used to transform the organization and overcome barriers to needed change.

For those less than convinced of the urgent need to transform the U.S. healthcare delivery system, a few statistics and a review of recent events may be instructive. For example, World Health Organization statistics from 2013[5] showed U.S. per capita healthcare costs to be second only to those of Norway and second only to the tiny Pacific Tuvalu islands in fractional consumption of national gross domestic product at 17.1%,[6] with total health spending growing from $2 trillion in 2005 to $3.8 trillion in 2014. Although these much higher expenditures might be justifiable if the vast majority of dollars yielded consistently high value care, such appears to be far from the case. Indeed, it has been estimated that up to 30% to 50% of healthcare spending in the United States is "pure waste."[7,8] A 2008 PricewaterhouseCoopers report[9] examined the issue of healthcare spending waste in detail, estimating that slightly more than half of the $2.2 trillion spent on healthcare in the United States at that time was wasteful. Major contributors included practicing defensive medicine (redundant, inappropriate, or unnecessary tests and procedures), excessive healthcare administrative costs, and the cost of conditions that are considered preventable through lifestyle changes (obesity, tobacco consumption). The authors of the report correctly recommended addressing these three major cost drivers by facilitating healthier individual behaviors; attacking overuse, underuse, and misuse of tests and treatments; and eliminating administrative or other business processes that add costs without creating value.

Not only have higher expenditures on healthcare in the United States failed to translate into higher overall quality, but also key quality and system performance indicators showed that the United States is actually lagging behind other developed nations.[10] This is due in no small part to limited access to primary care services, with nearly

46 million individuals representing 16% of the U.S. population living without health insurance in 2005, with a significant proportion (13.4%, 42 million) lacking health insurance for the entire year in 2013.[11] Unfortunately, underpayments for primary care, preventive care, chronic disease management, and care coordination, combined with high medical school debt and perceptions of primary care practice burdens, have combined to create a shortage of primary care physicians that contributes to limited patient access to care. Recent trends consistently show that U.S. medical school graduates increasingly eschew primary care[12] for specialties in which their care duties are more focused and payments for care and procedures are higher.

The unsustainable nature of the growth in healthcare expenses is further reinforced by data showing progressively increasing numbers of Medicare beneficiaries accumulating at the same time that the number of workers paying into the Medicare system is declining.[13] Among the factors contributing to healthcare expenses that have prompted calls for government action is the wide variation in use of tests and treatments without evidence that higher expenditures are associated with higher quality,[14,15] and even some evidence of an inverse correlation.[16,17] The impact of the primary care provider shortage on costs and quality[18] and the urgency of taking action to address the problem are underscored by the evidence that primary care is generally associated with better preventive care,[19,20] lower preventable mortality,[21] and similar quality with lower resource consumptions than specialty care for certain conditions, such as back pain,[22] diabetes, and hypertension.[23]

Unfortunately, the public debate regarding the preferred approaches for moving toward meaningful, beneficial, and enduring health reform remains mired in partisan political rancor fueled by powerful special interest groups with vested interests in the status quo. This has the effect of obscuring, distorting, distracting, and delaying discussion of the real and substantive issues that need to be worked out. In the meantime, our healthcare iceberg is still melting. Surveys such as those conducted by the Commonwealth Fund[24] have made it clear that the public wants change to address healthcare quality, access, and costs. Desired changes included organizing care systems to ensure timely access, better care coordination, and improved information flow among doctors and with patients. Respondents also wanted health insurance administrative simplification and wider use of health information systems. Since there is compelling evidence that the status quo is not sustainable, it is important to look at potential drivers of change that will help us redesign care so that quality is a system property supported by appropriate and meaningful use of HIT.

Drivers of Change to Promote a More Productive Industry

Although this chapter focuses on strategies for combining change leadership, practice assessment, process redesign, and HIT to assist practitioners in optimizing care quality and value, it is important to cite a few additional writings and events that highlight problems with the existing healthcare delivery system, underscore the urgency of healthcare system redesign, and serve as powerful drivers of change that have also informed our suggested approaches. For example, the Institute of Medicine (IOM) has commissioned several books describing a number of pervasive and critically important defects in the U.S. healthcare delivery system and recommended strategies for addressing them. Two of the most important of these books, *To Err Is Human: Building a Safer Health System*[25] and *Crossing the Quality Chasm: A New Health System for the 21st Century*,[26] shone a bright light on the defects in the current system and how such defects compromise the nation's ability to ensure the consistent delivery of high-quality care to all. Such defects result in care that is far too often fragmented, ineffective, error-prone, unsafe, inefficient, expensive, inaccessible, delayed, disparate, or insensitive to patient needs and preferences. The IOM also emphasized the reality that humans cannot be error free, and indicated that the healthcare delivery system must be fundamentally redesigned, not just repaired, if meaningful gains in quality are to be achieved.

Much has also been written in recent years about the essential role of HIT in repairing some of the pervasive and critically important defects in the U.S. healthcare delivery system. Here again, the IOM did pioneering work, publishing and subsequently revising a book on computer-based patient records,[27] describing what would afterwards be more commonly referred to as electronic medical records (EMRs) and electronic health records (EHRs) as essential to both private and public sector objectives to transform healthcare delivery, enhance health, reduce costs, and strengthen the nation's productivity. However, the IOM also correctly identified many barriers to widespread implementation of EHR systems and predicted the need for a "major coordinated national effort with federal funding and strong advisory support from the private sector"[26] to accelerate needed change.

Some have estimated that approximately $80 billion in annual savings can be expected out of an estimated $2 trillion total (4%) from widespread implementation, optimization, and appropriate use of HIT,[28,29] although a 2008 Congressional Budget Office (CBO) report[30] underscored the degree to which this number may be sensitive to a number of assumptions and factors. The report also highlighted the current perverse incentives built into healthcare financing and delivery in which "the payment methods of both private and public health insurers in many cases do not reward providers for reducing some types of costs—and may even penalize them for doing so."[30] On the other end of the savings prediction spectrum, it has been estimated that if healthcare could produce productivity gains similar to those in telecommunications, retail, or wholesale industries, average annual spending on what is currently considered waste in healthcare could be decreased by $346 billion to $813 billion.[28] It is this combination of the potential for significantly lowering wasteful spending, the evidence that the right combination of HIT and institutional culture can lead to important gains in quality and value,[31] and the urgency of needed change that has prompted healthcare organizations and federal government officials to "bet on EHRs"[32] by making funding available to physicians and hospitals to improve quality through HIT.

The "Game Changers"

The federal government placed its "bet" by introducing a new and powerful driver for HIT adoption and appropriate use on February 17, 2009, when President Obama signed the Health Information Technology for Economic and Clinical Health (HITECH) Act, a large component ($31.2 billion gross investment, $19.2 billion net of expected savings) of the much larger ($787 billion) economic stimulus package known as the American Recovery and Reinvestment

Act (ARRA) of 2009.[33] The HITECH Act made the IOM recommendation for a major coordinated national effort with federal funding a reality, with $29.2 billion ($17.2 billion net) available starting in 2011 for use as incentive payments to Medicare- and Medicaid-participating physicians and hospitals that use certified EHR systems in a "meaningful" way.

ARRA also provided for the creation of two advisory committees under the Federal Advisory Committee Act (FACA) that would be charged with making recommendations to the National Coordinator. Both of these advisory committees have since been formed and are constituted in a way that is consistent with the IOM's recommendations for involvement of experts from the private sector. The Health IT Policy Committee was given the responsibility of "making recommendations on a policy framework for the development and adoption of a nationwide health information infrastructure, including standards for the exchange of patient medical information,"[34] while the Health IT Standards Committee has been charged with making recommendations "on standards, implementation specifications, and certification criteria for the electronic exchange and use of health information,"[34] with an initial focus on the policies developed by the Health IT Policy Committee.

With codification into law of the National Coordinator for Health IT, improved funding for the Office of the National Coordinator (ONC), the passage of ARRA and the HITECH Act into law, and the appointment of the Health IT Policy Committee and the Health IT Standards Committee, energy turned to defining the goals, objectives, measures, and criteria by which physicians and hospitals will qualify for payments for meaningful use of HIT, along with the standards needed to support the goals for MU. ARRA authorized the Centers for Medicare and Medicaid Services (CMS) to reimburse physician and hospital providers who are meaningful users of EHR systems by providing incentive payments starting in 2011 and gradually phasing down over five years. Meanwhile, physicians and hospitals not actively using an EHR in compliance with the MU definition by 2015 are subject to financial penalties under Medicare.

It is important to emphasize that MU does not mean simply having an EHR system in place and in use. MU requires physicians and hospitals to progress through a series of increasingly demanding sets of behaviors, proceeding from EHR use to capture and exchange data, then to improve care processes, and finally to achieve improved patient health outcomes. Payment for MU Stage 1 started in 2011 and required eligible professionals (EPs) to use certified electronic health record technology (CEHRT) in a manner that met specific measures for electronic data capture and sharing with a focus on five healthcare priority areas:

- Improving quality, safety, efficacy
- Engaging patients and families
- Improving care coordination
- Improving population and public health
- Ensuring adequate privacy and security protections for patients

Meeting the measures for Stage 1 MU was challenging but the majority of EPs who registered for the program were able to implement 2011 Edition CEHRT, attest for MU and receive incentive payments. Along the way, they expressed significant concerns about the complexity and lack of clarity of the MU and Certification Final Rules, the accuracy and limited relevance of clinical quality measures (CQMs) for some specialties, and the challenges of submitting attestation data or getting answers to questions. Additional concerns centered on the usability of EHR systems to deliver workflow-integrated approaches to data capture and sharing required to demonstrate MU. Of particular concern to physicians and congressional leaders was the lack of interoperability of CEHRT systems three years and tens of billions of dollars into the program. These concerns prompted a greater emphasis on advancing interoperability in Stage 2.

Meanwhile, CEHRT developers and vendors lamented that the time, effort, and resources required to plan, develop, test, certify, release, and assist customers in implementing CEHRT left them unable to apply proper focus on EHR usability or innovation to improve care. This problem was exacerbated by the complexity and late timing (September 2012) of the release of the Stage 2 MU Final Rule and the 2014 Edition EHR Standards and Certification Final Rule, followed by the challenges of developing, testing, and certifying 2014 Edition CEHRT.

The considerably greater challenges of developing, delivering, implementing, and utilizing 2014 Edition CEHRT for Stage 2, which was scheduled to begin in 2013 for some EPs, resulted in several CMS actions. First, CMS allowed a third year of Stage 1 attestation in 2013 for those who first attested in 2011. CMS subsequently relaxed its 2014 full-year reporting period expectation for ongoing incentive program participants, allowing reporting for a single quarter. For circumstances in which delays in the availability of 2014 Edition CEHRT did not allow an EP, eligible hospital (EH) or Critical Access Hospital (CAH) to fully implement 2014 Edition CEHRT, CMS also allowed for the use of 2011 Edition, 2014 Edition, or a mix of 2011 and 2014 Edition CEHRT to meet MU requirements in 2014.

Recognizing the ongoing challenges to fully implementing 2014 Edition CEHRT by the start of the 2015 reporting periods, CMS published an additional Proposed Rule[35] modifying the MU program for 2015–2017, which was combined with the MU Stage 3 Proposed Rule and finalized on October 16, 2015, with a 60-day comment period, becoming effective December 15, 2015. The addition of a comment period to a Final Rule was unusual but necessitated by the passage of the Medicare Access and CHIP Reauthorization Act of 2015 (MACRA) soon after the two Proposed Rules were published. Because MACRA called for the MU program to be incorporated into the Merit-Based Incentive Payment System (MIPS) and that separate MU EP payment adjustments cease by the end of 2018, the 60-day comment period allowed for input regarding the provisions related to the incorporation of MU into MIPS.

The Final Rule modified the MU program for 2015–2017 in several helpful ways, including (1) relaxing the 2015 reporting period (which requires use of 2014 Edition CEHRT) from a full 12 months to any consecutive 90-day period, enabling successful attestation for those who could not fully implement 2014 Edition CEHRT by January 1, 2015; (2) changing the reporting period for EHs and CAHs from the fiscal year to the same calendar year reporting required for EPs; (3) removing more than 10 measures that CMS believed to be topped out, duplicative, or redundant; (4) easing measures that required patient action not under the direct control of the EP (e.g., patient-initiated secure messaging); and (5) creating a single, synchronized

MU stage ("Modified Stage 2") for all program participants. Having all MU Incentive Program participants on the same stage simplified the program and promoted concurrent implementation and use of the same CEHRT functionalities by all, such as sending and receiving electronic Summary of Care Documents.

These challenges and subsequent modifications of the MU Incentive Program for 2015–2017 underscored the complexity of building a nationwide technical and human infrastructure for HIT-enabled care transformation from volume to value. However, the flexibility and openness to feedback demonstrated by CMS and ONC predicts continued positive progress toward the Triple Aim goals (patient experience and outcomes, health of the population, reducing per capita costs of care) desired by all.

Success in the national effort to use HIT to transform health and healthcare requires sustaining the engagement and vitality of the health professions workforce. This was tested by how CMS responded to comments received in response to the CMS MU Stage 3 Proposed Rule[36] and the 2015 Edition HIT certification criteria, 2015 Edition base EHR definition, and ONC Health IT Certification Program modifications, which were finalized[37] in the fourth quarter of 2015.

The major strengths of the Stage 3 MU Final Rule include (1) a single definition of MU; (2) continued synchronization of all EPs, EHs, and CAHs to a single stage; (3) further consolidating the number of measures to eight (though there are measures within measures, which approximately doubles this number); (4) allowing but not requiring electronic prescribing of controlled substances to count in states where it is permitted; (5) reinforcing the broad range of allowable approaches to implementing clinical decision support; (6) flexibility in public health and clinical data registry reporting; (7) allowing messages sent to patients to count for the secure messaging measure; and (8) allowing for patient access to their records through ONC-certified application programming interfaces (APIs; e.g., smartphone "apps").

Some of the main criticisms and concerns that have been voiced about the Stage 3 MU and 2015 Certification Final Rules include (1) dissatisfaction with the continued reliance on highly prescriptive process measures, expensive and time-consuming to build for vendors, and not permissive of flexible and/or innovative workflows for providers; (2) continued emphasis on process measures over patient outcomes that foster "check the box" mentality over attention to improving out-comes; (3) the hope of decreased physician burden implied by limit-ing Stage 3 to eight objectives was replaced by disappointment when closer inspection showed that six of the eight objectives include two or three measures that must be reported; (4) the limited time EHR developers have from publication of the Final Rule (2015 Q4) to implementing 2015 Edition CEHRT to support Stage 3, especially for those seeking to attest for the 2017 reporting period; (5) the large number of 2015 Edition CEHRT certification requirements (22 of 60) that are not required for MU, raising concerns about diverting EHR developer resources and attention away from usability and innovation; (6) the pressure EHR developers will felt to release 2015 Edition CEHRT in time to support MU Stage 3 in early 2017, even if it means prioritizing certified functionality over usability, innova-tion, and workflow integration; (7) the requirement for certain patient actions, patient-generated data, or data from nonclinical settings that are outside the direct control of EPs, EHs, and CAHs, including the use of consumer apps and APIs that are not yet broadly available and in use; (8) challenges to small EP offices in conducting a robust secu-rity risk analysis and acting on the results; (9) the need for creation of a centralized repository of national, state, and local public health agencies and clinical data registries that support data submission; (10) the need to address problems with data validity, infrastructure, and workflows required to support mandatory electronic reporting of elec-tronic CQMs by 2018 when attestation will no longer be an option; (11) anticipated time and usability challenges of meeting new require-ments for clinical information reconciliation (problems, medications, allergies); and (12) the full-year reporting period for all but first year Medicaid MU participants in 2018, the first required year of Stage 3.

Although the first five years of the MU Incentive Program have not resulted in sufficient progress to enable full replacement of pro-cess measures with patient outcome measures, they have clearly cata-lyzed more widespread adoption and use of CEHRT than would have been likely otherwise. It also means that many physician practices and healthcare organizations are now equipped with the HIT infrastruc-ture, EHR proficiencies, electronically stored clinical data, clinical decision support tools, and data analytics capabilities to measure and improve the quality and value of care for individuals and populations.

These capabilities will be critically important to provider and organizational readiness to respond to forces that are rapidly driving shifts in payment from volume to value. A clear example of this can be found in the January 2015 announcement by the U.S. Department of Health and Human Services (HHS) of its "Better, Smarter, Healthier"[38] campaign (Better Care. Smarter Spending. Healthier People). In this campaign, HHS sets clear goals and timelines for shifting Medicare reimbursements from volume to value, by tying 30% of traditional (fee-for-service) Medicare payments by 2016— and 50% by 2018—to quality and value through alternative payment models (e.g., accountable care organizations [ACOs] or bundled payment arrangements).

In addition, HHS intends to use programs such as the Hospital Value Based Purchasing Program and the Hospital Readmissions Reduction Program to tie 85% of all traditional Medicare payments to quality or value by 2016, and 90% by 2018. HHS further seeks to extend these goals beyond the Medicare program through the creation of a Health Care Payment Learning and Action Network, working with private payers, employers, consumers, providers, states and state Medicaid programs, and others to expand alternative payment models into their programs.

The importance and urgency of moving from volume to value, participating in alternative payment models, and continuing to focus on MU of CEHRT was also reinforced by the April 2015 U.S. Senate passage of H.R. 2—Medicare Access and CHIP Reauthorization Act (MACRA) of 2015,[39] which passed with overwhelming bipartisan support in both chambers. This so-called "doc fix" legislation, signed into law (Public Law No: 114-10) two days later, permanently repealed the previous sustainable growth rate (SGR) formula that adjusted Medicare payments to physicians, replacing it with modest increases in Medicare physician reimbursement for five years starting in July 2015. Importantly, the law also combined and streamlined several quality, value-based payment, and MU incentive programs into a single new Merit-based Incentive Payment System (MIPS). Under MIPS, the Secretary of HHS is instructed to use the categories of quality, resource use, clinical practice improvement activities, and MU of CEHRT in determining performance. Incentive payments will also be available beginning in 2019 for physicians who participate in alternative payment models such as ACOs and meet certain thresholds.[40]

So notwithstanding one's feelings about the transition from paper to electronic systems and the merits and methods of the MU Incentive Program, "the ship has sailed" on the required transformation from volume to value, and HIT will be essential to payment for proving and improving the quality and value of healthcare going forward. As originally articulated in the HITECH Act, expectations for MU will continue to focus on the capture and exchange of health-related data using CEHRT to improve care processes and patient health outcomes. MACRA reflects a progressive emphasis on quality as reflected by clinical outcomes, so physicians and practices will do well to continue to focus on conditions that are common, important, preventable, costly, and highly amenable to treatment. Examples include diabetes mellitus, hypertension, hypercholesterolemia, smoking, obesity, preventive care services, safer medication prescribing in the elderly, and prevention of venous thromboembolism in surgical patients.[41] Efficiency and safety measures will likely continue to include avoidance of preventable emergency department visits and hospitalizations; decreasing inappropriate use of imaging studies; computerized provider order entry; use of evidence-based order sets; advanced electronic prescribing; barcode medication administration; device interoperability; multimedia support; advanced clinical decision support use; and external electronic data reporting on quality, safety, and efficiency.

Developing a Plan

Although the financial incentives available from the HITECH Act may have been sufficient to help providers and systems justify the capital expenditures required to implement and make meaningful use of EHR systems, it is the long-term payment reform outlined in the preceding section that creates a sustainable business case for managing information electronically and improving outcomes. MACRA consolidated the various quality incentive programs and the financial penalties for failure to achieve and sustain MU into a system that incorporates MU into a broader set of performance categories that determine incentive payments and negative payment adjustments.

We recommend that providers focus squarely on improving patient care quality, something that all health professionals resonate with and are individually committed to, and further begin to focus on value—the cost of achieving high-quality care. Physicians should be frequently reminded that they have a shared responsibility for quality,[42] that their participation in EHR system configuration is essential to achieving the organization's quality goals, and that having HIT is insufficient unless it is used in a meaningful way in an organizational culture strongly committed to quality, safety, and collegiality. By quality we mean the six elements described by the IOM in its *Quality Chasm* report:[26] care that is consistently patient centered, effective, safe, timely, efficient, and equitable. This emphasis on quality (especially safety), collegiality, and support for those at the front lines of care is what enabled John Nance's fictional St. Michael's Memorial Hospital to make its transformational journey to quality in *Why Hospitals Should Fly*,[4] and it provides a road map for how each of us can use our CEHRT to accelerate the transformation of our own hospitals and office practices in alignment with our main rationale for doing so, namely, ensuring that high-quality, high-value care is consistently available for all.

Although hospital executives, practice leaders, and front-line providers are increasingly mindful of the importance and urgency of acting on their responsibilities and opportunities for improving care quality while containing costs, they may also be currently using HIT systems and support structures beset with some of the same defects as the healthcare system they were intended to support, even several years into the MU Incentive Program. Such systems may have been designed and implemented without adequate clinician input, making them a poor fit for health professionals at the point of care. The systems may also still not "talk to each other," either through product integration, interfaces or interoperability mechanisms, requiring redundant data entry and risking introduction of errors of commission or omission that threaten patient safety, care effectiveness, workflow efficiency, or service timeliness. Physicians also quickly learn to ignore systems that do not respond quickly or reliably enough for their needs, and develop workarounds that enable them to justify ignoring or underusing HIT systems or foregoing training opportunities even when they are available and encouraged.

Engaging physicians and convincing them of the importance of HIT to achieving shared organizational quality goals is a crucial early step that will increase the likelihood that they will be "willing to strive"[43] to achieve meaningful EHR use. Assessing organizational HIT readiness[44] is also important, as is ensuring that HIT systems are designed, built, validated, tested, and implemented with clinician input. We encourage design strategies that improve usability by decreasing the reading, writing, navigating, and thinking load[45] to the minimum necessary to improve the user experience and help clinicians make and execute optimal care decisions.

To speed care transformation and create a high-reliability organization that inspires the trust and satisfaction of patients and providers, HIT strategists should create, prioritize, and execute plans reflecting awareness of and responsiveness to the critical success factors and potential failure paths of major IT system implementations,[46–52] incorporate approaches that encourage adoption and regular use of EHR systems,[43] and manage the activities required by busy health professionals, taking into consideration the ongoing stressful care transformation process. Boiled down to its bare essentials, a successful journey to qualifying for meaningful EHR use requires building a successful three-tier care transformation framework (Figure 3.1) and then assessing and assisting users in moving from basic to advanced EHR use (Figure 3.2).

The foundational requirement in an EHR system-enabled care transformation framework (Figure 3.1) is an EHR system that works. This means that the IT staff and EHR implementation team

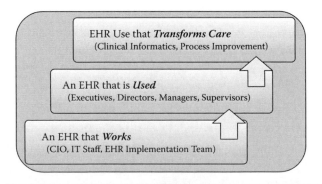

Figure 3.1 Electronic health record system-enabled care transformation framework: Stepwise goals and change leaders.

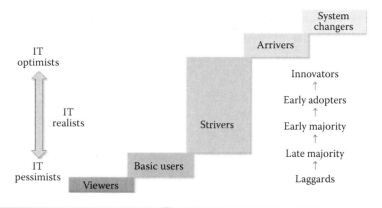

Figure 3.2 Attitudes regarding use of information technology and stages of EHR use.

combine to complete the IT technical infrastructure and build tasks required to deliver an EHR system that functions according to agreed on user requirements and is dependable and responsive. The second requirement is an EHR system that is used. This outcome is fundamentally dependent on the leadership and culture of the organization. Responsibility for physician engagement and alignment around a shared quality agenda,[42] accountability all the way to the board of directors, and elimination of "normalization of deviance"[4] from important policies and procedures regarding EHR training and use in patient care are all critical to quality and MU. All of these depend on the combination of formal organizational leadership and the building of a culture in which coworkers support each other in MU and correct themselves and each other when deviance from standards for appropriate use are observed. The third requirement is an EHR system that transforms care, which requires the clinical informatics leadership, expertise, and resources to formulate and execute the principles and strategies for use of HIT and EHR systems to accelerate continuous process improvement and care transformation.

At the individual EHR user level, it is important to recognize the differences between people with regard to their attitudes about change and the adoption of new technology, as well as factors (incentives and inducements) that affect their willingness to strive to progress from simple data viewing and basic EHR use to become highly competent users and even system changers (Figure 3.2).[53] Those with an EHR system already in place have most likely already identified the 15% or so of those IT optimistic individuals in their organization who are best characterized on the Rogers' technology adoption curve[54] as innovators or early adopters of IT. Supported by appropriate payment policy but otherwise with minimal encouragement, these individuals can be counted on to strive to become highly competent EHR users and will spontaneously help build enthusiasm for EHR adoption and MU by others as well. With appropriate training and support, some of these folks will become EHR champions or superusers who can be relied on to help other users make progress, try out enhanced EHR features and functionalities, or serve on EHR advisory committees.

Roughly two-thirds of the individuals in an organization can be expected to use the EHR early on only if it is communicated by leadership as a clear expectation, with monitoring and accountability. The early majority represents about half of this group and is more accepting of change than the more skeptical late majority. Understandably, executives can generally get behind expectation setting with accountability only when it is clear to them that the organization has installed an EHR that works, making it reasonable to hold people accountable for EHR training and regular, appropriate use.

However, inevitably the organization will be left with approximately 15% of its people lagging behind. These so-called laggards[54] often simply prefer the old way of doing things. They tend to be suspicious and critical of new approaches. In some cases they not only prefer the status quo but may also inadvertently disrupt the change process or even deliberately "poison the well" for others trying to lead or implement sorely needed organizational change. Without the input of considerable energy from others, laggards are unlikely to use the EHR or to use it appropriately until it has become the way almost everyone else is doing their work. For some, they will use the EHR only when the old way (e.g., paper, transcription, verbal orders) is no longer provided as an option. Rarely, some would rather leave an organization than adopt the new technology. Informatics experts and clinical leaders commonly struggle to decide how best to deal with these individuals. At one end of the spectrum, they may either accept or manage the clinician's unwillingness to adopt and use an EHR by allowing full exemption from EHR use (paper documentation with post-encounter document scanning and indexing), accepting "EHR light" use (dictation and transcription, viewing and signing results), or providing EHR-competent scribes. At the other end of the spectrum, employed laggards may face financial penalties or termination from employment if they are persistently unwilling or unable to become regular and meaningful users of the EHR system, while nonemployed laggards may face suspension or revocation of admitting or consulting privileges.

There are many trade-offs in any approach to resolving the problems associated with laggard noncompliance with EHR training or use expectations. Our advice is to set reasonable expectations and accountability for EHR use in advance and then measure, monitor, and enforce the expectations consistently. This should be done independent of rank, experience, or extent of push back about the adequacy of the system for use, particularly if other physicians and staff are consistently able to use the same EHR system to safely and effectively deliver similar care for similar patients using reasonable workflows. Failure to do so will simply teach others that foot dragging or negative behaviors are acceptable and effective ways of resisting needed change, while decreasing the morale of those who have exhibited the professionalism and dedication to strive to become competent and meaningful EHR users.

Assessing and Redesigning Your Practice

"Every system is perfectly designed to get the results it gets."[55] Although this is a sobering comment in light of the defects in the U.S. healthcare delivery system described previously, it also suggests the path to improved quality in healthcare—by carefully redesigning care, we can expect better results. The challenge is to identify resources and implement strategies that allow us to regularly deliver to our patients what Berwick and colleagues have termed the "triple aim"[56] of better experience of care (patient-centered, effective, safe, timely, efficient, and equitable), better health for the population, and lower total per capita costs. Although front-line clinicians may feel they have limited ability to influence healthcare redesign at a macro level, each local care team working closely and regularly with each other to provide care to a specific group of patients constitutes a clinical microsystem that, through a process of practice assessment and redesign,[57–62] can expand access,[60] improve effectiveness, advance safety, enhance patient and staff satisfaction, decrease waste and waiting, and leverage HIT to automate otherwise cumbersome manual processes. The

Dartmouth Institute for Health Policy and Clinical Practice maintains a comprehensive and useful set of clinical microsystem resources on its website,[61] including *Clinical Microsystem Assessment Tool*[62] and *Clinical Microsystem Action Guide.*[63]

Another rich source of useful information and tools for assessing practices and improving care delivery systems is the Institute for Healthcare Improvement (IHI) website.[64] Particularly relevant and helpful resources include improvement methods,[65] presentation handouts from previous annual international summits on redesigning the clinical office practice,[66] and white papers,[67] including topics such as going lean in healthcare,[68] engaging physicians in a shared quality agenda,[42] transforming care at the bedside,[69] and improving the reliability of healthcare.[70]

Finally, numerous resources are available from a number of professional organizations and societies to assist in developing strategies and plans for selection, implementation, and use of HIT and EHR systems to improve quality and achieve MU. For example, the Health Information and Management Systems Society (HIMSS) offers useful conferences, educational programs, information, and resources in a wide variety of areas spanning the spectrum of healthcare reform, EHR systems, clinical informatics, IT privacy and security, interoperability, IT standards, ambulatory information systems, and financial systems.[71] Likewise, the American Medical Informatics Association (AMIA)[72] provides programs and resources to support the effectiveness of healthcare industry professionals in using information and IT to support patient care, public health, teaching, research, administration, and related policy. Specialty societies have also made useful resources for EHR selection, implementation, and MU available, such as the Center for Practice Improvement and Innovation at the American College of Physicians[73] and the Center for Health IT at the American Academy of Family Physicians.[74]

Information Technology Strategies to Use Gains from Meaningful Use to Improve Quality and Value

Once the hospital or office practice leadership has shaped its culture and systems so that physicians and staff can be counted on to use clinical information systems regularly and appropriately, the next issue is to determine the HIT and EHR features and functionalities that are necessary or desirable, not only for MU, but also to support other quality initiatives, practice improvement activities, resource use, and readiness to participate in alternative payment models. As explicit CMS incentive payments for MU sunset and MU become an important but more integral part of consolidated incentive payments for outcomes, EPs, EHs, and CAHs will need to continue to ensure that they have the CEHRT in place and in regular use to meet the goals, objectives, and measures developed by the Health IT Policy Committee as part of the ARRA and HITECH Act, such as the current objectives and measures listed for EPs for MU Stage 2,[75] but it is important to be mindful that these are likely to be updated for 2015–2017.[35] Recognizing that the details and thresholds for specific objectives are in flux, we outline strategies for achieving these MU goals, objectives, and reporting requirements, which we believe will be relevant regardless of the details of the final objectives and measures. Also, rather than detailing the differences between provider and hospital objectives and measures, we will emphasize the system features and functionalities that need to be in place and used to qualify for MU and to be ready for future payment models. Note also that in the lists to follow, we use an asterisk (*) to signify that an item is no longer a separately reported measure but required as part of another measure. In addition, we have italicized items that have been proposed for removal for 2015–2017.[35]

Policy Priority 1: Improve Quality, Safety,
Efficiency, and Reduce Health Disparities

The care goals for this health outcomes policy priority are to (1) provide the patient's care team with access to comprehensive patient health data, (2) use evidence-based orders sets and computerized provider order entry (CPOE), (3) apply clinical decision support (CDS) at the point of care, (4) generate lists of patients who need care and use the lists to reach out to patients, and (5) report to patient registries for quality improvement and public reporting. The objectives include expectations for electronically capturing in coded format information to allow tracking and reporting on key clinical conditions. To that end and for each patient, qualifying providers and hospitals will be expected to:

- Use CPOE for medication, imaging, and laboratory orders
- Implement drug–drug, drug–allergy, and drug–formulary checks
- *Maintain a current problem list
- Use electronic prescribing for permissible prescriptions
- *Maintain an active medication list
- *Maintain an active medication allergy list
- *Record demographics (race, ethnicity, gender, insurance type, primary language)*
- Record advance directives (hospitals only)
- *Record vital signs (height, weight, blood pressure)*
- Calculate and display body mass index (BMI)
- *Record smoking status*
- *Incorporate laboratory/test results into EHR as structured data*
- *Generate lists of patients by specific conditions*
- *Report quality measures to CMS
- *Send patients reminders per patient preference for preventive/ follow-up care*
- Implement five clinical decision support rules related to four or more clinical quality measures, relevant to specialty or high clinical priority
- *Document progress note for each office encounter*

Electronically capturing these data in a structured format is critical to ensuring that the EHR database contains the necessary information for reporting quality measures to CMS, such as the percentage of:

- Diabetics with A1c under control
- Hypertensive patients with blood pressure under control
- Patients with low-density lipoprotein (LDL) cholesterol under control
- Smokers offered smoking cessation counseling
- Patients with a recorded body mass index (BMI)
- Orders entered directly by licensed healthcare professionals through CPOE
- Patients older than age 65 receiving high-risk medications
- Patients older than age 50 with colorectal cancer screening
- Female patients older than age 50 receiving an annual mammogram

- Patients at high risk for cardiac events on aspirin prophylaxis
- Patients receiving flu vaccine
- Percent of lab results incorporated into EHR in coded format
- Medications entered into EHR as generic when generic options exist in the relevant drug class
- Orders for high-cost imaging services with specific structured indications recorded
- Claims admitted electronically to all payers
- Patient encounters with insurance eligibility confirmed

To meet the Stage 2 objectives and report the measures, we recommend the following EHR functionalities (supported by a practice management system or third-party vendor solutions where relevant) be installed and operational:

- Structured data entry mechanisms acceptable to users for entering patient demographics, advance directives, orders, problems, medications, allergies, vital signs, relevant history (e.g., smoking status), and interventions (e.g., smoking cessation counseling)
- Functioning interfaces from the laboratory and radiology information systems to the EHR for receiving results
- E-prescribing capability that includes drug–drug, drug–allergy, and drug–formulary checks
- Clinical decision support functionality (calculating and displaying BMI, creating clinical decision rules)
- Registry functionality with actionable views and communication tools (secure messaging for reminders)
- EHR data mining and reporting tools

Policy Priority 2: Engage Patients and Families

The care goal for this health outcomes policy priority is to provide patients and families with timely access to data, knowledge, and tools to make informed decisions and to manage their health. To demonstrate MU in Stage 2, providers and hospitals will be expected to:

- Provide patients access to view, download, or transmit health information

- Use information stored in CEHRT to identify and provide patient-specific educational materials
- *Provide patients with a clinical visit summary for each encounter*
- Implement a mechanism for patients to send secure messages to the EP's practice

Assessing the degree of patient and family engagement will entail reporting the following Stage 2 measures to CMS, including the percentage of:

- Patients who have access to view, download, or transmit health information, as well as patients who actually do so
- Patients who are provided with or who have access to patient-specific educational resources identified by CEHRT
- Encounters where a clinical visit summary was provided
- Patients with patient-initiated secure messages sent to the EP's practice

To meet the Stage 2 patient and family engagement objectives and report the measures, we recommend the following functionalities be installed and operational:

- EHR-supported workflows that result in capture of relevant information to populate the clinical encounter
- The ability at the point of care to electronically transmit educational materials to the patient from within usual EHR workflows (e.g., electronically send to the patient portal rather than print handouts)
- A secure, EHR-linked patient Web portal with the capability to support selective EHR chart views (e.g., problem list, medication list, allergies, lab results), secure messaging, condition-specific educational resources, encounter summaries, and an option for the patient to have a personal health record (PHR)

Policy Priority 3: Improve Care Coordination

The care goal for this health outcomes policy priority is to exchange meaningful clinical information among professional healthcare teams. The Stage 2 objectives for care coordination are to:

- Send summary of care records with transitions out to other providers, with a threshold for electronic exchanges using specified mechanisms (e.g., Direct Protocol)
- Perform medication reconciliation at transitions of care into the care of the EP, EH, or CAH

The care coordination reporting requirements for Stage 2 include the following:

- Percent of encounters where medication reconciliation was performed
- Percent of outbound care transitions where a summary of care record is sent by any modality, and the percent sent electronically

To meet the Stage 2 care coordination objectives and report the measures, we recommend the following functionalities be installed and operational:

- An EHR-integrated secure clinical messaging solution that includes Direct Protocol functionality and allows secure sending and receipt of consolidated clinical document architecture (CCDA) formatted clinical summaries, messages, and electronic chart documents to other patient-authorized entities, whether or not the external entity has an EHR system in place
- An audit system to record and report instances of exchange of health information, including summary of care records shared, as well as the context in which they occur (e.g., admission, discharge, transfer, referral, follow-up)
- Medication reconciliation functionality that allows for recording of medication changes between visits and at transitions of care, as well as incorporating evidence of fill history to capture medications prescribed but not filled and medications added or changed by other providers

Policy Priority 4: Improve Population and Public Health

The goal of this health outcomes policy priority is communication with public health agencies. The Stage 2 objectives for improving population and public health are to:

- Submit electronic data to immunization registries where required and accepted (EPs)
- Submit electronic syndrome surveillance data to public health agencies according to applicable law and practice (EHs)

The population and public health reporting requirements for Stage 2 include the following:

- Report up-to-date status of childhood immunizations
- Percent of reportable laboratory results submitted electronically

To meet the Stage 2 population and public health objectives and report the measures to CMS, we recommend the following EHR functionalities be installed and operational:

- Immunization recording tools that capture all relevant immunization data in a structured manner to support reporting to state immunization registries and CMS
- An interface from the EHR to the external immunization registry in regions where actual submission of immunization information is required and can be accepted
- Auditing tools for reporting on all structured data (e.g., lab results) submitted electronically to public health entities

Policy Priority 5: Ensure Adequate Privacy and Security Protections for Personal Health Information

This health outcomes policy priority seeks to ensure privacy and security protections for confidential information through operating policies, procedures, and technologies and compliance with applicable law. It also works toward the goal of providing transparency of data sharing to patients. The Stage 2 objectives for privacy and security protections include the following:

- Compliance with HIPAA privacy and security rules
- Compliance with fair data sharing practices set forth in the national privacy and security framework[76]

The privacy and security protections reporting requirements for Stage 2 are to:

- Demonstrate full compliance with the HIPAA privacy and security rule[77]
- Conduct or update a security risk assessment and implement security updates as necessary

To meet the Stage 2 privacy and security protection objectives and report the measures to CMS, we recommend the usual organizational IT technical approaches for safeguarding patient information (e.g., firewalls, virtual private networks, intranets, data encryption (including encryption of data at rest), prevention of protected health information (PHI) data storage on local devices, strong authentication) and strong organizational policies and procedures for identity proofing, user authentication, and authorization, as well as for preventing, detecting, and taking action on instances of suspected breaches in patient data privacy, confidentiality, and security. In addition, we recommend the following EHR functionalities be installed and operational:

- EHR system configuration to support strong user authentication and role-based privileges
- Use of EHR functionalities to "hide" information that a particular user is not authorized to view under any circumstances (e.g., highly confidential documents, sensitive charts)
- Activation of "break the glass" tools (where appropriate) to warn users in advance of potentially unauthorized chart or information access, with options to record a reason for seeking access (e.g., emergency), enhanced auditing of those who proceed, and additional scrutiny of those who do not
- Activation of auditing tools to enable tracking of all relevant details of EHR system access, chart access, patient data and document viewing, modification, deletion, storage, printing, and transmission
- Ability to facilitate delivery and electronically record delivery of privacy practices notices to individual patients
- Creation of automated reports using filters that have a high signal-to-noise ratio, creating a short list of individuals that are highly likely to have accessed patient data inappropriately, rather than a long list of individuals, most of whom accessed charts appropriately

Meaningful Use: The Road Ahead

This chapter was written during a period of great flux in the MU and EHR certification programs. Three proposed rules were finalized, including: (1) electronic health record incentive program modifications to MU in 2015 through 2017[35]; (2) the CMS MU Stage 3 proposed rule,[36] and the ONC 2015 Edition HIT certification criteria, base EHR definition, and HIT certification program modifications.[37] While the full implications of these Final Rules will be revealed over the next several years, it is clear that HHS, CMS, and ONC have employed various regulatory and policy levers to drive interoperability, simplify and synchronize the MU program, align MU reporting periods, improve various aspects of clinical quality measurement and reporting, focus on clinically relevant outcomes, and promote alternative health models and alternative payment systems. While CMS has announced that it intends Stage 3 to be the final stage of the MU incentive program, inclusion of MU as one of the four performance categories of MACRA ensures that the objectives and measures included in the Stage 3 Final Rule will continue to drive how CEHRT is used to advance the overarching goals of the HITECH Act and MU program.

Although the details of the Stage 3 program may change further as CMS weighs the comments it received following publication of the Final Rule and incorporates the Meaningful Use program into the Merit-Based Incentive Payment System (MIPS), EPs, EHs, and CAHs can anticipate following:

- By 2018, everyone will be on the same stage of MU (Stage 3), regardless of how long they have been in the program.
- There will be only one set of objectives, measures, and thresholds.
- All MU participants will be required to use 2015 Edition CEHRT.
- Everyone will have the same calendar year reporting period (with the possible exception of Medicaid Year 1 EPs).
- MU quality measure reporting will be simplified by alignment with other quality measure programs, such as the Physician Quality Reporting System (PQRS) and Hospital Inpatient Quality Reporting (IQR).
- Quality measures will not be proposed in the MU reporting program itself. Instead, quality measures will be incorporated

annually in the Inpatient Prospective Payment System (IPPS) and Physician Fee Schedule (PFS) rules where Hospital IQR and PQRS are defined.

- Electronic submission of Clinical Quality Measures (eCQMs) will be required (with some exceptions).
- A number of measures will be removed for individual reporting because they were deemed to be topped out, redundant, or duplicative.

MU will focus on eight objectives, several of which have multiple measures that must be reported but not all will require exceeding the threshold:

1. Protect Patient Health Information
2. Electronic Prescribing
3. Clinical Decision Support
4. CPOE
5. Patient Electronic Access to Health Information
6. Coordination of Care through Patient Engagement
7. Health Information Exchange (HIE)
8. Public Health and Clinical Data Registry Reporting

EPs, EHs, and CAHs will do well to continue to focus on leveraging HIT to capture and share data, advance clinical processes, and improve patient outcomes. They will benefit from expanding their use of CPOE and evidence-based order sets, focusing their EHR clinical documentation in a manner that facilitates identifying and closing gaps in care, e-prescribing discharge medications, managing chronic conditions using patient lists and population health management tools, utilizing robust clinical decision support at the point of care, having specialists report data to external registries, and implementing closed-loop medication management, including electronic medication administration records and computer-assisted medication administration.

As engaging patients in their own care can facilitate goals for quality and value, health professionals and organizations will benefit from providing access for all patients to a personal health record, a patient Web portal populated with health data in real time, or APIs offering secure patient–provider messaging capability, providing patient-specific educational resources in common primary languages, recording patient preferences, documenting family medical history, and uploading data from home monitoring devices. Care coordination will benefit from being able to retrieve and act on electronic prescription fill data, production and sharing of an electronic summary care record for every transition of care, and medication reconciliation at each transition of care from one health setting to another.

Continued engagement around population and public health objectives will facilitate bidirectional exchange of immunization histories and recommendations from immunization registries, receiving health alerts from public health agencies, and providing sufficiently anonymized electronic syndrome surveillance data to public health agencies with the capacity to link to personal identifiers. Privacy and security protection will become increasingly challenging in this time of increasingly sophisticate cyberattacks, and must be balanced with the need to access PHI for clinical care and the generation of summarized or de-identified data when reporting data for population health purposes.

To drive quality and value from today into the future, providers and hospitals should be routinely using CDS for national high-priority conditions, achieve medical device integration, and deploy multimedia support for imaging technology. Patients should have access to online self-management tools, be able to complete online health questionnaires, upload data from home health devices, and report electronically on their experiences of care. Health information exchanges of various types should facilitate access to comprehensive patient data from all available and appropriate sources; enable use of epidemiologic data in clinical decision making; and allow for automated real-time surveillance for adverse events, near misses, disease outbreaks, and bioterrorism. Clinical dashboards and dynamic and ad hoc quality reports should also be routinely available. Privacy and security goals include providing patients with an accounting of treatment, payment, and healthcare operations disclosures on request, as well as minimizing the reluctance of patients to seek care because of privacy concerns.

In closing, we are reminded once again that our healthcare iceberg is melting. For all the risks associated with change and all of the unintended consequences of the MU incentive program, failing to adopt and meaningfully use EHR systems risks leaving our patients behind, while the healthcare system they depend on and those who financially support it strain under the weight of inconsistent quality, excessive waste, and unsustainable cost increases. Though imperfect, we see the MU incentive program and the various federal agencies promoting the safe and effective use of HIT as powerful catalysts for needed change. We also see provider payment reform as reflected in MACRA as necessary for durable change, by transitioning a significant fraction of payment away from volume and procedures and instead rewarding HIT–powered improvements in quality, value, and outcomes. Although EHR systems are also far from where they need to be to optimally support effectiveness, efficiency, interoperability, safety, and health information exchange, many are good enough to make continued striving to implement and use them reasonable and worth including in incentive programs going forward. It's "quality time"—time to keep moving on the journey to transform care.

References

1. Kotter J, Rathgeber H. 2006. *Our iceberg is melting: Changing and succeeding under any conditions.* New York: St. Martin's Press.
2. Kotter J. 1996. *Leading change.* Boston: Harvard Business School Press.
3. Park T, Basch P. 2009. *Wedding health information technology to care delivery innovation and provider payment reform.* Washington, DC. Available at: http://www.americanprogress.org/issues/2009/05/health_it.html.
4. Nance J. 2008. *Why hospitals should fly—The ultimate flight plan to patient safety and quality care.* Bozeman, MT: Second River Healthcare Press.
5. *Health expenditure per capita (current US$).* The World Bank, 2015. Available at: http://data.worldbank.org/indicator/SH.XPD.PCAP.
6. Health expenditure, total (% of GDP). The World Bank, 2015. Available at: http://data.worldbank.org/indicator/SH.XPD.TOTL.ZS.
7. O'Neill PH. 2006. Testimony in hearings before the Senate Committee on Commerce. Senate Committee on Commerce. 109th Congress, 2nd session. Washington, DC.
8. Milstein A. 2004. Testimony in hearings before the Senate Committee on Health, Education, Labor, and Pension. Senate Committee on Health, Education, Labor, and Pension. 108th Congress, 2nd session. Washington, DC.
9. PricewaterhouseCoopers Health Research Institute. 2008. *The price of excess: Identifying waste in healthcare spending.* Dallas: PricewaterhouseCoopers.
10. Ginsburg JA, Doherty RB, Ralston JF Jr, Senkeeto N, Cooke M, Cutler C et al. 2008. Achieving a high-performance health care system with universal access: What the United States can learn from other countries. *Ann Intern Med* 148:55–75.

11. Smith JC, Medalia C. Health Insurance in the United States: 2013. U.S. Department of Commerce, Economics and Statistics Administration, U.S. Census Bureau. Available at: http://www.census.gov/content/dam/Census/library/publications/2014/demo/p60-250.pdf.
12. Brotherton SE, Etzel SI. 2008. Graduate medical education, 2007–2008. *JAMA* 300:1228–43.
13. Kaiser Family Foundation. 2009. *Medicare beneficiaries and the number of workers per beneficiary.* Menlo Park, CA: Henry J. Kaiser Family Foundation.
14. Fisher ES, Wennberg DE, Stukel TA, Gottlieb DJ, Lucas FL, Pinder EL. 2003. The implications of regional variations in Medicare spending. Part 2. Health outcomes and satisfaction with care. *Ann Intern Med* 138:288–98.
15. Fisher ES, Wennberg DE, Stukel TA, Gottlieb DJ, Lucas FL, Pinder EL. 2003. The implications of regional variations in Medicare spending. Part 1. The content, quality, and accessibility of care. *Ann Intern Med* 138:273–87.
16. Baicker K, Chandra A. 2004. Medicare spending, the physician workforce, and beneficiaries' quality of care. *Health Aff* (Millwood) *Suppl Web Exclusives* W184–97.
17. Gawande A. 2009. The cost conundrum. *The New Yorker,* June 1.
18. Zerehi MR. 2008. How is the shortage of primary care physicians affecting the quality and cost of medical care? Philadelphia: American College of Physicians. White Paper.
19. O'Malley AS, Forrest CB. 2006. Immunization disparities in older Americans: Determinants and future research needs. *Am J Prev Med* 31:150–58.
20. Lewis CE, Clancy C, Leake B, Schwartz JS. 1991. The counseling practices of internists. *Ann Intern Med* 114:54–58.
21. Macinko J, Starfield B, Shi L. 2003. The contribution of primary care systems to health outcomes within Organization for Economic Cooperation and Development (OECD) countries, 1970–1998. *Health Serv Res* 38:831–65.
22. Carey TS, Garrett J, Jackman A, McLaughlin C, Fryer J, Smucker DR. 1995. The outcomes and costs of care for acute low back pain among patients seen by primary care practitioners, chiropractors, and orthopedic surgeons. The North Carolina Back Pain Project. *N Engl J Med* 333:913–17.
23. Greenfield S, Rogers W, Mangotich M, Carney MF, Tarlov AR. 1995. Outcomes of patients with hypertension and non-insulin dependent diabetes mellitus treated by different systems and specialties. Results from the medical outcomes study. *JAMA* 274:1436–44.
24. How SKH, Shih A, Lau J, Schoen C. 2008. *Public views on U.S. health system organization: A call for new directions,* The Commonwealth Fund, 11:1–15.
25. Kohn L, Corrigan, J, Donaldson, MS, eds. 2000. *To err is human: Building a safer health system.* Washington, DC: National Academies Press.

26. Committee on Quality Health Care in America IOM. 2001. *Crossing the quality chasm: A new health system for the 21st century.* Washington, DC: National Academies Press.

27. Dick RS, Steen EB, Detmer DE, eds. 1997. *The computer-based patient record: An essential technology for health care.* Rev. ed. Washington, DC: National Academies Press.

28. Hillestad R, Bigelow J, Bower A, Girosi F, Meili R, Scoville R et al. 2005. Can electronic medical record systems transform health care? Potential health benefits, savings, and costs. *Health Aff* (Millwood) 24:1103–17.

29. Walker J, Pan E, Johnston D, Adler-Milstein J, Bates DW, Middleton B. 2005. The value of health care information exchange and interoperability. *Health Aff* (Millwood).

30. Girosi F, Meili R, Scoville R. 2005. *Extrapolating evidence of health information technology savings and costs.* Santa Monica, CA: Rand Corporation.

31. Chaudhry B, Wang J, Wu S, Maglione M, Mojica W, Roth E et al. 2006. Systematic review: Impact of health information technology on quality, efficiency, and costs of medical care. *Ann Intern Med* 144:742–52.

32. Halamka JD. 2006. Health information technology: Shall we wait for the evidence? *Ann Intern Med* 144:775–76.

33. American Recovery and Reinvestment Act of 2009. In: 111 ed. USA, p. 407. Available at: http://healthit.hhs.gov/portal/server.pt?open=512 &objID=1325&parentname=CommunityPage&parentid=1&mode=2.

34. Health Information Technology Federal Advisory Committees. 2009. Washington, DC: U.S. Department of Health and Human Services.

35. Medicare and Medicaid Programs; Electronic Health Record Incentive Program-Modifications to Meaningful Use in 2015 Through 2017. Department of Health and Human Services, Centers for Medicare & Medicaid Services, April 15, 2015. Available at: https://federalregister .gov/a/2015-08514.

36. Medicare and Medicaid Programs; Electronic Health Record Incentive Program-Stage 3 and Modifications to Meaningful Use in 2015 Through 2017. Available at: https://www.federalregister.gov/articles/2015/10/16 /2015-25595/medicare-and-medicaid-programs-electronic-health -record-incentive-program-stage-3-and-modifications.

37. 2015 Edition Health Information Technology (Health IT) Certification Criteria, 2015 Edition Base Electronic Health Record (EHR) Definition, and ONC Health IT Certification Program Modifications March 30, 2015. Available at: https://federalregister.gov/a/2015-06612.

38. Better, Smarter, Healthier: In historic announcement, HHS sets clear goals and timeline for shifting Medicare reimbursements from volume to value. U.S. Department of Health & Human Services. January 26, 2015. Available at: http://www.hhs.gov/news/press/2015pres/01/20150126a .html.

39. H.R.2—Medicare Access and CHIP Reauthorization Act of 2015. Public Law No: 114-10 (04/16/2015), US Library of Congress. Available at: https://www.congress.gov/bill/114th-congress/house-bill/2/text.

40. HIMSS Fact Sheet: Medicare Access and CHIP Reauthorization Act of 2015 (MACRA). Health Information and Management Systems Society, April 23, 2015. Available at: http://www.himss.org/Resource Library/genResourceDetailPDF.aspx?ItemNumber=41882.

41. Meaningful use. 2009. Washington, DC: U.S. Department of Health and Human Services. Available at: http://healthit.hhs.gov/portal/server .pt?open=512&objID=1325&parentname=CommunityPage&parentid =1&mode=2.

42. Reinertsen JL, Gosfield AG, Rupp W, Whittington JW. 2007. *Engaging physicians in a shared quality agenda.* IHI Innovation Series white paper. Cambridge, MA: Institute for Healthcare Improvement.

43. Zaroukian MH, Sierra A. 2006. Benefiting from ambulatory EHR implementation: Solidarity, Six Sigma, and willingness to strive. *J Healthcare Inf Manag* 20:53–60.

44. Health information technology donations: A guide for physicians. 2008. Chicago.

45. Rucker DW, Steele AW, Douglas IS, Coudere CA, Hardel GG. 2006. Design and use of a joint order vocabulary knowledge representation tier in a multi-tier CPOE architecture. *AMIA Annu Symp Proc* 2006:669–73.

46. Ash JS, Berg M, Coiera E. 2004. Some unintended consequences of information technology in health care: The nature of patient care information system-related errors. *J Am Med Inform Assoc* 11:104–12.

47. Ash JS, Sittig DF, Poon EG, Guappone K, Campbell E, Dykstra RH. 2007. The extent and importance of unintended consequences related to computerized provider order entry. *J Am Med Inform Assoc* 14(4):415–423.

48. Koppel R, Wetterneck T, Telles JL, Karsh BT. 2008. Workarounds to barcode medication administration systems: Their occurrences, causes, and threats to patient safety. *J Am Med Inform Assoc* 15:408–23.

49. Koppel R, Leonard CE, Localio AR, Cohen A, Auten R, Strom BL. 2008. Identifying and quantifying medication errors: Evaluation of rapidly discontinued medication orders submitted to a computerized physician order entry system. *J Am Med Inform Assoc* 15:461–65.

50. Harrison MI, Koppel R, Bar-Lev S. 2007. Unintended consequences of information technologies in health care—An interactive sociotechnical analysis. *J Am Med Inform Assoc* 14:542–49.

51. Koppel R, Metlay JP, Cohen A, Abaluck B, Localio AR, Kimmel SE et al. 2005. Role of computerized physician order entry systems in facilitating medication errors. *JAMA* 293:1197–203.

52. Koppel R. 2005. What do we know about medication errors made via a CPOE system versus those made via handwritten orders? *Crit Care* 9:427–28.

53. Miller RH, Sim I, Newman J. 2004. Electronic medical records in solo/small groups: A qualitative study of physician user types. *Medinfo* 2004:658–62.

54. Rogers EM. 2003. *Diffusion of innovations.* 5th ed. New York: Free Press.

55. Batalden P. 1984. *Every system is perfectly designed to get the results it gets.* Available at: www.dartmouth.edu/~cecs/hcild/hcild.html.

56. Berwick DM, Nolan TW, Whittington J. 2008. The triple aim: Care, health, and cost. *Health Aff* (Millwood) 27:759–69.

57. Godfrey MM, Nelson EC, Batalden PB. 2004. Assessing your practice: The green book. Dartmouth College, Institute for Healthcare Improvement.

58. Godfrey MM, Nelson EC, Batalden PB. 2005. Assessing, diagnosing and treating your inpatient unit. In *Clinical microsystems greenbooks.* 2nd ed. Hanover, NH: Dartmouth College.

59. Godfrey MM, Nelson EC, Batalden PB. 2005. Assessing, diagnosing and treating your outpatient specialty care practice. In *Clinical microsystems greenbooks.* 2nd ed. Hanover, NH: Dartmouth College.

60. Murray M, Tantau C, eds. 2002. *Improving patient access to care—Primary care.* 2nd ed. Lebanon, NH: Trustees of Dartmouth College.

61. *Clinical microsystems.* Hanover, NH: Dartmouth College.

62. Johnson JK. 2003. *Clinical microsystem assessment tool.* 2nd ed. Lebanon, NH: Dartmouth College. Available at: http://dms.dartmouth.edu/cms.

63. Godfrey MM, Nelson EC, Batalden PB, Wasson JH, Mohr JJ, Huber T et al. 2004. *Clinical microsystem action guide.* 2nd ed. Hanover, NH: Dartmouth College.

64 IHI.org. A resource from the Institute for Healthcare Improvement. Cambridge, MA: Institute for Healthcare Improvement.

65. IHI.org. Improvement methods. Cambridge, MA: Institute for Healthcare Improvement.

66. 10th Annual International Summit on Redesigning the Clinical Office Practice. 2009. Cambridge, MA: Institute for Healthcare Improvement.

67. IHI.org. White papers. Cambridge, MA: Institute for Healthcare Improvement.

68. Institute for Healthcare Improvement. 2005. *Going lean in health care.* Cambridge, MA: Institute for Healthcare Improvement.

69. Rutherford P, Lee B, Greiner A. 2004. *Transforming care at the bedside.* IHI Innovation Series White Paper. Boston: Institute for Healthcare Improvement.

70. Nolan T, Resar RCH, Griffin FA. 2004. *Improving the reliability of health care.* IHI Innovation Series White Paper. Boston: Institute for Healthcare Improvement.

71. Health Information Management and Systems Society. *HIMSS topics and tools.* Chicago: Health Information Management and Systems Society.

72. American Medical Informatics Association. Bethesda: American Medical Informatics Association. Available at: www.amia.org.

73. Center for Practice Improvement and Innovation. 2009. *Electronic health record systems.* Philadelphia: American College of Physicians.

74. Center for Health IT at the AAFP. 2009. Leawood, KS: American Academy of Family Physicians.

75. Office of the National Coordinator for Health Information Technology. Step 5: Achieve Meaningful Use Stage 2. Available at: http://www.health it.gov/providers-professionals/step-5-achieve-meaningful-use-stage-2.

76. Office of the National Coordinator for Health Information Technology. 2008. *The nationwide privacy and security framework for electronic exchange of individually identifiable health information*. Washington, DC: Office of the National Coordinator for Health Information Technology.

77. Office for Civil Rights. 2003. *OCR privacy brief: Summary of the HIPAA privacy rule*. Washington, DC: U.S. Department of Health and Human Services.

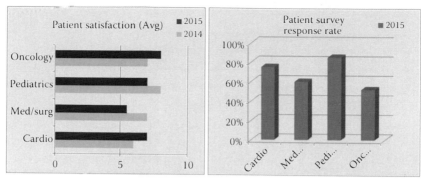

In-patient care area	# Patients daily (Avg)	% Change prev. year	Beds	Capacity rate	Days over capacity
Cardio	50	(2%)	60	83%	5
Med/surg	120	35%	125	96%	20
Pediatrics	42	20%	60	70%	10
Oncology	35	3%	45	78%	8
Total	247		290		43

Figure 11.1 Hospital patient volume and satisfaction.

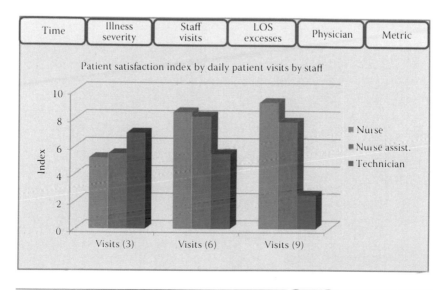

Figure 11.2 Multidimensional cube.

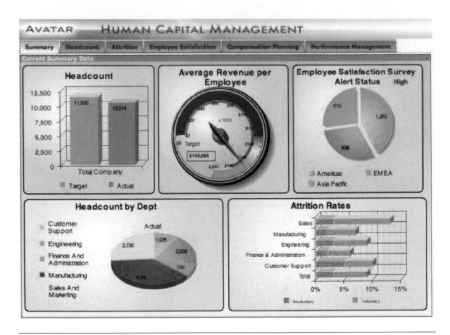

Figure 11.3 Clearly designed employee analytic dashboard. (From http://www.dashboards -for-business.com/dashboards-templates/business-intelligence/business-intelligence-executive -dashboard; Domo, Inc., http://www.domo.com.)

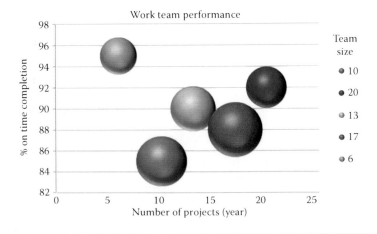

Figure 11.11 Bubble chart depicting workforce team performance.

Figure 11.12 Heat map that illustrates areas of hard-to-fill job vacancies. (From Wanted Analytics, http://www.wantedanalytics.com.)

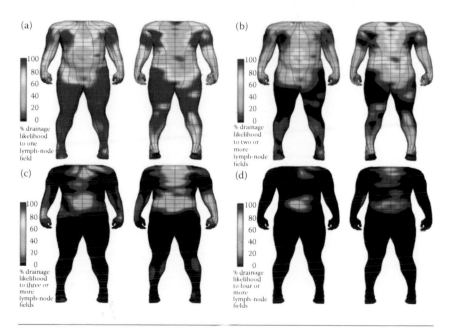

Figure 11.13 Three-dimensional visualization of lymphatic drainage patterns in patients with cutaneous melanoma. (From Reynolds, H., Dunbar, P., Uren, R., Blackett, S., Thompson, J., and Smith, N., Three-dimensional visualisation of lymphatic drainage patterns in patients with cutaneous melanoma, *Lancet Oncol* 8:806–12, 2007 (Figure 1), http://www.thelancet.com/journals/lanonc/article /PIIS1470-2045%2807%2970176-6/fulltext?rss=yes.)

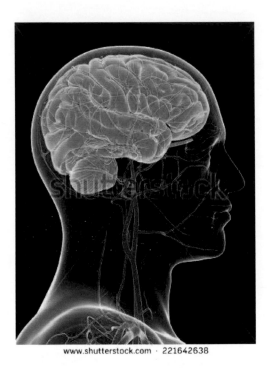

Figure 11.14 Computer tomography image. (From Shutterstock, http://www.shutterstock.com /pic-221642638/stock-photo-medical-illustration-of-the-brain-and-head-arteries.html.)

4

A PROJECT MANAGEMENT FRAMEWORK OF HEALTHCARE INFORMATICS INITIATIVES

CHRISTI RUSHNELL AND MARY BEATTIE

Contents

No one would debate that healthcare organizations are under increased pressure to perform. Healthcare costs continue to skyrocket out of control. Information technology systems are seen as one way to streamline processes and take costs out of a healthcare organization. However, healthcare information systems, specifically clinical information systems, are some of the most complex systems to install. Couple that with the changes in processes necessary to realize the potential savings in expenses and improved quality and safety, and you have one of the toughest projects in any industry to manage.

Solid project management methodologies exist, and if incorporated into the installation process for healthcare information systems, the result should be a more successful launch of an application and greater probability for a successful use of the application integrated into the clinical or business process workflow.

This chapter examines a methodology for project management in a healthcare setting focusing on the life cycle of a project as well as methodologies for incorporating process improvement techniques into a project to receive the most value from an implementation.

Project Management for Healthcare

Project Management Definition

Project management is a formal management discipline, dating as far back as the 1950s. The discipline consists of planning, organizing, and managing resources to reach the successful completion of specific goals and objectives.[1] Although the formal adoption of methodologies started in the 1950s, the use of project management dates back much further. Engineers and architects managed their projects without the formal Gantt charts and Program Evaluation and Review Technique (PERT) diagrams that today's practitioners are so used to. Although there are a variety of definitions, the most common is to look at a project as a temporary endeavor, *one that has a distinct beginning and end*, undertaken to create a unique product, service, or result. Projects and operations differ primarily in that operations are ongoing and repetitive, whereas projects are temporary and unique.

Healthcare Project Environment

The discipline of project management is utilized by all types of industries. The construction and software industries, specifically, have adapted many of the formal methodologies to meet their particular needs. Healthcare, by contrast, has been slow to adapt to the formal methodologies available. However, if any industry needs formal methodologies for managing temporary endeavors, it is the healthcare industry; the fast pace of healthcare change calls for a more streamlined project management approach.[2] In the healthcare informatics arena alone there are so many projects to complete, and the informatics projects are competing with patient care–focused projects, aging building improvement projects, and new revenue-producing service lines. Not unlike other industries, healthcare organizations have long-term risk and financial consequences for project delays, making the successful management of all projects an absolute necessity.

Healthcare is a highly regulated industry, and managing this regulation takes a concerted effort. Managing healthcare information technology projects assists an organization to meet its operational and financial goals. For most project managers, the typical triangle of constraints of time, finances, and resources is enough of a challenge. In healthcare information technology, a fourth constraint comes into play: regulations, whether they come from the state level or national level, must be considered in every project. Adding in the fourth area of focus changes the traditional triangle to a rectangle; however, including regulation as a formal constraint allows a project team to focus on all four areas equally (Figure 4.1).

Formal project management skills allow an organization utilizing proven standards on practice to receive proven results. A project's

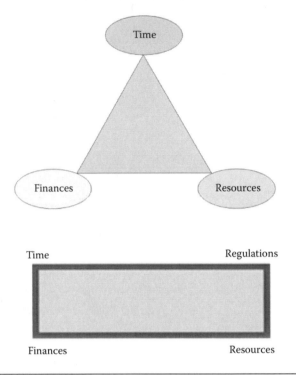

Figure 4.1   Constraints in managing healthcare information technology projects.

success is not always guaranteed if project management principles are utilized; however, without those standards, failure is almost certain.

Project Methodology

Completing project work can be accomplished in a variety of ways, so much so that not having a common, agreed on methodology can often lead to confusion for the project team as well as operational leadership expecting to see results. Adopting a common framework and educating all departments to that methodology streamlines the work effort and ensures that everyone working on a specific project is following the same script. It serves as a guide to the organization as it selects its projects, project teams as they plan the work, management as they supply the required oversight, and sponsors and customers as they collaborate in the design and delivery of new business and change. A commonly utilized methodology is outlined in the Project Management Institute's (PMI®) *A Guide to Project Management Body of Knowledge (PMBOK® Guide)*. It should apply equally well to and meet the requirements of projects large and small. The remainder of this chapter addresses project management methodologies, utilizing PMBOK as a baseline approach.

This chapter describes the process a project manager should use during the five established phases of every project: initiating, planning, execution, managing and controlling, and closeout. As readers go through this chapter, a description of each phase, tasks, and deliverables is suggested. Following this methodology will provide consistency and repeatable processes to help ensure successful project management.

In defining this methodology, we hope to reach the following goals:

- Establish common points of reference vocabulary for talking and writing about the practice of project management
- Increase the awareness and professionalism of good project management by those responsible
- Establish a common collaborative environment where everyone engaged in project work recognizes and understands what is required and the importance of key factors for improving project results

Project Management Office

Before going much further, a good project manager must understand the role a project management office can play in his or her success. Although not a mandatory office, and in healthcare, often not a formal department, a Project Management Office (PMO) is a valuable resource to a project manager. A PMO will have a structure in place to organize projects and manage the project pipeline to reduce the amount of time spent analyzing projects that should not be considered or do not align with strategic objectives. They will keep a complete project portfolio, reducing the number of redundant projects undertaken by various business units. Doing so gives the organization a better understanding of true project resource commitments. Better prediction of the impact of projects on ongoing future operations will help managers avoid making commitments that could jeopardize future results. Understanding the true cost of projects is a first step toward managing that cost. Alignment with other organizational oversight committees will allow for proper alignment with financial and quality functions. Benefits management and postproject benefits assessment will lead to processes that ensure that predicted benefits are actually realized. Using standard, repeatable, and reliable project practices allows better communication, and more important, better control and predictability of project outcomes. Project failures will be reduced; cost and schedule overruns will be reduced. Projects must employ standards that bring them to completion with quality and efficient use of resources; these standards should be tested and modified continuously to ensure that they contribute positively toward that end. For many larger healthcare organizations, projects are a constant where a strong PMO is a way to ensure productivity gains, not losses, are the norm.

Project Life Cycle Phases

Each project phase section of the document is organized as follows:

Overview
Tasks (table)
Deliverables

Phase I: Project Initiation

Overview

Generally, healthcare organizations are composed of people who are highly creative and full of energy. These people deal with everyday issues that range from the insignificant to saving patient lives, so they can be quite creative in conceiving solutions to the problems they face. Hopefully, they present these solutions to the PMO as potential projects.

Projects come about for a variety of reasons and can present themselves at any time. Projects may differ in the degree of benefit that they can bring to the organization, and cost can vary from the very small to the very expensive. Management generally recognizes that great care must be taken in considering which projects to embrace and which to defer. Therefore, most organizations eventually discover that they need a process that will allow them to choose among the project candidates.

The section process occurs during the very first stage of the project life cycle: initiation. The initiation phase is that time in the life cycle of a project when the project idea is defined, evaluated, and then approved by an executive committee or other review group. The project management profession has learned that this process works best when the strategic mission; justification for the project; its significant deliverables, risks, and estimated costs, resource requirements, and other significant information about the project are documented and reviewed in a formal manner. This process provides the executive review group, the project sponsor, and other stakeholders an opportunity to validate the project's potential benefits and costs. In a project management office environment, these project requests are generally reviewed against the project portfolio for further discussion of the right fit with other project initiatives.

The initiation phase provides benefits that include the following:

- Serving as a guide for the project team as they determine and articulate key aspects of a proposed project that will help in the decision process
- Development of a business case that helps ensure that the organization chooses the best projects that meet its needs and that chosen technology projects will be a successful fit for the organizational needs
- Development of a charter that promotes an early collaboration between the project sponsor, the customer(s), and the project team. Early establishment of a good relationship among these key project contributors can help ensure healthy collaboration later in the project
- A well-written business case to establish and communicate clearly what is being proposed, expected benefits, the technical approach to be taken, and how project deliverables fit into ongoing operations

The initiation phase is a success when it leads the organization to select the most pressing business issues for resolution and to choose effective technology to resolve them, and ensures that the organization makes a good investment that is consistent with its long-term strategies.

Activities

The following is a list of key activities necessary for successful development of a business case and initiation of a project.

1. Establish a project sponsor/leader. Every aspect of a project requires someone to guide it, and the initiation phase is no exception. The project sponsor, who may ultimately be different than the project owner or manager, is responsible for defining the purpose of the project and its goals and objectives; gathering strategic and background information; determining high-level planning; and estimating budgets, schedules, and high-level resource requirements for the life of the project. The project owner will coordinate resources and activities to develop and complete the business case and any other materials required for project approval. Since it generally takes more than one person to fully develop a business case, a team of individuals may be required to research, create estimates, and perform other work necessary for the business case document. This team may not actually carry out the project once approved.

> **Task: Establish a Project Sponsor/Leader**
>
> Select a project sponsor or leader.
> Select team members to assist with initiation phase activities.

2. Identify sponsor role and responsibilities. The project sponsor is the single individual, generally at an executive level, who is responsible for the strategic direction and financial support of a project. The project sponsor must have the authority to define project goals; secure resources, from both a financial and a human resource level; and resolve organizational and priority conflicts. Lack of project sponsorship can be a major contributor to project failure, so this role is a key factor in the success of every project.

   Project sponsor responsibilities include the following:

   • Champion the project from initiation to completion
   • Guide the development and articulation of the project business case

- Present the overall vision and business objectives for the project
- Secure final funding and resourcing for the project
- Serve as executive liaison to key stakeholders (e.g., senior management, business owners, and stakeholders)
- Support the project team

Task: Identify a Sponsor

Identify sponsor roles and responsibilities.
Obtain acceptance of project accountability from project sponsor.
Sponsor understands his or her role and is engaged.

3. Define the business need or opportunity. The statement of need or identified opportunity should explain, in business terms, how the proposed project will address specific needs or opportunities within the organization. This statement cannot be general but instead must be specific as to the issue being addressed.

   This information allows an organization to determine how much of its resources (including dollars required as well as people's time) to put into the project. This allows the business decision to be made based on how well the project is expected to meet the business need identified or take advantage of the opportunity.

Task: Define the Business Need or Opportunity

Identify the business need or opportunity.
Determine the resource requirements of the business need or opportunity.
Determine how the business need or opportunity will address the problem.
Determine what would happen if no change is made.
Document the business need or opportunity and its detail in the business case.

4. Identify business objectives and benefits. Every project has a requirement for an investment of time, money, or both. Business objectives define the results that must be achieved for a proposed solution to effectively address the business need or opportunity. Business objectives should be written so they are clearly identified as the immediate reason for investing in the project. Objectives are quantifiable success factors against

which the organization can measure how well the proposed solution addresses the business need or opportunity.

Task: Identify Business Objectives and Benefits

Determine business objectives to ensure they support the business need or opportunity.
Identify process improvement opportunities.
Identify benefits of meeting business objectives.
Use SMART (specific, measurable, achievable, realistic, and time-sensitive) business objectives.
Determine financial cost savings and quality of service improvements.
Document the business objectives and benefits in the business case.

5. Ensure alignment with strategic mission and vision. Every project that an organization commits to must be aligned with its mission and vision to effectively support its business strategy. Many organizations have made use of project portfolio management as a key process in project selection and oversight, which provides for each project to be reviewed for alignment with strategic business goals, selecting only those projects that are best fit for the organization. This works best when health information technology (for technology projects) and business end users partner as part of the process.

Task: Ensure Alignment with Strategic Mission and Vision

Review the organization's strategic business plan.
Review information technology's strategic business plan.
Review business owner or department business plan.
Review current business and technical environment to avoid duplication and ensure fit.
Review project business need and objects to ensure alignment with strategic business plans.
Document how the project is aligned with organization, department, and information
technology strategic vision in the business case.

6. Identify and engage key stakeholders. Stakeholders are defined as individuals and organizations that have a vested interest in the success or failure of the project. During the initiation phase, stakeholders often provide assistance to the project team to define, drive, change, and contribute to the definition of scope. Stakeholders can be key to the success of the project through their buy-in and participation.

To ensure project success, the project team must identify key stakeholders early in the project. As "customers," their needs and expectations must be clearly defined and managed throughout the life cycle of the project. Stakeholders who are not supportive of project goals must be either made into supporters or, at the very least, brought to a place of passive agreement to the project.

Task: Identify Key Stakeholders

Identify internal stakeholders (internal to the organization).
Identify external stakeholders (external to the organization).
Determine stakeholder needs and expectations.
Document key stakeholders in the business case.
Establish a plan to manage key stakeholder expectations throughout
the project life cycle.

7. Determine cost–benefit and schedule estimates. Projects are often part of a larger product life cycle. For example, when a new financial or clinical system is put into place, it is understood that the system will require maintenance and occasional upgrades over its lifetime, will involve operational or support costs, and at some point will be replaced with yet another system. Therefore, the true cost of the overall product must include both the implementation and ongoing operational and maintenance costs.

During the initiation phase, it is important to compare alternative approaches, including full product life cycle costs rather than just project implementation costs. This provides the organization with a true picture of the cost of ownership and demonstrates how the solution provides the greatest value over its lifetime.

Cost–benefit: For the business case, estimate all one-time costs, such as development; acquisition or purchase of hardware, software, middleware, licenses, and leases; implementation costs, including project implementation, professional services, or other resource costs, and then total the costs so that they can be monitored throughout the course of the project life cycle and beyond into operations. Examples of these costs may include the following:

- Maintenance
- Required enhancements
- Upgrades
- Ongoing operation expenses

Calculating the anticipated benefits of the project includes considering tangible and intangible operational benefits, cost savings, cost avoidance, and other benefits that may be identified. These estimates of cost and benefit will determine the anticipated cost savings, revenue gain, and other benefits that are expected to result from the project.

Next, determine how the project will be funded. The project sponsor will play a key role in helping to secure appropriate funds and resources for the project. While this process varies from one organization to the next, it is common for an organization to have a financial budget that may include projected projects, or those previously identified as critical to the organization's strategic vision, as well as a pool of funds that may be discretionary. In some organizations, projects may be funded by the phase of the project so that each phase is evaluated independently and future funding is driven by the success of the project in meeting its anticipated objectives. Projects may be funded from a variety of sources, including internal and external sources, so be sure to indicate the amount of funds required, their primary source, and any special caveats or requirements of each contributor.

It is also recommended that the operational funding resources, those resources that will continue to fund the operational expenses once the project is complete, be identified along with the details of the costs. It is important that all financial considerations, for both implementation and ongoing support of the project, be clearly identified.

Schedule: The initiation phase of most projects does not generally include specific scheduling or schedule planning. While there should be general agreement on the scope of the project, specifics regarding implementation are not generally available in this phase. For this reason, it is usually not expected that anything more than a high-level schedule be provided. This should be made clear in the business case.

The high-level schedule information should include critical tasks, their expected duration, major decision points such as go/no-go decisions, and milestones. Milestones are major events that are identified as completed or not completed on a specified due date. Larger projects, those of lengthy duration or having multiple parts, are done in phases (e.g., evaluation, configuration, activation, etc.). Phasing should be defined in the schedule and make clear the tangible output of each phase. If the project is to be completed in a single phase, it should be clearly defined that way with an explanation as to why the single phase is the most appropriate approach.

Projects may also be planned for a staged implementation approach or one where different parts of the project are delivered at different times. These should be clearly defined as part of the project schedule, with specific deliverables and success criteria for each stage. Generally, each stage must be successfully deployed before the next stage is delivered.

Usually, late or overbudget projects that are seen as failures are actually only estimating failures. This can happen when estimates, usually made in the early stages of a project, are based on inadequate or incomplete data and are used as the expected final. This is a major risk to any project and requires that the initiation phase be clearly defined and articulated as estimates only. One successful approach to mitigating this risk is to update the estimates at each phase of the project. This can even be incorporated as a deliverable at the end of each stage to set an expectation for management and provide valuable reviews to ensure the project still has full support from the organization. Insistence that unreasonable cost and time targets be met only results in a dispirited project team, unhappy customers, poor-quality outcomes, and yet another project failure.

Task: Determine Cost and Schedule Estimates

COST

Estimate one-time costs, including development, acquisition, and implementation.
Estimate maintenance and ongoing operational costs expected after project completion.
Determine anticipated benefits of the project (including tangible and intangible benefits,
 revenue generation, cost savings, cost avoidance, and other benefits).
Explain funding, including funding resources, percentage by resource (if multiple
 resources apply), and any caveats or requirements of each funding source.
Identify the level of confidence in the estimates.

SCHEDULE

Identify high-level tasks for the project, their duration, decision points, and milestones.
Describe the phases of the project, what each phase will deliver, or explain why phasing is
 not appropriate.
Identify the level of confidence in the estimates.
Document project costs and schedule in the business case.

8. Identify potential risks. Every project is full of risks that can be expected or may arise during the course of the project. It is prudent to perform and document an initial risk assessment to identify, quantify, and establish contingencies and mitigation strategies for high-level risks that could adversely affect the outcome of the project.

A *risk* is usually regarded as any unplanned factor that may potentially interfere with successful completion of the project. A risk is not an issue. An *issue* is something you face now, whereas a risk is the recognition that a problem might occur. By recognizing potential problems, the project team can plan in advance how to deal with these factors.

It is also possible to look at a positive side of risk. A risk may be seen as a potentially useful outcome that occurs because of some unplanned event. In this case, the project team can attempt to maximize the potential of these positive risk events should they occur.

Task: Identify Key Potential Risks

Identify high-level risks, both positive and negative.
Assess impact and probability of risks occurring.
Establish contingency plans and mitigation strategies for identified risks.
Document key potential risks and contingency plans/mitigation strategies in the business case.

Initiation Phase Deliverables

Business Case   The business case is a business proposal. It is a statement of the opportunity with details about the problem it solves, the solution it provides, the cost of the solution, and expected benefits. Once the project sponsor, key stakeholders, and others involved in the project (e.g., departmental business owners, information technology staff, financial representative, privacy and security officer) accept it, the business case is presented to upper management (or a group appointed by them) for review and approval.

If the project is approved by a project steering committee or other appropriate review group, the initiation phase is ended and planning begins. During planning, the project team, along with additional staff as needed, will begin the work of creating the project charter and other project planning documents.

Phase II: Project Planning

Overview

Project planning follows the project initiation phase and is one of the most important stages in project management. Project planning is not a single activity or task, but instead is a process that takes time and attention. Project planning defines the project activities needed to complete the project and how those activities will be accomplished. Time spent up front planning the project, identifying needs of the project and project team, and the structure for organizing and managing the project saves countless hours of confusion and rework in the execution and controlling phases of the project. Without proper planning, time and cost estimates are generally at risk even before the project starts.

Proper planning will result in:

- A clearly defined charter
- A detailed and well-defined project scope
- More detailed cost and schedule for the project and a higher confidence level of previous estimates
- A list of defined deliverables and delivery dates
- An organized work plan

- Project sponsor, team, and management acknowledgment of work to be accomplished
- A framework for review and control

Without proper planning, a project's success will be left to chance. The project team will have limited knowledge of its tasks and expected outcomes, project activities may not be well defined or in proper sequence, and resource requirements or skill sets required will not be identified or defined. Even if the project is finished, it may not be seen as a success because the expectations and deliverables were not clearly defined. Planning will involve identifying and documenting the project's scope, specific tasks, project schedule, risk and risk mitigation plans, quality requirements, and staffing needs. The planning process is not complete until as many of these details as possible are identified and addressed.

The planning process should include the following steps:

- Estimating the size of the project
- Estimating the scope of the project
- Estimating the resources required to complete the project
- Documenting a schedule with tasks to be completed and sequencing
- Identifying risks and a high-level mitigation plan
- Determining quality indicators

All of these steps are needed to complete the project plan. The planning process may take several iterations and may change throughout the planning process until a final plan is completed; however, the plan must be complete before the next project phase is initiated.

Activities

The following is a list of key activities required to plan a project.

1. Assign a project manager. Every project needs a leader. Without a leader, project activities are left to vacillate, unorganized, undocumented, and without drive. Assigning a project manager should not be underestimated in its importance. The skills the project manager offers are a major contributing factor to the success or failure of the project. The project manager is seen as the face of the project and, as such, will be

a direct reflection of the department's commitment and competence in project management. A project manager's responsibilities generally include the following:

- Making day-to-day decisions on critical project issues, specifically keeping the project within its scope, schedule, and budget
- Managing project resources
- Providing direction, leadership, and support to project team members
- Maintaining project documentation (e.g., project charter, scope, schedule, budget, requirements, and testing)
- Managing planning and control of project activities and resources
- Developing and managing contracts with vendors
- Reporting project status and issues to the project sponsor and executive (oversight) committee(s)
- Providing teams with advice and input on tasks throughout the project
- Resolving conflicts
- Influencing stakeholders and team members to get buy-in on decisions that will lead to success

Taking these responsibilities into account, it is easy to see that a project manager must be able to perform at a leadership level for the project team and cannot be selected based on function or longevity within the organization, but rather for his or her project management, organizational, and leadership skills. The following skills should be considered when selecting a project manager:

- Project management skills and experience
- Interpersonal and team leadership skills
- Business and management skills
- Strong communication skills
- Experience within the project's technical arena
- Respect and recognition among peers

Project managers who are selected to lead a project but were not involved in the initiation phase must review the project initiation phase documentation to get a clear picture of the project.

Remember, the initiation phase defined the business need or opportunity and set the foundation for all future project work.

Task: Assign a Project Manager

Assign a project manager.
Project manager reviews business case and other initiation phase documents.
Project manager establishes the project planning team.

2. Develop the project charter. Once the project is approved and a project manager assigned, a project charter should be developed. Much of the information for the charter will come from the business case.

3. Define product/project scope. The project scope will define what is, or is not, to be included in the project. Scope statements should be as concise as possible. If the project is to produce a product, a product scope may be created. If not, a project scope is appropriate. Remember:

   - Product scope is a description of the product or service that is produced as an outcome of the project.
   - Project scope is a statement of the work required to create and implement the product or service as well as the work required to manage the project.

   Project scope is documented at a high level in the project charter. It should include a discussion of the proposed solution and the business processes that will be used. Scope statements are generally written at a high level, with the detail described later in the charter document.

Task: Define Project Scope

Identify what is included in the project (expected deliverables).
Identify what is not included in the project.
Determine the general approach used to complete the project.
Document the project scope in the project charter.

4. Define project objectives. Project objectives are the specific goals of the project. These objectives, when properly defined and met, lead to the accomplishments outlined in the business objectives. While business objectives relate to the goals and objectives of the organization, project objectives relate specifically to the immediate goals of the project. For example,

the project goal "implement a new time-tracking system" has no value in and of itself. That goal brings value to the organization only when it leads to accomplishment of the business objective (e.g., "reduce costs and improve productivity through improved resource management").

Project objectives are used to establish project performance goals—planned levels of accomplishment stated as measurable objectives that can be compared to actual results. Performance measures should be derived for each specific goal and should be quantified to ensure the project is meeting its objectives. Using SMART (specific, measurable, achievable, realistic, and time-sensitive) goals is the best means of setting project objectives.

Project objectives can be described in two ways.

- *Hard objectives* relate to the time, cost, and operational objectives (scope) of the product or service. Was the project on time? Within budget? Did it deliver its full scope?
- *Soft objectives* relate more to how the objectives are achieved. These generally include overall customer satisfaction, team satisfaction, quality of outcomes, and so forth.

Focus should be on the full set of project objectives, both hard and soft, to lead to a more complete project success. Focus only on hard objectives can lead to a completed project but one that is less than successful because the customer and project team are not satisfied or accepting of the final product.

Task: Define Project Objectives

Define SMART project objectives as they relate to business objectives.
Define stakeholders' expectations for success.
Document project objectives in the project charter.

5. Identify project constraints and assumptions. All projects have constraints, or limiting factors, that need to be identified in the planning phase of the project. Every project has some limitations, whether people, money, time, equipment, regulatory requirements, or business limitations. Although these may be adjusted up or down, they are considered fixed resources by the project manager and form the basis for managing the project.

Additionally, certain elements relevant to a project are assumed to be essential. For instance, it is assumed that the organization will make resources, both budget and human resources, available to the project manager. These assumptions need to be defined and acknowledged before the project moves to the next phase.

The project charter must include an acknowledgment of project constraints and major assumptions. These defined items are an essential part of the project.

Task: Identify Project Constraints and Assumptions

Identify limiting factors (people, money, time, and equipment).
Describe major project constraints.
Describe major project assumptions.
Document project constraints and assumptions in the project charter.

6. Determine procurement and sourcing strategy. Most organizations will not be able to supply all the necessary resources needed to complete a project, and therefore they must purchase these from outside vendors. Entering into a contract with an outside vendor is a necessary part of the project. Therefore, developing a procurement and sourcing strategy that identifies those needs as part of the planning phase of the project can avoid unnecessary delays later in project activation.

   When to procure:

   Make-or-buy analysis: This is a simple method to determine the cost-effectiveness of creating a product in-house compared to the cost of buying the product or having it produced from an outside vendor. All costs, both direct and indirect, should be considered when performing a make-or-buy analysis. These costs should be compared with each other, reviewed with the project team, and a final decision made based on pros and cons of each option. There may also be opportunity to lease versus purchase certain resources, and again, the pros and cons of each option should be fully discussed in consideration of the project or product to be delivered. Many of these decisions will be based on the length of need for the item or service, as well as the overall cost. It is important to plan a schedule that includes time for whichever option is selected.

How to procure (contract types):

Fixed-price or lump-sum contract: This is a contract that involves paying a fixed, agreed on price for a well-defined product or service. Products should be well established and the requirements well defined to reduce the risk of purchase.

Cost reimbursement contract: This contract type refers to a reimbursement to the vendor for the actual cost of producing the product or service. Costs within the contract are classified as direct (e.g., salaries to staff, development or building of the product) and indirect (e.g., vendor overhead costs, research and development costs, etc.). Indirect costs are normally based on a percentage of direct costs.

Unit price contract: The contractor is paid based on a preset amount for each unit (e.g., $10 per item produced) or unit of service (e.g., $50 per hour of service). The contract equals the total value of all the units purchased.

How much to procure: Procurement of products or services should be planned based on the project schedule. For example, how much supply is needed at the beginning of the project, later in the project, or after the project is complete? Budget availability is another important consideration: When will budget dollars become available for the purchase of needed supplies or services? It is also important to consider in the contracting negotiation phase that opportunities to reduce purchase price may be driven by the time and amount of purchase of these resources.

Task: Determine Procurement and Sourcing Strategy

Determine what to procure.
Determine when to procure.
Determine how to procure.
Determine how much to procure.
Document the procurement details in the project plan and charter.

---

7. Develop project schedule/work plan.

Develop a work breakdown structure (WBS): The WBS is designed to break the scope of the project into multiple steps required to deliver the project with all the objectives previously defined. Remember in the business plan that a very high level plan was presented to articulate the major milestones needed to achieve the expected outcomes. The WBS further breaks down the activities into manageable ones and includes durations, work effort, and resources.

Identify activities and sequencing: The WBS reflects activities associated with the overall design of the project, its requirements, design, implementation, testing, training, operationalization, installation, and maintenance. The project manager is responsible for facilitating and documenting identification of all top-level tasks associated with a project, and then assembling the appropriate resources to ferret out the details of the top-level tasks.

WBS tasks are developed by determining what needs to be done to accomplish the project objective. The choice of how detailed the WBS becomes is subjective and reflects the preferences and judgment of the project manager based on his or her experience with similar projects. As levels of the WBS become more detailed, the scope, complexity, and cost of each subtask become more accurate. The lowest level tasks, or work packages, are independent, manageable units that are planned, budgeted, scheduled, and controlled individually. However, while the project manager must be sure the appropriate level of detailed planning is done, creating a work plan that is too large and unmanageable creates unnecessary risk to the project.

In addition to identifying the tasks needed to reach project objectives, the order in which tasks must be completed is equally important. Activity sequencing involves dividing the project into smaller, manageable components (activities) and then specifying their order of completion. When creating the WBS, this may be simultaneously done so that the WBS is created in a logical sequence that makes sense to the project team.

Identify activity dependencies: The WBS creates a hierarchy of tasks and task relationships. Each task group rolls up into a higher level group until all tasks are complete and ultimately project objectives are attained. Activity dependencies exist when tasks must be completed in order, or when one task must be completed before other tasks can begin. These are task dependencies (or constraints) and must be included as part of the overall project schedule.

Develop project schedule or work plan: After all project activities are identified, including their order of completion and dependencies, a project schedule or work plan can be created. The project schedule/work plan provides a detailed representation of tasks, milestones, dependencies, resource requirements, task duration, work effort, and deadlines. The project's master schedule links all tasks on a common timescale so that the full duration of the project to reach project objectives is clearly defined. The schedule/work plan should be detailed enough to show each task to be performed, who is responsible for that task, when it is expected to begin and end, and the full duration of the task.

Task: Develop Project Schedule/Work Plan

Identify activities and sequencing to complete the project.
Estimate each activity's duration, work effort, dependencies, and resource requirements.
Determine activity dependencies.
Create the project schedule/work plan.

8. Establish milestones. A successful project includes milestones or key activities that must be completed throughout the project. These milestones are used as checkpoints to ensure the project is progressing at a satisfactory level. The project manager will use the milestone events as a means of communicating project status with the project sponsor, and executive committee project milestones are recorded in the project plan and charter.

   Phase exit criteria are deliverables, approvals, or events that must occur before the project team is allowed to declare that phase complete. These are marked as milestones and reviewed with the team, executive steering committee, and project sponsor for agreement.

   Phase entrance criteria are materials, personnel, approvals, or other matters that must be available before the project team can begin the next phase. In some cases, project managers may need to get approval from the project sponsor and executive committee before moving forward to the next phase if budgeting or project approval is contingent on project progress and realignment with strategic business goals.

Task: Establish Project Life Cycle Phase Checkpoints

Establish milestones with clearly defined planned dates to measure progress.
Establish entrance criteria for each phase.
Establish exit criteria for each phase.

9. Develop human resource requirements. In every project, a finite set of resources will be needed to complete the project. Once the project schedule is complete and resources are assigned to each task, the overall work effort needed to complete the project becomes evident. Generally, resources are a limited commodity and may require augmentation from external resources. One of the primary roles of the project manager is to identify all the required skill sets needed to complete the identified tasks in the project schedule/work plan and then to acquire the people with those skills throughout the life cycle of the project. Resource planning then becomes the documented process to execute tasks in the order in which they are required to deliver the product required.

   Identify required skill sets by role: It is helpful in the planning process to develop a list of skills required, first for execution of the project and then for execution of each task. This skills list may then be used to determine the type of staff required for the task. It is helpful to create a roles and responsibilities document that generally describes responsibilities of key roles within the project. After assigning individuals to these roles, the project manager should review these roles with team members so that each individual understands expectations throughout the course of the project.

   Acquire project team members: Organizations vary in the way in which resources may be assigned to a project. Some organizations may have a resource pool of available individuals who may be used for projects. Other organizations select from the entire organization to fill project roles. Regardless, understanding the skills needed to fill the needs of the project is essential.

The project manager has a primary role of securing necessary resources to complete the project, taking advantage of and maximizing skilled labor that is available. The project manager will be responsible for identifying any skills that are required by the project tasks but not available within the resource pool, and to build a plan that realistically accounts for those skills or lack thereof. Skill sets may not be the only deciding factor in assigning resources to the project team. The project manager must also ensure that team members will work well together and that conflicts are managed throughout the project life cycle. Additionally, team members may come and go throughout the project and may be part of the team only for the short time in which their skills are needed. Should available resources be unable to fill the required skill sets needed for the project, the project manager may have an option to hire the necessary talent or contract services to perform the work.

Update project schedule/work plan (e.g., load resources): Using the project tool provided by the organization, it is essential to capture the tasks and work assignments for each resource. This is a critical part of the planning process to ensure tasks have the appropriate level of resources, as well as ensuring the resources are available during the task duration to complete the task. This should be documented in the project plan.

Create human resource plan documents: The resource plan should consist of roles and responsibilities, to include project sponsor, executive steering committee, project manager, team leaders, and team members. Additionally, a hierarchal representation of how each team member is accountable should be constructed and reviewed with the team to ensure a clear understanding of communication and escalation paths.

Task: Define Project Organizations and Governance

Identify required skill sets by role.
Assign/acquire project team members.
Update project schedule/work plan (e.g., load resources).
Create human resource plan documents.
Resource plan is accepted by project sponsor, team members, and executive committee.

10. Identify other resource requirements. External to the human resource requirements, all project teams require the tools to perform their tasks successfully. In scheduling resources, the project manager must ensure that both people and equipment necessary to support the project team are available simultaneously. As part of the project schedule/work plan, the project manager must ensure all resources are available as needed.

Workspace requirements: The project manager must recognize the needed workspace for people and equipment. It is desirable for all project team members to be housed in the same location whenever possible to facilitate interaction and communication. Team spirit and synergy are enhanced and chances for project success are increased when everyone is close together. Although this may not always be feasible, it is a goal worth striving toward.

Infrastructure, equipment, and material needs: In addition to workspace, equipment for the team should be included in the resource plan. Ensuring the availability of equipment at critical points in the project is key in planning a successful project. In some cases, there may be a need to procure and store equipment as part of the project; space must be made available for receiving, processing, and eventually deploying these products. When considering equipment, it is imperative that team members have the tools to do their jobs, so if additional equipment is needed for the team members, it should be part of the resource plan and secured as early as possible.

Update the resource plan document.

Task: Identify Other Resource Requirements

Determine facility needs.
Determine infrastructure, equipment, and material needs.
Update the resource plan document.

---

11. Refine project cost estimate and budget. Budget planning is done in parallel with project schedule/work plan development. Remember, in the business case development, high-level budget planning was performed. During the project

schedule planning, resource requirements are refined and budget adjustments may be identified. This is a crucial process in making sure that all costs associated with the project are identified and, if costs exceed the initial approved budget, that there is opportunity for review with the project sponsor and executive committee.

Budgeting serves as a control mechanism whereby actual costs can be compared with and measured against the project budget. The budget is a constraint that must be continuously managed and reported on with the plan sponsor. When a project schedule begins to slip, cost is proportionally affected. When project costs begin to escalate, the project manager should revisit the project plan to determine whether scope, budget, or schedule needs adjusting.

To develop the budget, the applicable cost factors associated with project tasks are identified. The development of costs for each task should be simple and direct and consist of labor, material, and other direct costs. The cost of performing a task is directly related to the personnel assigned to the task, the duration of the task, and the cost of any nonlabor items required by the task.

Budget estimates are generally obtained from the people responsible for managing the work efforts. They provide the expertise required to make the estimate and provide buy-in and accountability during the actual performance of the task. These team members identify people or labor categories required to perform the work, and multiply the cost of the labor by the number of hours required to complete the task. Determining how long the task performance takes is the single most difficult part of deriving a cost estimate. The labor costs should factor in vacation time, sick leave, breaks, meetings, and other day-to-day activities. Not including these factors jeopardizes both scheduling and cost estimates.

Nonlabor charges include such items as material costs, travel, cost of capital purchases, leasing fees (if applicable), software licenses, and other variable costs associated with tangible items.

All of this information is captured in the project budget and should be included as part of the business plan and project charter.

Task: Refine Project Cost Estimate and Budget

Identify the applicable cost factors associated with project tasks. The development of costs for each task should be simple and direct and consist of labor, material, and other direct costs.
Identify people or labor categories required to perform the work and multiply the cost of the labor by the number of hours required to complete the task.
Include nonlabor charges.
Include all one-time and recurring costs.
Baseline approved project budget.

12. Risk analysis. As discussed in the initiation phase, a risk is any factor that may potentially interfere with successful completion of the project. A risk is not a problem: a *problem* is a situation that has already occurred; a *risk* is the recognition that a problem might occur. By recognizing potential problems (risks), the project manager can attempt to avoid or minimize their occurrence through proper planning or mitigation.

    Risk analysis is a formal process for identifying potential problems, the probability of their occurrence, and actions that will minimize the chances of their occurring or minimize their impact to the project. In most cases, the project team will identify risks throughout the development of the project schedule.

Task: Risk Analysis

Identify potential project risks.
Assess impact and probability of risks occurring.
Determine a risk response, including any contingency plans.
Record risk data in the risk analysis plan document.
If a project management tool is used, document the risks and mitigation plans in the tool.

13. Develop a quality management plan. Providing a quality product or service is essential to every project. Often this most important aspect is left out of the project planning phase or does not have a documented plan with important customer acceptance. The purpose of using a good quality management plan is to ensure products and services meet the business plan

objectives. Quality management consists of three very distinct processes: quality planning, quality assurance, and quality control.

During the business case planning, metrics to measure project success should have been established. These metrics should be documented and periodically measured throughout the course of the project. Additionally, during the development of milestones, key deliverables should be identified. Many times these milestones can be quantified and also serve as quality measurements.

The project team should discuss quality standards and how best to meet those. Product acceptance criteria should be part of the project planning and reviewed at routine intervals.

Successful quality processes always strive to see quality through the eyes of the end user (customer). Customers are the ultimate judges of the quality of the product they receive and will typically judge a project by whether or not their requirements are met. To ensure delivery of a quality product, the project team should ensure that requirements are addressed at each phase of the project.

Task: Develop a Quality Management Plan

Define the quality standards that pertain to this project.
Describe how the project team is to meet those quality standards.
Define the audit process and schedule that will be used in the project to evaluate
  overall project performance.
Define the process that will ensure that customer requirements are met.
Document the quality plan as part of the overall project plan.

14. Determine issue management strategy. The purpose of issue management is to provide a mechanism for organizing, maintaining, and tracking the resolution of issues that cannot be resolved at the individual level. This plan should consist of issue reporting, escalation path, tracking and reporting, and assigning priority to each problem. This important process should enable the project team to report issues quickly without waiting for other formal communication methods, and provide the project manager with a means of quickly assessing and addressing issues that may jeopardize the project.

> **Task: Issue Management Strategy**
>
> Determine issue management approach.
> Define reporting and escalation procedures.
> Define process for issue resolution.

15. Managing scope change. Project scope management is a critical part of every project. Remember the mention of scope creep above, which can easily jeopardize a project. Having an established change policy and methodology for processing change requests is critical to every project manager. Often the project management office will have a documented change process that can easily be followed. It is imperative that the project team be educated on this process.

> **Task: Managing Scope Change**
>
> Define process for identifying and documenting change requests.

16. Develop a project communication plan. Communication planning is a critical part of every project. Information exchange across all those involved in the project is essential. From the project team members to the project manager, from the project manager to the stakeholders and executive committee and ultimately to the customer, communication is a critical success factor for every project. The communication plan, therefore, must identify which people need what information, when it will be needed, and how they will get it. Communication is the cornerstone of how work gets done among different parties within a project and must be free-flowing. Communications planning should incorporate how information will be shared and when it will be shared; set expectations for status reporting, issues management, problem resolution; and so forth. The communication plan should include defined steps to communicate with regularity with the project team, stakeholder, and executive committee, and provide a feedback mechanism for the customer and any end users that may be impacted by the product or service being developed, and may include marketing representatives as

resources. This information is documented in the communication plan.

Task: Develop a Project Communication Plan

Determine who needs what information and when.
Determine how to communicate information (memo, e-mail, weekly/monthly meetings, etc.).
Document in the communication plan.

17. Develop a project plan. The *project plan* is completed in the planning phase of a project and includes all the components discussed so far. For large projects, a team may be dedicated for the single purpose of creating the project plan, while smaller projects will likely be developed as part of the project whole. Project plans should be completed in cooperation with the project sponsor, key stakeholders, project manager, and team members, and ultimately reviewed with and approved by the customer.

    The project plan is never a static document, but rather an iterative process. Each element of the plan is regularly reviewed for changes and refinements, based on further analysis and decisions made in developing other plan elements. This refinement also develops buy-in from the project team and stakeholders. However, once the project plan is finalized, any additional changes or adjustments must go through the change management process. It is critical to get buy-in to the project plan from the involved parties prior to actually starting the project. Approval of the plan commits the resources needed to perform the work.

    ### Task: Develop Project Plan

    Consolidate outcomes from planning phase activities.
    Develop the project plan document; have it reviewed and gain approval.
    Distribute the project plan according to the communication plan.
    The project plan is completed and approved.

Deliverables

Project Plan The project plan is a formal, approved document used to manage and control project execution. It is a compilation of text and stand-alone deliverables created during the initiation and planning stages. The level of detail should be appropriate for the scope, complexity, and risk of the project.

The following is a list of key components usually included in a project plan.

- Project charter
  - Project overview
  - Business objectives
  - Scope statement
  - Project objectives
  - Constraints and assumptions
  - Project deliverables and milestones
  - Project procurement and sourcing strategy
  - Project cost estimate and budget
- Project plan
  - Work breakdown structure (WBS)
  - Project schedule/work plan
  - Risk analysis
  - Quality management plan
- Project organization and governance
  - External resources
  - Internal resources
  - Roles and responsibilities
- Issue management
- Scope management
- Communication plan

Once the project manager completes the project plan, it should be reviewed and approved by the project team, including the business owners, project sponsor, and executive committee. The level and extent to which the plan will be reviewed is based on the size of the project as stated in dollars or period of time. Ultimately, the review process allows for executive management buy-in and approval of the plan. Once the project plan is approved and signed, the project manager is given the authority to complete the current project efforts and enter into the execution phase.

Phases III and IV: Project Execution and Monitoring and Controlling

Overview

A project manager's responsibilities and skills really begin to be taxed once the execution phase starts. Because a project manager is responsible to internal and external stakeholders, the project team, vendors, executive management, and others, the visibility of the position is intensified because many of these people will now expect to see and discuss the resulting deliverables that were detailed in the planning phase. As a project manager, it is important to stay at the appropriate management level and not become task oriented beyond managing the overall project. Micromanaging at the project manager level will most certainly alienate the resource team and distract the project manager from the real goal of keeping the project moving forward and achieving its objectives on time and within budget.

Once a project moves into the project execution, and monitoring and controlling phases, the project team and the necessary resources to carry out the project should be in place and ready to perform their tasks. At this point, the team members should be well prepared for the tasks ahead of them, recognizing their role and responsibilities, how to identify and report issues, and what quality control measures are in place, and be ready to move forward with confidence. The project plan should be complete and a baseline established from which to measure any variances that may occur. The project team should be focused on the project at hand and have confidence in their leader, the project manager.

Executing the project plan simply means taking the project schedule and completing the task. Monitoring and controlling the project is the primary responsibility of the project manager, in concert with the project team. Activities should be carried out effectively and efficiently, ensuring that measurements against project plans, specifications, and the original project feasibility concept continue to be collected, analyzed, and acted on throughout the project life cycle. Particular attention must be paid to keeping interested parties up to date with project status, dealing with procurement and contract administration issues, helping manage quality control, and monitoring project risk. This is an important time for the project manager to be sure the team is working effectively together and achieving the desired results.

Project control involves the regular review of metrics and status reports to identify variances from the planned project baseline. These variances are determined by comparing the actual performance metrics from the initiation phase to the metrics achieved during project execution. Variances caught early and addressed immediately will help keep the project on track. The project schedule, including timing and resource alignment, may need to be periodically adjusted should unexpected problems or issues occur. In some cases, change management processes may need to be invoked to realign the schedule, resources, or budget. For example, a missed milestone date may require adjustments in resources for overtime or additional staff, which may result in budget overages. Project control also includes taking preventative action in anticipation of possible problems.

Activities

The following is a list of key activities required to execute, and manage and control a project:

1. Communication. The project communication plan is an important factor in the execution, and monitoring and controlling phases. Team members must effectively communicate with their team leader or project manager to keep the project on target. The project sponsor, internal and external stakeholders, and business partners expect to be kept informed of how the project is progressing. To that end, the project manager may employ several levels of communications:

   • The project manager should stay in constant communication with the project team, both formally and informally. Informal discussion is sometimes the best way to determine team morale, true project status, looming difficulties, and so forth.
   • Meeting minutes should be made available to stakeholders along with any "to do" lists that may have been generated during the meetings.

- Routine (monthly) status reports should be offered to the project sponsor and other stakeholders as a means of providing a general overview of project status. These are generally generated by the project management tool being used.
- A high-level project plan should be accessible to all stakeholders. This may be accomplished by providing access to a project management tool or providing routine updates.
- Joint project reviews are a good way to bring visibility to all areas of the project. They provide an opportunity to discuss important issues and make management decisions on the project with input from several sources. Joint project reviews can involve the project manager, project team members, project stakeholders, and department management, depending on the issues being discussed.

Task: Communication

Ensure that the communication plan is being executed as planned. Revise the communication plan based on feedback received from stakeholders and project team members.

2. Risk management. Identifying new risks, monitoring known risks, and developing/implementing contingency plans are key tools for successfully completing a project. Part of controlling a project during the execution, and monitoring and controlling phases is to have implemented the risk management process developed in the planning phase. This process is a key component of project planning and should be kept current until the project is closed.

Risk management plays a vital role in the management of technology projects because the solution may include undeveloped or unproven technologies that may be critical to the infrastructure. For that reason, technology project managers must continuously monitor for unforeseen problems and be able to work with the project team quickly to identify potential solutions. These types of projects generally carry the highest level of risk and require the most skilled project team and project manager.

Task: Risk Management

Document all known risk in a project management tool.
Include a risk summary in the regular status meetings—monthly status report.
Providing consistent and ongoing evaluation of risk items and development of risk strategies.
Identify new risks (e.g., risk assessment).
Evaluate new and existing risks (e.g., potential project risks).
Define/refine risk response strategies.
Conduct regular follow-up risk assessments based on magnitude of the project.

3. Schedule management. It is important for the project team to understand at all times exactly where the project stands with respect to the schedule (i.e., is the project ahead of or behind schedule?). The process used to communicate task status and then overall project status is critical to depicting current work efforts accurately and ensuring schedules are maintained.

   Each team member or team leader should be expected to provide updates, including notes, quality issues, and work comments, for each of his or her responsible tasks in a project management tool. This real-time update provides invaluable information to fellow team members and the project manager for addressing schedule, quality, issues, and risks associated with the project.

   Schedule control is one of the most difficult but important activities within the project control phase. The project schedule can be affected by any number of issues, including resource issues, funding, and vendor performance external influences, among others. The ability of a project manager to manage the schedule and keep the team focused is a critical part of his or her responsibilities.

   Schedule issues may come from a variety of sources, but schedule changes should be dealt with consistently. If a potential schedule problem occurs, the problem should be immediately investigated and the cause determined quickly. Once the schedule problem is uncovered, an immediate plan should be created for correcting the problem in the shortest allowable time with the least impact. The promptness with which this occurs may directly affect the ability to recover with minimal amount of impact; however, every schedule change should be analyzed for potential risk to the project and overall budget.

It is standard practice to baseline the schedule at the start of the project. This allows all schedule changes to be displayed against the original project schedule/work plan. If schedule slippage becomes significant, adjustments to the baseline may be advisable. Any change to the baseline should be done only after the change management process has occurred.

Every project is constrained by its scope, schedule, and budget; however, stakeholders may see meeting the schedule as the prime imperative. If this is the case, change control for the schedule and communication of the change is imperative to keeping the customer and stakeholders satisfied. It is a good idea for project managers to hold regular project schedule/work plan reviews with the team and to update stakeholders as frequently as may be needed to ensure their comfort level with the project. Large or complex projects may have several schedules being managed at a deliverable or functional level; therefore, having the "owners" of these schedules meeting at regular intervals is critical to the overall project schedule remaining on track. The project manager is responsible for integrating these project schedule/work plans and making them understandable for all of the project's stakeholders.

Task: Schedule Management

Collect and validate schedule status.
Validate work effort to ensure that the schedules are accurate.
Conduct regular project schedule/work plan review. meetings. Large or complex projects may require more frequent meetings.
Identify potential schedule problems.
Investigate potential schedule problems and uncover the cause as soon as possible.
Develop a plan for correcting schedule problems in the shortest allowable time with the least impact.
Make the customer aware whenever a schedule change occurs.
In the event of severe schedule slippage, re-baseline the project schedule/work plan.

4. Document work results. Work results are the end results of each task. To stay on schedule, each work effort should be updated to show when it is completed, any issues associated with the work effort, quality indicator results, work effort required, and costs. The project management tool should be updated with this information to allow appropriate performance reporting.

Tasks: Document Work Results

Project deliverables are produced and work products are tracked.

5. Scope management. Project scope should have been specifically stated as part of the project charter, and therefore contains the requirements of the project. Scope management is thus ensuring that all elements in the scope are carried forward so that any changes that could impact the scope, either to increase or to limit scope, are immediately addressed. Scope control, therefore, is avoiding scope creep as well as controlling scope reduction.

Scope changes will come from the perceived need for a change in a project deliverable that may affect its functionality and in most cases the amount of work needed to perform the project. A scope change is critical.

Scope changes most likely will require a change in project funding, resources, or time. All scope change requests should be submitted in writing and must be approved by the project sponsor, stakeholders, and customer. A committee that consists of stakeholders from all areas of the project should be willing to convene and discuss the potential change and its anticipated impact on the project. This group of stakeholders should be a predefined cross section of people who will have the ability to commit their interests at a strategic management level. Once a decision is made to increase or reduce scope, the change must be authorized by all members of the committee. Any changes that are agreed on must be documented and signed as a matter of formal scope control.

For technology projects, scope control is critical, especially when producing a product. It is not uncommon when team members are doing their development testing or implementation work for them to try to get creative or give the customer something other than, or in addition to, the original stated requirements. Doing any work that is outside or beyond the stated work, as called out in the original requirements, is considered scope creep.

Task: Scope Management

Identify potential scope change.
Evaluate impact of potential scope change.
Determine if additional project funds, resources, and time will be required.
Ensure that the scope change is beneficial.
Convene a committee to review the scope change.
Update planning documents with scope change.
Communicate change to the project team.

6. Quality management. Quality control involves monitoring specific project results to determine if they comply with quality standards and seeking ways to eliminate unsatisfactory results. It is expected that quality control be performed throughout the course of the project. Quantifiable results, such as deliverables, and management results, cost and schedule performance, should all be part of quality control. In some organizations a specific group of staff may be assigned to do quality control for projects, although this is not a requirement for quality management to be in place.

Task: Manage Quality

Monitor specific project results to determine if they comply with relevant quality standards and to identify ways to eliminate causes of unsatisfactory results.
Establish quality management awareness and a training program.
Project team members accept responsibility for quality.

7. Budget management. Budget management is a critical part of the project manager's responsibility. If the project has been appropriately planned in the initiation and planning phases, the necessary budget to complete the project is available. The

project manager, then, must ensure that costs do not exceed those approved, and he or she must follow a strict change control process. Often, budget overages are not the result of a single issue but rather a compilation of smaller problems that accumulate over time. Staying on budget is often seen as the most critical constraint for a project and must be managed accordingly.

Cost control involves understanding why budget variances occur, in both the positive and the negative. It requires the same diligence in management as scope control, schedule control, and quality management. Setting budget limits and monitoring variances must be done early in the project and repeated often. Budget problems tend to compound themselves if left unattended. On a technology project, more money could be spent trying to fix budget, scope, or schedule issues near the end of a project than should have been spent on the entire project. In many cases the budget is a fixed amount, so if other actions fail to bring the project's costs into budget alignment, the scope must be reduced.

Task: Manage Costs

Monitor cost performance to detect variances.
Document variances between the scheduled and actual costs.
Inform appropriate stakeholders about authorized changes.

8. Issue management. Issue management is the process of organizing, maintaining, and tracking issues and their resolution. Issue management should consist of controlling issues identified through the course of the project, prioritizing to ensure those issues with the greatest risk of impact to the project are worked on first, and using sound problem-solving techniques to reach resolution.

   The issue management process should give everyone involved with, or affected by, the project a way to report issues or problems. Usually a project management tool is provided to capture issues, but something as simple as a shared Excel worksheet will provide the same level of documentation. Some issues may remain throughout the project if they are determined to be of minimal impact, and the cost to resolve the issue will pose risk to the project. In some cases, issues may be escalated to the executive team if they are of great significance or pose risk to the schedule, scope, or budget.

Task: Issue Management

Maintain a repository of project issues.
Review issues on a regular basis.
Track all issues until they are resolved.

9. Conduct update meetings. The project manager plays a key role in the communication process and, as such, is required to coordinate a number of communication opportunities or meetings. The project team should meet routinely to provide an opportunity to update the work effort, communicate problems and issues, and understand the overall project schedule, budget, and quality. Additionally, the project manager is responsible for communicating outside the project team, with stakeholders, both internal and external, the project sponsor, and the executive oversight committee. Communication may take the form of an informal review or may be a formal process, based on the size and complexity of the project.

A standard requirement of all projects is to provide status reporting. Although the format and frequency of these reports may vary, they should include specific information to address project constraints of scope, budget, and schedule, along with risks, issues, and quality controls. For reports to be accurate, however, team members must update the project tool.

Communication should be directed to three distinct audiences:

Project—Status meeting includes the lowest level of detail and provides an opportunity for the project team to discuss the current state and for the project manager to discuss the overall project status, issues, and to escalate problems or risks. For large, complex projects with multiple project teams, this level of meeting should be about bringing the teams together for a collaborative update.

Sponsor—Sponsor meetings are a venue for the project manager to discuss key project issues and escalation points with the sponsor. The sponsor is generally there to help resolve key or organizational issues and provide general direction to the team.

Executive steering committee—The executive steering committee meeting is intended to be a forum for the committee to evaluate the overall progress of the project and hear updates specific to scope, schedule, and budget. If the sponsor is part of the executive steering committee, these meetings may be combined to avoid duplication.

Task: Conduct Update Meetings

For large or complex projects, each project team leader conducts a weekly status meeting with his or her team.

The project manager conducts weekly status meetings with team or team leaders.

Conduct monthly meetings with project sponsor, including providing status reports.

Conduct monthly executive steering committee meeting using status report to identify key issues.

10. Review project life cycle checkpoints. The project manager, along with the project sponsor, executive committee, and stakeholders, ensures the project is progressing appropriately by reviewing key milestones and critical checkpoints throughout the project. In some cases, completion of a phase may require approval to move to the next phase of the project.

Task: Review Project Life Cycle Checkpoints

Review exit criteria and associated deliverables of completed phase.

Review deliverables and milestones.

Failing projects are stopped or corrective action is taken.

On-track projects are authorized to continue.

11. Administer vendor contracts. The project manager is responsible for management of vendor contracts throughout the duration of the project. Vendor management

includes ensuring the vendor is delivering quality services on time and within the cost constraints agreed on. The project manager must be responsible for the vendor, as he or she is for internal resources, and must obtain the same information from the vendor as he or she would from other project team members.

Contract administration is the process of ensuring that the vendor's performance meets contractual requirements. This is accomplished by monitoring the vendor's performance, obtaining progress reports and project plan updates, inspecting for quality, and approving deliverables.

Setting up procedures for contract control is vital to dealing with unexpected situations during project development, testing, and implementation. Without procedures in place, issues can go unresolved or result in project delays. It is important that the project manager have a strong communication plan with the vendors during the course of the project.

Task: Administer Vendor Contract

Project managers will also be responsible for tracking, reviewing, and analyzing the performance of contractors on a project.
Participate in oversight and review of any contract changes that will affect the project.
Ensure vendor adherence to application development and project management methodologies.

12. Update project documents. During the execution, and monitoring and controlling phases, the project plan is implemented and may be changed as needed. Modifications may be needed as a result of work still to be done, changes in scope, resource changes, or other unforeseen circumstances.

Assuming project baselines were created, changes may be necessary to formally reflect approved changes. Project documentation should include updates to the budget baseline, schedule baseline, risk documents, and project tool.

Task: Update Project Documents

Revise project plan baselines (through formal change control process).
Revise other project documentation as needed.

Deliverables

Project Status Reports   Routine status reports should communicate the following:

- Current schedule status
- Significant accomplishments for the current reporting period, including deliverables and milestones
- Planned activities for the next reporting period
- Financial status
- Present issues, concerns, and risks

Updated Planning Documents   Deliverables in this stage include consistent and updated planning documents, such as the project schedule, budget, scope, issues, risks, communication plan, etc.

Project-Specific Deliverables   Deliverables and milestones identified during the planning phase of the project and documented in the project charter should be documented as to their completion date and any issues remaining from the deliverable.

Phase V: Project Closeout

Overview

The last major stage of a project's life cycle is project closeout. The project closeout is completed once all defined project tasks and milestones have been completed and the customer has accepted the project's deliverables.

When planning for the closeout, the project manager should consider that, even though all project tasks may be closed, the project closeout cannot occur until there is formal acceptance by the executive committee, project sponsor, and key stakeholders. Documentation presented for the closeout meeting should include evidence of all project deliverables and acceptance of those deliverables, remaining open project issues and recommended action plan for closure, and a formal acknowledgment document.

Key activities to be conducted as part of the project closeout should include return of resources to their primary positions, closeout of any financial requirements, including internal budget review, and outstanding requirements from the vendor. A formal review meeting to identify lessons learned throughout the project should be conducted and documented in the project management tool. Project documents should be finalized and archived as part of the project closure. Finally, always celebrate project successes with the project team, stakeholders, and affected parties.

Activities

The following is a list of key activities required to close out a project:

1. Conduct a final acceptance meeting. The issue of primary importance with project closure is the acceptance of the product or project by the customer. The best way to secure this is by holding a final meeting with all necessary stakeholders to review the product delivered against the baseline requirements and specifications. Any deviations from the established baseline should have been documented and approved, but it is still necessary to document any variations from the scope, schedule, or budget for stakeholder review.

   The final deliverable of this meeting should be an acceptance statement created by the project manager describing the project's final deliverables and requiring the stakeholders' signatures.

Task: Conduct Final Acceptance Meeting

Obtain formal acceptance from stakeholders and executive committee.
Evaluate the project to determine if business and project objectives and benefits were achieved.

2. Conduct a final contract review. Vendor contract closure is another critical process in closing out a project. Vendor meetings should be conducted to finalize acceptance testing of the product and to verify all terms of the contract have been met. Contracts may have been for the duration of the project or may be extended to include operational coverage well beyond the terms of the project.

   Contracts can be brought to closure for a variety of reasons, including contract completion, early termination, or failure to perform. Regardless, closure of the contract term, even if it is beyond the scope of the initial project, should be performed.

Task: Conduct Final Contract Review

Review the contract and related documents.
Validate that the contractor has met all of its contractual requirements.
Resolve contractor variances and issues.
Terminate the current contract.

3. Conduct outcomes assessment. An outcomes assessment meeting is an essential part of closure for the project team. It provides an open discussion to review project strengths, weaknesses, and challenges. The project team is able to put closure to any remaining open issues and discuss opportunities for improving the project process.

The outcomes assessment meeting should include the project team, sponsor, stakeholders, and vendors. Items of discussion should include customer satisfaction, final budget, scope and schedule reviews, open issue review, and risk review. It is equally important for the team to provide feedback for what went well in the project and opportunities to improve the process.

A final project report is generally completed to document the full project through all phases, ending in a final review of the triple project constraints of scope, schedule, and budget. This report should also include recommendations from the team for improving the project and specifically improving project processes. Sharing this report among other project managers is a key to continuing to improve project methodology in the organization.

Task: Conduct Outcomes Assessment

Document project successes and failures.
Determine the extent to which business and project objectives and benefits were achieved.
Compile lessons learned.
Complete the final project report.

4. Conduct knowledge transfer. All documentation that has anything to do with the product itself (including design

documents, schematics, technical manuals) that has not already been turned over to operations should be completed and turned over during an operational transition meeting.

All documentation pertaining to the project should be compiled. This includes contracts, meeting minutes, project plans, charter, and other materials not archived in the project tool. Generally the project management office maintains all materials related to projects. Summary documentation, such as technical specifications, technical documentation, operations manuals, and the like, will be turned over to the operations group. Project documentation should be stored in an archival fashion, either through the project tool, on CD, or in a project binder for future reference. Contracts should be archived as a part of the project unless it is to be maintained for operational purposes, in which case a copy should be retained with the project documentation and the original turned over to operations.

Task: Conduct Knowledge Transfer

Turn all documentation related to the product over to operations.
Confirm all end users have been adequately trained.
Create an archive for project documentation.

Deliverables

Project Closure Document The project closure document summarizes the agreement with the project sponsor and stakeholders and confirms:

- The product meets requirements and specifications as outlined in the charter.
- Deviations are documented and approved with applicable action plans.
- Issues are closed or have been acknowledged with an action plan.
- Agreement to the project closure by the project sponsor and key stakeholders.

Final Project Report The final project report creates a historical look at the project and includes both planned and actual scope, schedule, and budget summaries. Any quality metric outcomes should be documented along with open actionable items. Final assessment documentation, including lessons learned, should also be included in the project report.

Conclusion

This chapter has reviewed the methodology a project manager should use during the initiating, planning, managing, controlling and executing, and closing stages of every project. The described phases, tasks, and deliverables suggested for each phase are only a proposed method for reaching a successful project implementation. Repeatable methodology more often than not leads to success.

This chapter was originally published in *Healthcare Informatics, Improving Efficiency and Productivity*, Taylor & Francis, New York, 2010.

References

1. Cleland DI, Gareis R. 2006. *Global project management handbook*, 1–4. New York: McGraw-Hill Professional.
2. HIMSS Project Management Task Force, Stetson N, Klinedinst JW. 2008. *Why have a project management methodology in healthcare? How to deliver successful projects*. Chicago: Healthcare Information and Management Systems Society.

5

NURSING ROLES IN THE IMPLEMENTATION OF CLINICAL INFORMATION SYSTEMS

TERRY MOORE

Contents

An electronic health record (EHR) is a standardized, efficient, and accessible way to provide information to clinical staff across the continuum of care. A clinical information system (CIS) is the foundation of the EHR. Most healthcare institutions have embraced the 1999 Institute of Medicine report *To Err Is Human: Building a Safer Health System*. This study identified that faulty systems or processes most commonly cause errors.[1] Follow-up studies from the IOM, *Crossing the Quality Chasm*[2] and *Keeping Patients Safe: Transforming the Work Environment of Nurses*,[3] address the role systems play in safe, quality care. Driving forces for CIS implementations include clear documentation, real-time access, timely execution of orders, and quality care consistent with best practice.[4] Successful implementation relies on identifying key clinical champions and defining their specific role in the implementation. While all clinical stakeholders are important to the implementation, nurses can play a unique role in each phase, and at every level, of the implementation. Including nurses in the selection, design, and implementation teams and giving them a significant role is one key to a successful implementation. Nurses can facilitate end-user engagement, enhance system design, provide education, sponsor change management, and effectively communicate to all other stake-holders. Because their focus is patient-centered care, they can support most clinical disciplines where tapping into this pool of experts is a recognized way to successful implementation.

Implementation Roles

There are many roles in a CIS implementation. Different levels of experience are needed and responsibilities vary for each role. As system implementation has many phases and each phase requires different knowledge and skills, the roles and responsibilities vary at each phase. The phases include system selection, design and go-live, and system optimization. Implementation roles include executive sponsor, project director, team leader, clinical system analyst, educator, and superuser.

One important team in the process is the executive steering committee, which assumes responsibility for the project, ensuring that the vision is identified and communicated, and escalated issues are resolved. The committee members provide top-down, visible support to the team members. Very often the chief nursing officer (CNO) and the chief information officer (CIO) co-chair this committee, and additional members attending this committee include the chief financial officer (CFO), chief medical officer (CMO), chief medical informatics officer (CMIO), and department chairs. The executive steering committee will resolve any issue that cannot be resolved by the project teams, where typically these issues relate to resources or budgeting concerns.[5] During the course of the project, the teams may need additional resources because some steps in the project plan may take longer than anticipated to complete. In addition, the team may uncover a more complicated process that could delay the go-live date. These issues will be resolved by the executive steering committee, led by the executive sponsor.

Executive Sponsor

Deciding who will be the executive sponsor is a critical step in the implementation. The CIO oversees the entire project, and the role of executive sponsor is one that bridges the gap between the technical and the clinical environments. The person in this role ensures that the clinicians are fully engaged in the implementation. The executive sponsor will help align system design with clinical outcomes and will establish implementation goals that will support the organization's mission, vision, and values. The sponsor will also determine strategic and business objectives, communicate the vision to stakeholders,[6] and help define the scope of the project, ensuring that mission-critical applications are given highest priority. Finally, the executive sponsor reports project progress to senior leadership and to the board of governors.

Project Director

The project director is responsible for overseeing all of the teams associated with the implementation. These teams will be application specific and can include such areas as clinical documentation, order entry, pharmacy, or radiology. Each team will have its own project plan with tasks and milestones that are specific to the application. There will also be some items, such as selecting point of care devices, system security, and printing options, on each of the plans that are common to all of the applications. The project director must be able to coordinate multiple project plans and ensure that milestones in the plans are met. Each of these plans must be synchronized across all applications so that common milestones are addressed once for all teams. Each of these plans will roll up to the main project plan for the entire implementation, where the responsibility of the project director is to ensure that the project milestones are met.

The project director must have the respect of end users as well as administrators, as they align the organizational goals to the project goals. This individual is generally a person who is comfortable with both the technical and clinical aspects of the system. The director will develop the project plan and direct every aspect of the project,[7] where his or her responsibility is to ensure that the team is meeting the project goals and following the project plan, which includes resolving issues within or across applications. Meeting project milestones, identifying regulatory changes that will affect the design, and monitoring the budget are key components of project direction, and the director ensures that an effective change management strategy is in place. While the executive sponsor will identify and communicate vision, it is up to the director to manage the teams and keep the vision aligned at all aspects of the project plan. Finally, the project director should be an active member of the project steering committee, reporting on project progress, team accomplishments, and issues, and will work with the vendor to manage the project timeline.

Team Leader

As there may be multiple applications and multiple teams in the implementation process, an additional role to be filled is that of team leader. This person fills the role of managing one application, or team; provides oversight to the individual application team; keeps the team members on vision and team goals aligned with the vision, and matches resources to each task.[7] The team leader generally reports to the project director and is responsible for the daily operations of the members of the application team. The team leader is generally well versed in departmental operations and has detailed knowledge of the application and can apply both a technical and a clinical focus to it. Part of his or her task is to assign a clinical system analyst to project tasks, ensuring the analyst has the competence to complete the assignment. The team leader will also coordinate with the other team leaders on duplicate tasks across the entire project, chair team meetings, provide updates to the project director, and resolve individual issues within the application and escalate to the project director those that cannot be resolved.

Clinical System Analyst

The application team is responsible for bringing the finished product to end users[8] and completing the tasks associated with the application project plan. Working together are representatives of all disciplines, including nursing, physical therapy, dietary, respiratory therapy, medical records, and finance. Members can be either permanent or ad hoc team members, where the permanent members of this team are called clinical systems analysts (CSAs).

The CSA reports to the team leader and focuses on workflow analysis, software requirements, and design of the application to meet organizational specifications.[6] The CSA conducts an assessment of existing workflow and the current operational process and receives education on the system from the vendor. The education will provide the CSA with knowledge of system functionality and how to design the system, where on completion, the analyst will be the expert on the application. In collaboration with clinical staff, the analyst will evaluate how the system can be adapted to meet clinical outcomes and departmental and organizational goals. The department manager, in collaboration with the project director, will identify resources for the evaluation, and the CSA will work with these resources, who will be experts on the current operational process.

Educator

New system implementation requires competent users. To ensure this, end users will need formal education to develop the skills to use the system because no matter how well designed the system is, if the end user does not learn the system, the implementation will fail. The educator will determine when training will be conducted,[5] and the project director, in collaboration with the executive sponsor, will identify the additional trainers, class location, and logistics. The selection of the staff to train end users will depend on the applications to be implemented, and the educator will have a detailed knowledge of how the system works and the operational process of the end users.

The project director and the educator will develop the education plan that determines logistics, such as number of educators, appropriate class size, process for scheduling end users, and identification of clerical support services. The educator will be responsible for development of lesson content, the process to measure competency, and skills validation. The lesson content will include both application procedures and workflow redesign, and the educational session will be concept based rather than task oriented. Ultimately, the emphasis will be on integrating technology and workflow.

Superuser

Another important member of the team is called a superuser. Superusers are peers who will help train and support their colleagues in the implementation process.[9] They are active members of the implementation team and will provide input into the design of the system. Superusers generally possess excellent communication skills, expert knowledge of department operations, and are coaches to their peers. The superuser, as nurse champion, facilitates communication in two directions: articulating nursing needs to the CSA and explaining technology solutions to the nursing staff.[10] Superusers help decrease dependence on the CSA, are a department-based resource, and have expert skills in the use of clinical applications.[11] The superuser should be flexible and understand the internal chain of command for resolution of issues. Additionally, he or she will provide input into policy revision and procedure redesign. The CSA will follow superusers through their workday and log each of the steps and document each task and how the task is completed. This will provide the basis for documentation of the current workflow. The CSA compares the current workflow and applies it to the design of the system, where the superuser offers guidelines for documentation, participates in system selection, completes system testing, and trains and supports his or her colleagues.[12]

The Phases of Implementation

Once the implementation roles are defined for the institution, it is up to the executive team to match the appropriate clinician to the role. Each role actively participates in all phases of the implementation. Nurses should have a prominent role as champions on the implementation team given their professional experience and knowledge.[10] Nursing roles include the CNO, informatics nurse specialist, nurse educator, and staff nurse. Involving nurses in education, go-live support, and system optimization is one of the key factors to success.[13] This concept is supported by a study that concludes that successful implementations are ones that are owned, sponsored, and championed by the nursing team.[13]

There are several phases in the life cycle of an informatics project: selection; implementation, which includes design and go-live; and postimplementation system optimization. In the selection phase, the focus is finding the right system for the institution. In the design phase, technology and workflow will be integrated to facilitate best practice, and in the go-live phase, support for new users of the system will be the priority. System optimization prepares the clinicians for less intense activities of maintenance and enhancements, where they will eventually fully own the system, with the project team transitioning to a supporting role.

System Selection

In the role of executive sponsor, the CNO has a strategic position in system selection. In collaboration with the CIO, CMO, CFO, and CEO, the CNO identifies and communicates the organizational vision for management of information.[14]

The CNO will be actively involved in selection and implementation of information systems, a policy that is supported by The Joint Commission (TJC), which requires nursing involvement in the selection process.[15]

The executive steering committee determines the budget for the project, identifies the participating disciplines, and approves the standards by which vendors will be evaluated. The committee will ensure that organizational goals are congruent with the system and evaluate the vendors from a macro perspective. By networking with their peers, the committee will be able to compare vendor solutions for systems that are functioning at similar institutions. The executive team will also approve the request for information (RFI) and request for proposal (RFP) documents. Members include administrators from nursing, medicine, pharmacy, information technology, operations, and finance.

Ideally, a nurse with clinical, informatics, and implementation experience is an ideal candidate for the role of project director given his or her broad background across a variety of processes in the healthcare spectrum. An informatics nurse specialist is a nurse who is formally trained in the practice of informatics. This involves the management and utilization of information and technologies. Responsibilities for this role include development of systems, research to support information systems, and making information systems usable for nurses.[16] The informatics nurse synthesizes informatics standards into every aspect of the implementation. With an American Nurses Credentialing Center (ANCC) certification in nursing informatics, project management certification, or as a Certified Professional in Healthcare Information and Management Systems (CPHIMS), the project director will have the knowledge and skills necessary for this role. The ability to follow a plan, identify barriers, and resolve issues is a common skill in nursing practice. The director has experience in managing multiple patient priorities that enables him or her to manage multiple application project priorities.

The project director completes the RFI and RFP documents. The director, in collaboration with directors from other disciplines, will identify requirements from a technical and clinical perspective, where functional requirements are included in these documents. He or she will also include information about the institution, such as number of beds, facility structure, annual admissions, and annual outpatient visits. This will allow the vendors to better prepare a proposal. Those vendors who cannot meet basic functionality are eliminated from the selection process.

Evaluation of the systems that make the first cut will give an end-user view of how the systems function in day-to-day operations. This will allow the selection team to further narrow down the field of systems. The final evaluation will ensure that patient-centered care is maintained through electronic documentation, improved accuracy of documentation, and clinical decision support.[15] The project director completes a functional needs assessment that details the necessary functions a system should have. The functions will be based on regulations, policy, and best practice. The director will then develop the assessment listing the key components for the system, specific to the institution, that identifies the "must haves" for the system (Table 5.1). For example, does the system allow standard tables/drop-downs across modules? The director will determine if this is a requirement or an option. Each system is evaluated by the functions, and a decision is made once all system evaluations are complete. The functional

Table 5.1 Example of a Functional Assessment for Clinical Documentation

SYSTEM FUNCTIONALITY—CLINICAL DOCUMENTATION	PRESENT YES/NO	REQUIRED YES/NO	DESCRIPTION/ COMMENTS
Does the system allow standard tables/drop-down menus across modules?			
Can documented information be pulled from encounter to encounter?			
Can documentation in all encounters update information in history?			
Does the system support multidisciplinary documentation?			
Are problem lists supported?			
Can documentation generate a charge to the financial system?			
Can documentation generate acuity?			
Can alerts be generated based upon documented fields?			
Can sets of information be required?			
Can documentation be set up to specific patient populations?			
Can documentation trigger orders?			
Can documented problems generate orders or interventions?			
Can problems be prioritized?			
Can the system prevent future documentation?			
Are there templates for progress notes, op notes, etc.?			

assessment is combined with other factors, such as cost and technical requirements, to identify the top choices. The next step is to identify the team to see the top choices in action. The director will coordinate the site visits and ensure that all disciplines are represented on the visit. Once the site visits are complete, and the assessments are made, the director will prepare a recommendation to the executive team.

The next step in the selection process involves the staff nurse and front-line direct caregivers. This is when the top vendors will come to the institution to demonstrate their system. The staff nurse as superuser can be a valuable asset at this stage. The team will want to see how the systems work in their own environment. Staff nurses will help prepare a script of the typical patient encounter at the institution. The systems should be evaluated across the patient care continuum and include the most common patient populations. The best way to accomplish this is to use the system to follow the patient experience through orders, documentation, and follow-up care. Enabling direct caregivers to walk through the system will provide an opportunity to "test drive" it. Designated staff nurses will become engaged in the selection process, where they will be the early adopters and help create a pool of superusers who will assist through the next steps of the implementation. Once the site visits and demonstrations are complete, the selection team will complete evaluations of each of the vendors and the director will compile the results and make a recommendation to the executive committee.

At this point, contract negotiations will be held. The project director will evaluate the contract for inclusion of requirements identified in the functional assessment. The chief counsel, CIO, CNE, and CFO will complete the negotiation team, and they will have the final decision and take all aspects of the selection steps into consideration. The signing of the contract will start the next phase, system implementation. See Figure 5.1 for a stepwise illustration of the entire process.

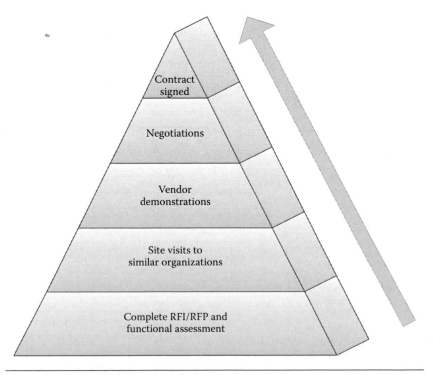

Figure 5.1 The steps of the system selection.

System Implementation: The Design Phase

After the contract is signed, the executive steering committee identifies the team for the implementation phase. The executive sponsors' primary responsibility is to facilitate end-user engagement in the design. The executive steering committee team will determine the scope of the project and identify which applications will be implemented first. The implementation team members will be assigned to each application based on their clinical expertise. The application team will assess the needs of the end users, and a formal needs assessment will capture their basic requirements for system functionality. The assessment will include collecting information needs, workflow process, and functional requirements, where the requirements indicate what must, must not, may, or should be included in the design of the system.[17]

The team should meet frequently with the superusers in this phase, during which the CSA designs the system and provides feedback on the design to the superusers. As executive sponsor, the CNO focuses on the administrative aspect of the design, keeping in mind the strategic goals, mission, vision, and values, making certain that the best candidate is assigned to the role of the project director.

Much of the high-level implementation activity is the responsibility of the project director. The director applies project management and informatics standards, integrating nursing science, computer science, and information science. Project activities include analyzing, testing, and implementing systems to support patient care. The project director will have communication, change management, and business and application knowledge,[16] and the director will guide the application teams through the steps of system design.

The director is also responsible for multiple teams and multiple applications. The scope of the project will determine the required skills of each CSA and the number of analysts needed per application. If the implementation consists of many applications, team leaders will be assigned to each application. The director ensures that the project plan is developed and that the team stays on track for the expected go-live date. Key milestones and target dates will be identified, and it will be the responsibility of the project director to keep the team on target. Ultimately, the CSA will follow the plan and complete the tasks in the application plan.

Success in system implementation will depend on the nurse having a prominent role in change management, with nurse champions on the team.[10] The CSA will review basic system functionality and match it to the clinician workflow, and will identify and review all departmental policies and procedures that relate to the implementation. He or she will evaluate the screens provided in the basic system and tailor them to end-user specifications. The CSA also collaborates with superusers to identify and incorporate best practices into the system, where system design should include standard terminology and required minimum data. Required data are the essential information that must be included for completion of the process. In this case, the user cannot leave a computer screen without entering the information. This guarantees that minimum data are collected.

The nurse in the CSA role documents the current operational workflow associated with the application, which takes place over several days in various ways. Workflow process analysis leads to a clearly defined diagram of how tasks are completed by the clinical staff. This step requires frequent interaction with the clinicians. These interactions include a formal interview to detail the step-by-step process needed to complete the task. Time to shadow the clinician is also necessary to verify the accuracy of the documented process. Superusers comfortable with the current documentation process will be the primary resources for documentation of workflow, where several episodes of shadowing are necessary. The CSA will follow the superusers through their workday and keep a log of the steps documenting what they do and how they do it, and complete the diagram of current process. The goal is to integrate the current best practice, new functionality, and technology into one seamless process.

Workflows will be created for each of the operational processes associated with the functions in each application. For nursing workflows, this will include the medication administration process, documentation of patient assessments, vital signs, intake and output, and care planning, where all details will be included. As each workflow is documented, the appropriate administrator will sign off to validate the accuracy of the documented workflow. The CSA will then compare the current process to the functionality in the system and will also take into consideration any new point of care devices or steps that will be added to the workflow at implementation. A proposed new workflow will be diagramed to show how the new system will change the process.

Figure 5.2 shows a typical new medication management workflow for a physician, pharmacist, and nurse after implementation of the CIS. The new process will build safety into each step with the addition of computerized physician order entry (CPOE), clinical decision support system (CDSS), point of care (POC) technology, and barcoding for medication administration (BCMA). Automated dispensing cabinets will improve turnaround time and provide another level of safety. For physicians, CPOE with CDSS will provide patient-specific recommendations to assist in making clinical decisions.[2] For nursing, it is important in this phase to recognize the implementation as practice redesign. Current processes and workflows will change in order to implement a new evidence-based practice model.[13]

The CSA designs the system based on the details in the new workflow. After completing the screen builds, data entry fields, and tables, the CSA compares the current process to the proposed new process, where the comparison of the two workflows will generate an impact analysis. The executive sponsor and appropriate department leaders then review and sign off on the new process and the impact analysis, which will be used to prepare the end users for the new system. It will form the key items to stress in education for the end users. The superuser will communicate the new process prior to formal education to better prepare the end users for the change, and will champion the new workflow as one that is beneficial to delivering patient care.[11] Holding regularly scheduled sessions with the superusers will provide them with the information to validate and communicate the change. Figure 5.3 shows the process for identifying and detailing the current process, proposed new process, and impact analysis.

On completion of the new workflows and revisions to the system, the CSA will start the testing phase and complete individual testing within each application. This will verify that the application build works as intended. Then the CSA will test across applications, where once the verification at this level is complete, the superusers will test for usability and accuracy. Testing should be integrated to include hardware, interfaces to ancillary systems, and the billing process. Testing new point of care devices will identify any network issues, and if the network is unreliable, the devices will not consistently be

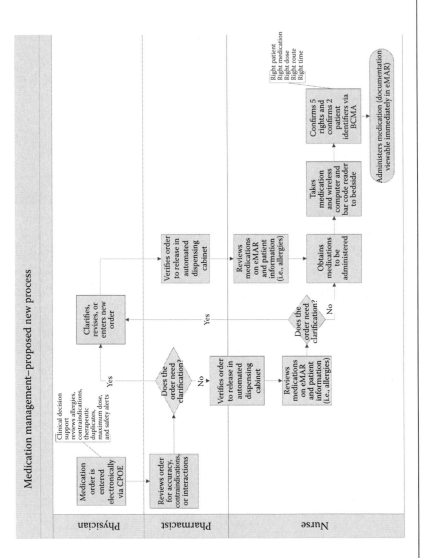

Figure 5.2   Medication management proposed new process for CIS implementation.

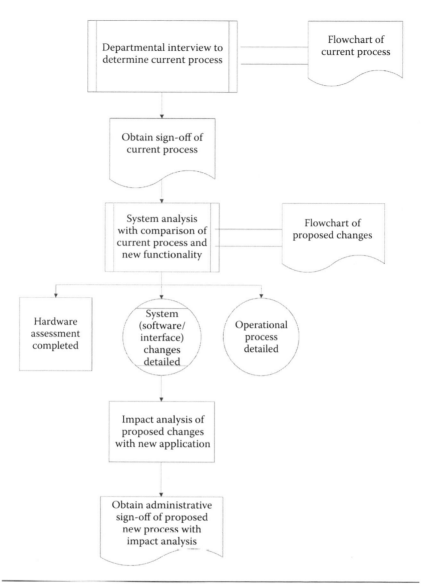

Figure 5.3 Process for current, proposed, and impact workflows.

available for the end user.[18] Superusers from all disciplines will participate in the final level of testing, and they will sign off on the workflow and screens. The project director then confirms all is ready to start training the end users.

Ideally, classes should start shortly before the staff is scheduled to begin using the system. Planning too far ahead may result in users

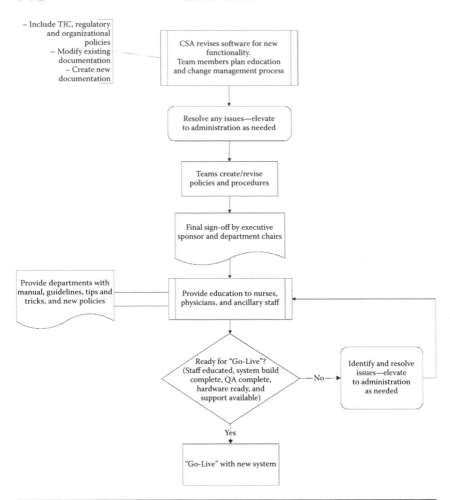

Figure 5.4   Steps in go-live phase of implementation.

forgetting what they were taught.[5] Together, the project director and the educator will develop the education plan. It should be kept in mind that classes should be scheduled at times that are convenient for the end users. This will require a large pool of educators who can conduct classes on all shifts, seven days a week. Managers will be responsible for maintaining minimum staffing levels on their units while sending staff to class, and the educator will select and train the class instructors. Super-users are generally excellent choices for instructors given their expert knowledge of the new workflows and the system. The educator will monitor class attendance to ensure the majority of users are educated prior to go-live, and completion of class will be mandatory prior to granting access to the system. Each attendee will be expected to demonstrate competency by completing a test on the new workflows and system, where once education is complete, the end users are ready to use the system. Figure 5.4 shows the process for the steps up to go-live, including education and issue resolution.

System Implementation: Go-Live

The go-live is the date on which the staff will begin using the new system. The date is one set by the executive team from the recommendation of the project director. Consideration for the decision includes availability of resources to support the go-live and organizational initiatives that could divert resources or attention from the go-live. At this point, education of end users must be complete and the system must have passed integrated testing.

The executive sponsor and project director must be sure that the support for go-live is adequate. Whether the go-live is a pilot on one unit or whole house, users must be adequately supported. This implies that requests for assistance must be responded to in real time and the entire implementation team will be available to support all users. The superuser will provide on-unit support for basic troubleshooting and resolution of operational issues[5] and will triage more complex issues to the support team stationed in a go-live command center.

During the go-live period, a log should be kept of all calls to the support team. The information that will be logged includes name and location of the caller, description of the issue, category of issue, responsible party, and resolution of the issue. The issues will be identified into three categories: operational, technical, or educational, where the category of the issue will determine who will be the responsible party to resolve. The issue log will provide a mechanism for trending analysis and will help the team to determine if they are isolated events or part of a more global problem. The log should be posted for all end users to view, which will allow them to see the response and to reach out to the responsible party with any questions. In the case of educational or operational issues, it can also help prevent the issue from occurring again by another user.

The support team located in the command center will be a combination of vendor support staff, CSA, team leaders, and the project director. Additional support will take the form of a roaming team of superusers on the units to resolve operational and educational issues. Support will be 24/7 and will remain in place for as long as calls are coming into the command center. The number of staff needed for support will decrease after the first week, and then the team should be able to transition the support to the superusers and normal support staff. The transition from active 24/7 support to standard support operations will be determined by the CIO, executive sponsor, and project director. Nursing administration will take the lead in establishing a team for ongoing operational support for the end users, where this support team will answer questions about documentation, provide advice on how to improve new workflows, and continue to log and trend issues. The post-go-live superusers will be well versed in the CIS and new processes.[19]

The executive sponsor and the members of the executive steering committee should have a visible presence during the go-live, in the command center and on the units. The executive sponsor and project director's responsibilities are to ensure that the transition for the frontline staff is seamless. The executive sponsor will empower the clinicians to take ownership of the system and the new process. Finally, the CNO should understand the impact of the implementation on all levels of the organization.[15]

System Optimization

Following the go-live period, the project team will begin the optimization phase, at which time they will evaluate enhancements to be implemented. These enhancements may be suggestions or noncritical issues from the issue log. They could also be items that were deferred during system design due to time constraints. The project director will prioritize the enhancements and the team leaders will implement the solutions.

The executive sponsor and the project director will determine the metrics by which the implementation will be measured. Some of the critical success factors include staff satisfaction, patient satisfaction, increased time at the bedside for the nurse, increased accuracy in documentation, the timeliness of information, and the accessibility of information. The pharmacy and pathology areas will measure turn-around time, number of clarifications, and number of prevented errors by clinical decision support alerts.

Staff satisfaction should improve with the implementation of more efficient and effective workflows. To measure this, a satisfaction survey should be conducted after some time has elapsed following the system rollout. Typical questions in this survey include ease of documentation, speed of response by the support team, and turnaround time for recommended changes.

Another way to evaluate success is to monitor the quality and completeness of documentation, where the minimum required data identified in the planning stage could be used as indicators for performance monitoring. Accuracy and completeness should be key elements considered. The evaluation should be simple since computerized data are more accessible and retrievable than handwritten documentation. Other evaluations should then be completed based on quality of documentation, assessment of national patient safety goals (NPSGs), TJC standards, and organizational policy. Completion of documentation, such as assessment and reassessment of pain, within specified time frames can be measured.

The executive steering committee will prioritize and allocate resources for monitoring the effect of implementation on the clinical workflow and patient outcomes. The implementation will also streamline and automate the process for reporting of public data. The team can use the driving forces for the implementation to assess their performance.[4] See Figure 5.5 for a stepwise illustration of the process.

Conclusion

The implementation of a CIS is a process that requires teamwork. Assembling the best teams will ensure a successful transition to new workflows, automated processes, and real-time clinical decision support, where the teams must represent all disciplines. The inclusion of nurses at all phases and in key roles of the implementation will help ensure for end users that the implementation will be patient centered. The selection phase will allow the team to see the systems in action being used by their peers. The design phase is the best opportunity to get buy-in from nurses and other disciplines, which includes

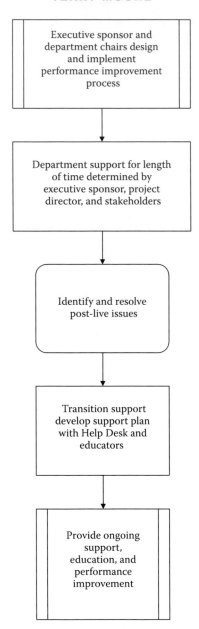

Figure 5.5   Post-go-live processes for system optimization.

understanding the current process and integrating technology into best practices to redesign clinician workflow. Education is a very important consideration in this phase.

To achieve a smooth go-live rollout, dedicated staff support by the implementation team is necessary. The team, in collaboration with administration, will decide the day the clinicians begin to use the new system, where well-trained and supported users should begin to utilize the new platform. In the optimization phase, the team will evaluate the implementation, where feedback will include a staff satisfaction survey. The team will monitor documentation for accuracy and completeness.

Implementation of a CIS should ultimately increase accessibility and improve the accuracy of documentation. In the end, an implementation is costly, time-consuming, and resource-intensive, but the return on investment should be worthwhile given the positive impact on clinical outcomes. Including new technology in the redesigned workflow will improve safety with real-time clinical decision support, improve quality with more complete documentation, and improve satisfaction by increasing nurse time at the bedside. Having nurses in key implementation roles will ensure that the patient is the primary focus of the implementation.

This chapter was originally published in *Healthcare Informatics, Improving Efficiency and Productivity*, Taylor & Francis, New York, 2010.

References

1. Kohn LT, Corrigan JM, Donaldson MS, eds. 1999. *To err is human: Building a safer health system.* Washington, DC: Institute of Medicine Committee on Quality of Health Care in America, National Academies Press.
2. Institute of Medicine Committee. 2001. *Crossing the quality chasm: A new health system for the 21st century.* Washington, DC: National Academies Press.
3. Page A, ed. 2003. *Keeping patients safe: Transforming the work environment of nurses.* Washington, DC: Institute of Medicine Committee on the Work Environment for Nurses and Patient Safety, National Academies Press.
4. Mustain JM, Lowry LW, Wilhoit KW. 2008. Change readiness assessment for conversion to electronic medical records. *JONA* 38:379–85.

5. Maffeo R. 2000. Project implementation: A tailored approach. *Semin Nurse Managers* 8:51–52.

6. Hassett M. 2006. Case study: Factors in defining the nurse informatics specialist role. *JHIM* 20:30–35.

7. Staggers N. 1998. Notes from a clinical information system project manager: Requisite survival skills. *Comput Nurs* 16:244–46.

8. Souther E. 2001. Implementation of the electronic medical record: The team approach. *Comput Nurs* 19:47–55.

9. Ball MJ., Hannah KJ, Edwards MJA. 1999. *Introduction to nursing informatics.* New York: Springer-Verlag.

10. Kirkley D. 2004. Not whether, but when. *JONA* 34:55–58.

11. Boffa DP, Pawola LM. 2006. Identification and conceptualization of nurse super users *JIHM* 20:60–68.

12. McNeive JE. 2009. Super users have great value in your organization. *Comput Inform Nurs* May/June: 136–39.

13. Murphy J. 2009. The best IT project is not an IT project. *JIHM* 23:6–8.

14. Brokel J. 2007. Creating sustainability of clinical information systems. *JONA* 37:10–13.

15. Simpson RL. 2007. The politics of information technology. *Nurs Admin Q* 31:354–58.

16. American Nurses Association. 2008. *Nursing informatics: Scope and standards of practice.* Washington, DC: American Nurses Publishing.

17. Brady M, Hassett M, eds. 2000. *Clinical informatics.* HIMSS Guidebook Series. Chicago: Healthcare Information Management and Systems Society.

18. Huvane K. 2008. Trouble at the bedside. *Healthcare Inform* 25:32–35.

19. Shedenhelm HJ, Hernke DA, Gusa DA, Twedell DM. 2008. EMR implementation and ongoing education. *Nurs Manage* July, 51–53.

6

ARCHITECTING TRANSITIONS TO A FULLY ELECTRONIC MEDICAL RECORD WITH EMPHASIS ON PHYSICIAN ADOPTION AND OPTIMAL UTILIZATION

JAMES F. KEEL, III
AND D. ARLO JENNINGS

Contents

The electronic medical record (EMR) is an electronic means for physicians and other clinical providers to review clinical results, place patient orders, and create appropriate electronic documentation. The EMR actions on the part of physicians include computer order entry (CPOE) and electronic documentation. CPOE is not keyboarding orders as free text into a word processor, but rather it is the process of retrieving orders from an electronic order catalogue by matching specific catalogue orders to the desired order intent as conceived. CPOE additionally provides the means to make available defined order sets that support integrated tasks into a common complex clinical action. The creation of electronic documentation is the physician's means of providing documentation of history and physical notes, consultations, procedures, operations, progress notes, and discharge summaries, prescriptions, and medication reconciliation. Much of this documentation is free text in nature, but requires adherence to standard formats.

Because the EMR deviates markedly from the traditional paper-based formats, the proposed transition to the EMR has commonly spawned significant physician resistance to the utilization of this new technology platform. This resistance, common with many new users of technology, is generally in reaction to a change in their daily routines forced on them by the use of the proposed technology. In 2009 approximately 10% of the 5000 plus hospitals in the United States had ventured into the world of CPOE. Two factors at that time inhibited a stronger adoption rate of CPOE: first, the expense of the implementation and second, a resistance to adoption on the part of stakeholders. However, following the federal Meaningful Use incentive program, there has evolved a strong national migration to CPOE in the hospital setting such that CPOE is rapidly becoming the standard instrument for executing clinical orders. Migration to a fully electronic record, including physician documentation, is not required by Meaningful Use, and as such is causing a continued lag in further EMR adoption. Nevertheless, physicians and hospital administrators are recognizing that without full EMR adoption, the clinical process remains split between paper and electronic environments, leading to losses in efficiency and effectiveness in the care of patients.

The implementation of the EMR creates added expenses to hospitals' bottom lines. These expenses derive from the considerable effort needed to effect this major cultural and clinical transformation, including planning, expectation setting, implementation of preparatory prerequisite applications, deployment of adequate computers for access, downtime contingencies, design and build of an electronic processes physicians will accept, education, go-live support, and management of post go-live requests for changes and updates. Each of these is discussed in some detail in this chapter.

The question remains as to how a hospital's information technology (IT) team should work with clinicians to orchestrate the best approach to ensure a well-functioning system that will be readily accepted by physicians and that works efficiently for clinical support staff. The IT team must include the position for a strong chief medical information officer (CMIO) to interface among the design and build team, the administration, and physicians to guide the transformation process and to provide clinical guidance to the design of the system. IT must also have experienced nurses on the informatics staff to help with design and build, but without physician input acceptance will be limited or completely denied. The ultimate success of the implementation depends on the interaction among the administration, support departments, and physicians. The hospital must then devise a project scope, develop a formal implementation plan, and budget appropriate resources, utilizing formal project management methodology. Finally the hospital administration must fully recognize that this is not "just another project." This type of transformation is unique and requires uniform leadership alignment, persistence, collaboration with medical staff, and an unwavering commitment to follow through with stated intentions.

Background: Perceptions, Costs, and Outcomes

The EMR transition presents a perception both challenging to administration and threatening to physicians. Hospital administrators react positively to moving in this direction because of the potential saving that might be gained and the potential reduction of medical errors.

Regarding potential savings, measurement of return on investment from the EMR is complex and fraught with pitfalls. Hospital executives may be tempted to significantly underestimate both capital and expense costs of implementation. Global changes in dashboard outcomes for the organization, such as length of stay, cost per case, mortality, and morbidities, are confounded by many factors, including shifting acuity, seasonal variations, adjustments in market share, impact from multiple other projects, changing reimbursement plans, and so on. In addition, reduction in medical errors, particularly those with harm, is commonly cited as a benefit of the EMR but is notoriously difficult to quantify, primarily because of problems inherent in voluntary reporting. Finally, hospital executives must keep in mind that the EMR transition will not be the final product to justify their goal for integration of information technology into the provision of healthcare. The EMR should be viewed as an evolving composite of many pieces that will form the foundation of an electronic underpinning to replace an antiquated and highly limited paper-based system. Although the final solution may be expected to facilitate and yield enormous improvements in hospital care, too much should not be expected of or attributed to this initial EMR implementation alone.

The EMR provides a foundation from which many improvements in data mining and clinical care will ultimately emerge. Nevertheless, a careful process should be put in place before implementing the EMR to facilitate a careful analysis of investment costs tied to clinical and operational outcomes.

Medical Error Reduction Proposition

Much has been written about medical errors and the EMR. The EMR has been touted to decrease medical errors by several mechanisms. On the surface, it eliminates errors and problems associated with misinterpretation of illegibility. Illegible notes, orders, and handwritten prescriptions have been documented to be a major source of errors. CPOE holds the potential to make orders more explicit and less vulnerable to misinterpretation resulting from errors in construction and syntax in the creation of handwritten orders. Furthermore, orders may be implemented more consistently as a result of properly imbedded clinical decision support at the point of order entry. This includes such devices as the attachment of commonly used appropriate order sentences to medication orderables, the development of computer-based order sets that may act as prompts to prevent errors of omission, and the judicious use of rules and alerts to guide safe and proper execution of orders. Although CPOE holds great promise for reducing medical errors in orders, it should be kept in mind that other processes for ensuring safe administration of medications, such as bar coding or radiofrequency identification tying patients to dose dispensing of medications may be equally important in this regard. Electronic documentation has the advantage of facilitating clear, legible communications in standard formats that can be viewed from any computer workstation. Transitioning entirely away from paper processes holds the promise of greater efficiency in workflows with improved effectiveness, giving physicians and nurses more time to spend with patient care. The EMR has the potential to do more than just decrease medical errors. The EMR may improve outcomes directly through the embedding of best practice standards in the form of decision support at the point of order, prescription, or documentation entry. It is tempting for the hospital and medical staff to grossly underestimate the resources necessary to design and build a complete EMR environment that will meet these expectations that are necessary to achieve the anticipated benefits of a successful implementation. Furthermore, these benefit assumptions have been challenged by conflicting reports in the literature that include wide ranges in outcomes following a transition to the EMR most likely resulting from variations in vendor technology, EMR design and build, and implementation strategies. Finally, measuring benefits from the EMR is a shifting proposition, owing to changes and improvements in hardware and software technologies that make prior reports of outcomes rapidly obsolete.

Preplanning for the EMR—Analysis and Documentation of Clinical Processes and Workflow: Current and Future State

To be successful, the process should begin with reengineering both clinical and business processes. This should always begin with a careful workflow analysis of all clinical processes from the bedside through all of the clinical support departments, both for the current state and as expected to be leveraged in future state.

As an organization, it is a must to think in terms of how physicians, nurses, clinicians, and clinical support staff work, and how a patient needs to be processed through the hospital, regardless of health issue, and inclusive of all clinical departments. Lean/Six Sigma methodology may be very useful in crafting a structured approach to design and implementation when coupled with formal project management.

- Initially an upfront systems analysis detailing workflow must be accomplished that will address current state and future state after implementation of any EMR application, a process that will require input from all relevant stakeholders.
- Workflow must be considered at all points in the clinical process. A detailed process and data flow diagrams should be designed for each clinical process, clinical unit, and clinical support department to indicate patient flow, patient data flow, and detailed workflow processes for all staff. Foremost, the patient must considered at the center of the process.
- The flow diagrams may now be used to examine weaknesses in the current environment and then pose possible solutions for improving patient care and data flow, creating new flow

diagrams. Comparing current state with the new flow diagrams allows users to easily visualize and become more creative in seeing new opportunities.

- Finally, a subsequent flow diagram may be constructed, depicting how workflow could be improved if electronic systems were in place to support the needed functionality. To achieve optimal process improvements, one must "get outside the box in thinking." This process provides an important time to pause and carefully consider, not to redesign the current system that already exists and will not meet future needs, but rather to think future, think workflow, think process, and think reengineering. Most of all it is critical to think in terms of optimal patient care.

Most healthcare organizations may be tempted to make the mistake of expending valuable resources redesigning what they are already doing, thereby missing this vital opportunity to reengineer processes and better leverage information technology. No organization can take advantage of computerized applications if the objective is to continue to do things the way they have always been done. Design teams must think outside the box, a point that needs to be stressed over and over to the team. Once current workflow, a desired workflow, and reviewed processes that must be reengineered have been defined, workflow may be aligned to the order entry applications design and build.

Methodology for Adoption of the EMR: The Transformation and Product

EMR implementation will be discussed from two distinct perspectives: (1) the Product, meaning the design and build of the application environment, and (2) the Transformation, meaning the preparation and process of transition of the clinical culture. Although the EMR impacts the entire hospital organization as a consequence of its downstream impact on all departments, in this chapter we focus primarily on the transformation necessary for the physicians and other providers who will be the users of the system. The strategies and processes described here are expected to be relevant whether the medical staff of the hospital in question is largely employed or practicing in independent practices.

Prerequisites

Before engaging in a discussion of the transformation, it is appropriate to describe a number of prerequisites regarding the computer system should be solidly in place before undertaking the implementation of any major component of the EMR. Also, certain clinical and departmental processes should be standardized to incorporate evidence-based best practice and limit unnecessary variability through the use of structured, standard protocols, procedures, and orders sets (usually on paper initially) before implementation. These concepts are very useful and are discussed subsequently in more detail.

Clinical Access to Computer Workstations

There must be ample access to computers for clinical care distributed in a way that supports efficient clinical workflow. This requires a structured walk-through of the nursing units and areas where physicians normally congregate to discuss patient care. This analysis will definitely mean adding additional computer workstations and telephones (if required) to ensure appropriate workflow. Using dual screens have been demonstrated to enhance workflow efficiency during the process of both order entry and electronic documentation, allowing the user to simultaneously review available clinical information on one screen while executing input on the other. Portable device solutions have demonstrated more utility in gathering patient data in the direct patient encounter setting. The adequacy of computer access points must be carefully assessed prior to a live roll out through careful inspections of the demand for computer terminals during peak rounding hours. Demand for computers will not decrease with any implementation. These observations should be followed by augmentation of those areas in the system that may become deficient with go-live. Observations should also be conducted to identify any areas that may need renovation to accommodate the required number of devices. Many hospitals and clinics were constructed well before the introduction of computer technology and as such there are often critical limitations in space for the deployment of computer technology and workstations. New devices and renovations should be budgeted, acquired, and deployed, with follow-up analysis to confirm the sufficiency of the remedy. It is critical to observe how physicians make rounds. If part of the patient chart is on paper, physicians will want a place to sit and enter information, where mobile access devices may not be first choice.

Downtime Procedures

There must be carefully designed downtime procedures, including appropriate backup software and workflow processes in place. All downtime solutions should be tested by regularly scheduled drills to ensure familiarity with downtime procedures and to identify potential gaps in the process. Having paper forms readily available, either printed or printable from the workstation, but secured during normal up time, will expedite continuing patient care by all providers during downtime occurrences.

Computer Authentication Login and Performance

Computer login efficiency and performance should be assessed and optimized with appropriate network, hardware, and software installations that will facilitate rapid screen-to-screen times. Computer processor utilization on the back end as well as user screen-to-screen timings on the front end should be monitored and reported at regular intervals. We learned no matter how fast the back end processing might be, the ease and quickness of screen response on the front end, in fact, defined the physicians' perception of satisfactory computer performance. Newer technologies are now available, such as mobile desktop platforms and badge login, that allow more rapid access to multiple applications to improve workflow efficiency.

Deployment of Departmental Clinical Support
Applications in Advance of CPOE

Prior to any EMR transition, clinical department-based applications that will support the deployment of orders and documentation downstream from the physician input should be implemented, fully tested, and functional. This includes laboratory, radiology, nursing documentation, rehabilitation services, respiratory care, nutrition services, and so on. Most importantly, medication process applications that will support pharmacy filling and verification functions, medication dispensing functions, and the electronic medication administration record should be live and functioning smoothly prior to CPOE to ensure a complete, safe, and effective medication delivery process. Finally, applications supporting surgery, emergency department services, scheduling, registration, and patient management are additional IT building blocks that are best implemented prior to moving to CPOE or to electronic documentation by providers. This will facilitate transition to a paper-free process that is necessary to capture critical efficiencies in workflows.

The Transformation

Preliminary Steps: Getting Physicians on the Computer in Advance of CPOE and Documentation

Part of preparing the medical staff for the EMR should focus on leading physicians to engage the computer in their daily clinical workflow. We facilitated this transition in two ways:

1. *Making the post-discharge chart available only via the computer.* This was accomplished by first implementing a robust document imaging product. We then transformed the processing of all medical records by our Health Information Management Department such that all paper documents from the inpatient record were scanned into the electronic medical record within 24 hours of discharge. This had the effect of requiring physicians to go to the computer to retrieve any patient's old record, whether accessing a chart for a patient returning for subsequent care or completing medical record postdischarge deficiencies. This change in workflow proved to be an extraordinary asset to physicians. First, physicians found that they could access the old chart in seconds instead of 20 to 40 minutes when evaluating return patients, thereby greatly improving their workflow. Second, physicians discovered that they could review and complete charts at any time from any location. The dividend from this transition was that all physicians not only became rapidly adept at using the computer, including keyboard and mouse point and click activities, but

also became familiar with navigation of the electronic patient record. A final and perhaps the most important dividend was that physicians for the first time experienced concrete benefits in their daily workflow directly attributable to the electronic patient record. This represented a first critical step in the pathway to adoption of the EMR.

2. *Making test results and patient data available online.* This step was accompanied by a simultaneous implementation to make all or nearly all results and documents immediately available in the electronic inpatient record in real time through direct feeds and interfaces with dictation/transcription, lab, electro-diagnostics, radiology, picture archiving and communication system (PACS), electronic medication record, home and in-hospital medication lists, vital signs, intensive care unit (ICU) flow sheet data, family contact information, active provider lists, and nursing documentation. Because of some remaining paper documents and lack of working interfaces among disparate vendor applications, it may not be possible to enter all information directly into the computer record. Nevertheless, these documents may be made available in the computer through the process of concurrent scanning. Clinical results on paper should be scanned in real time. Nonurgent documents may be scanned in twice per day to keep the computer information current. Once physicians became familiar with accessing patient information electronically, their ability to access comprehensive, fully up-to-date patient data through a single process from any location provides a second revolutionary improvement in their workflow. As a result, physicians quickly transitioned voluntarily from a paper to an electronic process for chart review in their inpatient rounds every day, no longer depending on the time it takes to search for and review the paper chart. This provided a second giant step in the movement toward adoption of a fully electronic medical record.

Development of Patient Care Pathways for Orders

CPOE enables the execution of discreet, legible, and robust orders, including preformatted order sentences and rapid deployment to downstream support services. The process of combining multiple orders into order sets with specifically tailored formats, based on the requirements of specific disease processes and workflows, allows for the introduction of standardization in the ordering process that incorporates best practice standards. The flexibility of the electronic system leveraged in this way also makes possible the ability of the system to rapidly evolve in the inclusion of the latest evidence-based recommendations. Order sets may be designed to support specific processes, such as admission and discharge, as well as complex transitions in care. Such order sets may be termed Patient Care Pathways or Plans of Care. Each organization should establish a department that is responsible for the development and updated maintenance of these plans. The process for creating them should be multidisciplinary and preferably physician led. Lean/Six Sigma processes are recommended for the development and maintenance of these plans, including value stream mapping and supporting data analytics.

This important transition may be expected to result in:

- Improved, highly refined, and streamlined order sets throughout the system, using a common style guide format familiar to all providers
- A comprehensive array of paper order sets, supporting admissions, consultations, titrations, and perioperative/procedure processes
- Improved efficiency in the day-to-day entry of orders
- Improved compliance in general use by all physicians
- Better compliance with best practice and evidence-based standards
- Improved patient outcomes with fewer complications, readmissions, and harm
- Improved financial performance
- Improved compliance with growing regulatory requirements in clinical practice

Physician Transformation

Physician Resistance   Understanding how to approach transformation successfully begins with an appreciation of the reasons physicians often resist the transition to the EMR. Some of the most commonly expressed concerns include the following:

- "It will take me too long to enter my orders and create my notes electronically."
- "I will be spending more time in front of a computer than in front of my patients."
- "We are just trading one system of errors for another."
- "There is conflicting literature on the efficacy and safety of computers in healthcare."
- "You're asking me to do the work of a secretary."

A review of the 2008 KLAS data shows how serious this issue of physician adoption has become. KLAS reported in 2008 that only 17.4% of hospitals greater than 200 beds had implemented CPOE at some level. At these sites, only about 60% of orders on average were entered using CPOE and, tellingly, only 3% of physician users reported increased satisfaction with the use of CPOE. Since that time, largely because of the requirements of Meaningful Use, adoption of EMRs to support patient care has exploded. Significant challenges to adoption and utility remain. However, this is related largely to hurried implementations with poorly designed systems associated with multiple vendors, poor options for interoperability, and failure to analyze current and future state workflows sufficiently. Success in creating a seamless, efficient, and effective EMR requires careful planning, workflow analysis, education, and implementation go-live support.

A Physician-Driven Project   EMR implementation failure may occur for several key reasons, but at the top of the list is failure to engage physicians in the process. *Hospital administrators, often pushing an IT-driven initiative from a business proforma, decide to implement EMR systems with insufficient involvement and collaborative cooperation on the part of the medical staff.* It is unwise to succumb to the notion that adequate physician engagement cannot be practically achieved. Physician involvement may be facilitated by the inclusion of physician champions very early in the formative process of decision making. *In fact, engaging primarily physician champions to initiate and drive the process toward the electronic record for reasons of improved patient care is by far the best approach to achieving medical staff adoption.*

Recommended Steps to Achieve a Successful Transformation

The Transformation of the medical staff may be broken down into a number of components, ranging from the development of an initial, basic understanding of the EMR process to the formulation of implementation strategies. These are discussed in the following paragraphs.

The Rationale for EMR Implementation   The first step in transformation is to help physicians and clinical support staff understand the rationale behind the decision to proceed with EMR adoption. This argument may be summarized as follows.

- The EMR resolves the chronic problem of deciphering physician handwriting that has plagued healthcare since its inception that can lead to countless errors.
- An appropriately built EMR system provides the opportunity for unmatched clarity and standardization in order entry and documentation format, which in turn removes much of the ambiguity found in handwritten orders and notes, even when they can be easily read.
- The EMR has the advantage of not being confined to one location and one chart, such that the chart can be reviewed, orders can be entered, and documentation can be created from any computer access point.
- The EMR represents not just the simple rote process of effecting the entry of orders and documentation of clinical events, but instead involves the deployment, notification, coordination, completion algorithms, checklists, and safety elements for all departments downstream. The EMR has now been demonstrated to shorten significantly the time of order implementation and clinical documentation in well-designed implementations. CPOE in particular has enabled critical improvements in clarity of order clarity, reliability, and speed of order transmission.
- Perhaps most importantly, the EMR holds the promise of leveraging true clinical decision support to influence clinical decision making. By deploying well-designed, evidence-based clinical order sets; appropriate rules and smart alerts that fire only when an unsafe or undesirable action is invoked;

and a series of prompts and reminders, such as prepopulating medication orders with the most commonly used medication order sentences, clinicians are provided with state-of-the-art decision support tools. These tools allow physicians to practice medicine at an enhanced level of performance not otherwise achievable.

- Finally, the EMR is one of the fundamental components that can make up a searchable clinical data repository, permitting analysis of practice patterns and resource utilization tied to clinical and financial outcomes. This process, in turn, creates the opportunity to engineer true continuous quality improvement.

Anticipated Impact of the EMR on Workflow Another early essential step in transformation is the building of a realistic expectation of how the EMR will impact physicians and staff, and a clear explanation of how it may be expected to affect workflow in their daily lives. The physicians should be made aware that they are likely to experience both improvements and difficulties with the new system. Anticipated advantages of the EMR include the following:

- Legibility and clarity of orders and clinical notes are improved, leading to fewer misinterpretations and fewer callbacks for clarification.
- Orders and notes may be entered and reviewed from any location, permitting physicians to provide care without calling the unit or waiting for someone else to finish with the paper chart.
- Well-developed Patient Care Pathways will be immediately available on the computer, obviating the necessity of locating needed order sets in drawers, or requesting staff to find more because the sets needed have been depleted.
- Physicians will have more decision support available to support safer and more effective order entry than is possible with the paper process.
- Physicians can expect more prompt action on orders with CPOE and electronic documentation compared with a paper process.

It is important, however, to be frank with physicians regarding perceived disadvantages of the EMR.

- Some electronic actions may take longer compared with paper processes, such as the login process.
- If the system is not carefully configured notes and orders may be more difficult to implement and locate in the computer. Proper configuration should facilitate intuitive processes for orders search and for locating all results and documentation.
- Orders may be accompanied by alerts and pop-up reminders that physicians may find annoying, impeding, and distracting. If poorly configured and implemented, these instruments will lead to alert fatigue and deterioration in patient outcomes.
- Physicians may find that they are vulnerable to new types of medical errors not present on paper, such as accidentally picking an incorrect, adjacent order from a pick list.
- Physicians will face the difficult task of learning a new and foreign method for completing very familiar tasks.
- Physicians have learned to think about problems and diagnostics through the act of writing. For those with a history of using paper processes, the adoption of the EMR is invariably associated with difficulty in assuring oneself that all considerations and actions have been correctly completed. For newer clinicians who have never encountered paper processes, the adoption seems perfectly normal.

Communicating an Appropriate Expectation   The goal of communicating expectations may be accomplished by an initial communication of the intention to move forward with EMR adoption through presentations in meetings, posters, emails, Intranet/Internet postings, mailings, and informal discussions. These efforts should be accompanied by the presentation of a series of scheduled, structured, live demonstrations of the EMR to all practice groups. Live demonstrations of the EMR processes by peers are invaluable in setting the stage for eventual acceptance by the broader medical staff. Many questions and much discussion may be expected along with suggestions for improving processes and, most critically, the creation of engagement.

Some groups requested follow-up presentations. As these presentations were rolled out, physicians' preconceived notions of the EMR (almost uniformly negative) were successively replaced by an educated and more realistic understanding of the actual facts of the matter. In this regard, the importance of being *brutally honest* about the expected impact on the workflow of the providers cannot be overemphasized. Overselling or overmarketing may be perceived as disingenuous, which could result in creating loss of confidence in those putting forward the effort. These initiatives to build understanding and an appropriate expectation will take a significant period of time. This time should be factored into the cost and the timeline. Any plan to minimize this component of the preparatory process is likely to lead to serious problems with adoption later in the course of the project.

Engaging Physicians in the Process   A very important step is the process of actively engaging practicing physicians with the EMR design and implementation processes. Often there is perceived reluctance to impose the EMR on physicians and request their time to help with implementation and maintenance. This reluctance must be overcome. With proper support and incentives, physicians are generally willing to step forward and become involved in many aspects of the project. Some of these aspects included participation in leadership roles, site visits, assistance with the design of orders, order sets/Patient Care Pathways, documentation note formats, assistance with the design of specialty-specific folders, and participation in EMR pilots and go-live support. In virtually every case, their participation may be expected to improve the execution of the project and led to improved adoption.

Physician Leadership

Any project of this magnitude and controversy will require strong leadership. The role of the physician leadership in the design and support of the EMR implementation is a critical element in the success of the project. If the implementation is to proceed with high adoption, the project should be led primarily by the physicians themselves. This begins with the need for a lead physician and a CMIO or leader in a similar role who is afforded the necessary time and resources to organize and lead the overall process effectively. The CMIO should enlist a group of interested physicians to form what may be termed an information technology clinical advisory committee to review and make formal recommendations to the hospital and the medical staff on clinical IT initiatives. This group will prove to be critical in both guiding the process and providing the most visible nidus of physicians to lead the initiative.

The chief and vice chief for medical staff must play pivotal roles in the leadership effort. Their clear and articulate understanding of the value of the EMR and their willingness to aggressively support the aim of the project is very important. These individuals, in turn, worked to provide the medical staff service lines and departmental clinical leaders, usually during meetings of the medical executive committee, with presentations and opportunities for input and decision making that directed the implementation.

Four Critical Questions for the Physician Leadership to Address: A Crossroad Decision for the Leaders   During this process the chief and vice chief of medical staff must address a number of critical questions to the medical administrative committee.

1. Whether they should endorse the decision to proceed with the EMR, how and whether to stage implementation components, and, if so, over what timeframe.
2. Whether EMR adoption should be mandatory or optional for all providers. In this regard, the leadership must be apprised of a comprehensive list of pros and cons. Careful deliberation of the patient safety risks inherent in a protracted dual process (paper and computer) will be inherent in any optional adoption strategy. A dual process represents an ongoing patient safety risk and workflow efficiency risk, not only for clinical review of orders and documentation, but also for the dual deployment of these modalities to downstream departments should an optional strategy be chosen. In general, a mandatory approach is preferred.
3. Whether the EMR should be implemented by a "big bang" or a sequential go-live process, again with consideration of the potential risk associated with dual ordering methods during a prolonged sequential approach. A big bang implementation

is generally felt to be the most effective approach to EMR implementations, but only if the necessary education can be provided proximate in time to the go-live and if the necessary "at-the-elbow" go-live support can be provided.

4. Whether physician education would be a sufficiently important factor in promoting a smooth and safe transition from paper to electronic order entry to justify requiring that EMR education be mandatory, including a requirement that all providers who intend to enter orders spend significant time in class. Again, a mandatory approach is recommended.

These questions may be bitterly debated in leadership meetings and in the hallways. Including physicians in the discussions and approval process is the best avenue to achieve the desired outcomes.

These decisions represent the most important ingredients in the recipe for a successful implementation of EMR components with full adoption by the medical staff. They incorporate the critical role of physician leadership with the necessary mandatory elements to bring along those members of the medical staff who inevitably would resist the transformation. Without these decisions, as has happened in many hospitals where optional participation was permitted, a significant percentage of physicians on staff would almost certainly have persisted indefinitely with paper processes.

In any major organizational change, there is usually a bell-shaped curve plotting willingness to adopt new technology against the number of providers. The curve typically ranges from a relatively small number of ready adopters to a much larger number of individuals who are less opinionated and assume a wait-and-see attitude, to the deeply entrenched, highly resistant, and, regrettably, highly vocal naysayers. The challenge is how to bring along even the most resistant elements without allowing the naysayers to convince the much larger group of "undecideds" also to become resistant to the proposed change. One element can prove critical in disabling an effective resistance to the EMR implementation: ensuring that the process is driven by and voted on by the elected medical staff leadership. Following the decisions of the medical staff leadership, rules and regulations may be amended to incorporate the mandatory components, including clauses that would specify accountability and accompanying consequences for noncompliance. A letter jointly signed by the administrative leadership (usually the CEO) and the medical chief of staff may be especially helpful in both setting expectations and ensuring compliance with education and adoption. In the final analysis, however, it will be the quality of the product, as defined by the software and hardware configuration as woven into workflow, coupled with effective education and go-live support, that will determine the success of the project.

Project Organization, Management, and Budget

In coordination with physician leadership, the hospital administration and board of directors must also be fully informed, engaged, and uniformly aligned in their commitment to the success of the EMR project. Their roles include ensuring the development of an appropriate organizational structure for project design and implementation, a credible scope of project, an implementation plan with milestones and oversight, an appropriate budget, and a large bully pulpit from which to engage and support the effort across the organization.

In terms of organizational structure, a number of teams, all utilizing formal project management methodology, should be created to address each of the core elements necessary for the design and implementation of the EMR. These include teams for:

- Computer access downtime
- Functionality (the design of build of the Product) performance
- Completion of all processes necessary for online viewing of results and documentation, whether directly entered into the computer software system, interfaced across to the system, or scanned into the system
- Completion of clinical process mapping for current and future state
- Transformation, including communications, education, policies, rules, bylaws, pilot strategy, education, and go-live support

Each team should be assigned an appropriate team leader and stakeholders. A scope document and plans should be developed and physician and administrative sponsors should be assigned for each team. The teams should be coordinated by an overall project plan, requiring sign off by identified executive and physician leadership sponsors. Team leaders should meet regularly to report on progress against the plan; to coordinate with other teams; and to raise, escalate, and track issues. The teams should in turn report to an EMR executive oversight committee consisting at a minimum of the CIO, the CMIO, the CMO, the COO, and the informatics project manager. This committee is responsible for general oversight, review of milestones, and issues resolution.

The EMR project must be supported by a solid budget. Because of the cost and complexity of the design and implementation, specific funding should be allocated to the project, based on the defined scope as determined by formal project management, including all software, hardware, and anticipated staffing.

The Product

CPOE

The CPOE Product consists primarily of all of the orders, order sets, rules, alerts, and formats forming the basis of the computerized order entry tool. The Documentation Product consists of those elements that support fast and complete clinical notes, including required document templates, supporting autotext and macros, and robust voice recognition software with voice command capabilities that enable preformatted documentation. The final product should be fast, elegant, and easy to use. In IT terminology, one could say the system must possess speed, intuitive usability, interoperability, and breadth of functionality. As stated earlier, if the Product does not work well, no amount of transforming will lead to adoption.

The most basic element of the build is the individual orderable. Each orderable contains within it a set of detail options and values, also known as order entry formats, that allow each order to be easily modified to suit individual patient needs. The rules for the construction of orderables are fairly simple, but clearly the design, build, and testing of this massive compendium of orderables demand a considerable effort to complete, depending on the amount of work preformatted from the vendor. Several key features that should guide a correct approach to orderable build are listed below.

Synonyms

First, orderables must be easy to look up, as they are generally not entered as free text, but rather are matched to the terms within a search catalogue. Stated differently, ease of look up means that as the provider begins typing in the name of an order, the search engine successfully matches and converts the provider's idea into a standard prebuilt order. This requires that each orderable name be listed under a variety of commonly used aliases or synonyms, mandating careful attention to completeness in the catalogue build. Consider, for example, an order for a CT of the Chest. This orderable can be listed variably with synonyms as "CT Chest," "Chest CT," "CT Thorax," and "Thorax CT." Thus, the orderable catalogue must be comprehensive to include nearly any order that may be imagined. In this approach, as the physician thinks of the name of the test, he or she may expect to get a positive match with a prebuilt orderable from any reasonable search.

Modification of Order Details

Modification of orders should be easy for physicians to complete and should have the fewest possible required fields for order completion. Some required fields are necessary to capture all relevant information to construct a clear and complete order. The number of required fields may be minimized using several techniques. One of the most important fields is a listing of prepopulated order sentences attached to each medication orderable. The most common sentences for all formulary and many nonformulary medications should be prebuilt so the provider may easily select the closest one to the desired order sentence required for the order, thereby avoiding the completion of additional required fields specifying dose, dose unit, route, and frequency. These prepopulated order sentences also serve another important function. They provide real time decision support at the point of order entry by prompting the provider to choose from the most commonly used and safest order sentences, thereby preventing errors by providers who may inaccurately recall a medication order sentence.

In the case of some orderables, many useful order details that would otherwise need to be completed by the physician may be pulled from information already present elsewhere in the system. For example, when ordering a radiology examination, relevant details for mode of travel, monitoring, oxygen support, nurse escort, pregnancy status, and others may be pulled from daily nursing assessments into the order details without querying the physician for this information. A more complete description of the design and build of orderables will depend on the format and software design from each particular vendor. Nevertheless, the point here is that the ease and speed of order entry, facilitated by a smooth search, and the inclusion of all relevant information within the order are critical components in the successful adoption of CPOE.

After successful order entry, efficient and effective order fulfillment must follow. The design and build of the downstream deployment of orders must include the clear and proper communication of the order intent, the provision of all necessary accompanying information, and careful design of processes needed to facilitate order completion and documentation. The design of these elements is best facilitated, as previously stated, by constructing a detailed analysis of current and future state workflow processes for each clinical support department.

Order Sets Design and Construction

Another necessary element in the build of the Product is the creation of a useful array of order sets based upon the Patient Care Pathway model. An order set may be defined as *a set of related orders required for the management of a series of integrated clinical tasks.* Common uses for order sets include the admission process, transfer, and pre- and post-operative processes, adapted to the needs of each specialty. In addition, diagnosis-specific order sets may be constructed. Others may be used to facilitate safety measures, such as immunizations or venous thromboembolism prophylaxis. Order sets may also be constructed to guide the administration of complex medications, such as titrated drip medications requiring additional orders for monitoring labs or titration algorithms. These may be additionally supported by relevant guidelines, reminders, supporting lab results, nomograms for administration, and dose calculators.

Occasional high-risk medications require the provider to address a list of indications and contraindications prior to use. These may be incorporated into required ordering formats for specific medications.

Other order sets may be constructed to support the performance of bedside procedures or the ordering of groups of related tests. Order set utility may be further enhanced by the inclusion of nested order sets and sequenced order sets. Clearly order sets are highly useful, not only for the purpose of saving time for the user, but also for the provision of real-time decision support to guide ordering precision, consistency, and reliability at the proper point along the continuum of care. Physicians from each service line or specialty should be involved in the construction, revision, and approval of all order sets that support CPOE.

Documentation: Provider Notes

Provider notes typically include progress notes, procedure notes, operative notes, history and physical notes, transition in care notes, consultation notes, and discharge summaries. Templates and supporting software must be configured to facilitate the efficient creation of each of these note types. That being stated, the end user should be able to leverage tools to further customize his or her notes to support the individual's requirements for documentation, down to the level of individualized, preconfigured physical examinations and procedural techniques. Creating global templates in an attempt to support all specialty notes and procedures hampers the ability of the individual user to adapt the notes to his or her workflows, creates cumbersome template searches for the end user, and becomes a long-term management challenge.

Note creation should be supported by state-of-the-art voice recognition software. Such software should include capabilities to support voice tracking with high fidelity, allowing the user to translate voice into text with a minimum of required editing across a broad range of accents. It should support robust range voice commands to format and prepopulate text easily. Appropriate tools that support ease of editing are to be expected.

Refining the Product: Usability Testing

Following design and build, the Product must be refined and polished prior to productive use. This critical phase involves extensive testing. A system as complex as the practice of medicine involves the assembly of many documentation requirements, more than 60,000 orders, each with numerous ordering options, and hundreds of order sets. Therefore, great care must be exercised to avoid errors and ensure the safe application of orders to patient care. In addition to customary unit testing, application testing, and integration testing, an additional category is recommended that is referred to as *usability testing*.

Usability testing consisted of creating realistic clinical scenarios to which end users are asked to apply configured electronic tools, using the hardware that will be used in production. For example, in the case of CPOE, scanned copies of thousands of handwritten paper orders may be tested by requiring users to translate these orders into electronic formats in a test environment. Testing may be conducted by informatics personnel converting these handwritten orders into electronic orders. Each user records on standard forms any difficulty or impedance he or she may encounter, however minor, to the successful computer entry of these orders. All such order defects are reviewed by a change control committee, charged with evaluating each complaint and recommending appropriate action to amend and improve the order. Usability testing may need to be conducted in waves, such that successive attempts are able to result in a product that performs nearly flawlessly with associated ease of use.

Education

Because CPOE and electronic note creation differ substantially from paper processes, and because many elements are not entirely intuitive, the issue of formally educating the medical staff and hospital staff must be carefully planned. Our education process began with the development of interactive computer-based training modules (CBT). CBT modules should be developed as short vignettes that can be used both for initial education and also as reference modules for later refresher tools. They were internally developed by our education staff and several physicians using a CBT software development tool. The CBT should be made broadly available via a direct link in the EMR and also via an Internet link for ease of access from the physician's home or office.

Education classes should be scheduled months in advance to permit physicians adequate time to adjust their clinical schedules. Classes should be scheduled as closely as possible to the go-live event to mini-mize memory loss of information acquired during the class. In gen-eral, no class should be scheduled more than four weeks in advance of go-live. Classes should be small, generally with no more than three providers per class. This allows a great deal of individual attention and facilitates directing education to the needs of a range of subspe-cialty requirements. The resulting schedule requires planning for a number of educators and concurrent classrooms at a range of available times throughout the day. Educators are optimally contracted from a national pool of experienced personnel. Available software products may be employed to help configure complex scheduling. Sufficient open classes should be held the final few days prior to go-live to accommodate stragglers and those needing to reschedule.

In general, classes should utilize a working format, wherein the phy-sician is required to actively engage in executing all steps of the pro-cesses with coordinated demonstration and proctoring support from the educator. The format of the classes should consist of the following:

- A brief introduction describing the intent and format of the experience to follow.
- A demonstration overview of the skills that the user will be expected to master.
- A working class may be divided into two phases. In the first, the user is expected to execute each individual keystroke, mouse click, and voice recognition command to effect entry of each required order and creation of each required documenta-tion. For this purpose, the physicians should each work from separate computer workstations. The educator should circu-late as necessary and maintain close communication with the physicians during the class to offer assistance and answer questions. Completed orders and documentation should be examined to ensure that the information is entered correctly.
- In the second phase, the physician is given time to practice using common orders, order sets, and note configurations that are relevant to his or her practice and specialty. This should include time to prepare individual favorite folder orders and customized note configurations, using both autotext/macros and voice commands.

Although admittedly tedious, by the time physicians had completed this classroom activity, they should be able to execute a broad range of basic EMR functions independently.

Beyond the education classes, it is useful to offer supplemental education in the form of an "open lab" to give providers and selected groups of physicians an opportunity to have additional assistance with order entry and note creation education specific to the needs of their specialty. Practice patients should be in an electronic training domain in order that providers would have the opportunity to work independently on their own for additional order entry practice both in the classroom and after class for additional practice opportunities. Educators were also stationed in the physician lounges who were available to help with questions and assist physicians with useful tips and tricks. By communicating an expectation that the go-live experience would be seriously challenging for those not sufficiently familiar with the order entry application, many physicians, concerned about the impact to their workflow, are likely to take advantage of these additional options.

Certified Medical Education Credit

Physicians are likely to question what offset is being provided to compensate them for lost time in their practice. One option is to apply for and provide a number of required hours or Category I Certified Medical Education (CME) Credit. Hours can be estimated both for time in the classroom and also for time spent learning during the implementation process itself with go-live. CME requirements may vary by state. Because providers are required to maintain a minimum number of CME hours for accreditation and licensing, this will prove to be an appreciated benefit for the trouble of going through the process.

Building Physician Favorite Folders

Because physician specialties tend to select from a limited range of commonly used orders, allowing physicians to build individual favorites folders containing frequently used or complex-to-build orders prior to go-live was expected to be useful. Training for favorites folder build was included in our physician education program. In addition, selected members of the medical staff assisted in the build of folders of orders specific to each of their clinical specialties. These folders were useful for assembling collections of specialty specific orders and also served as templates to assist some physicians in the construction of their personal favorites folders. To accommodate the need for physicians to build orders into their personal favorites folders, a technique was devised allowing physicians access to the Production Domain prior to go-live to build their favorites folders, but without allowing them to sign and implement orders until the scheduled go-live. Having a prebuilt favorites folder available to use on the day of go-live proved helpful and reassuring to many physicians.

The Pilot

Ultimately a structured physician pilot for CPOE is recommended to serve several purposes preceding the primary go-live. First, the pilot serves as a final proof of concept for the order entry and/or documentation process. This proof-of-concept will be closely watched by the entire medical staff as they observe their piloting colleagues' reactions throughout their transition for signs of failure or success. Second, the pilot serves as a final "polishing" of the Product to clear up any final identifiable defects in the build prior to the main go-live. Issues with orders and processes should be carefully recorded by informatics personnel assisting the pilot physicians and sent to the change control team for analysis and remediation. Finally, the pilot serves as a proving ground for workflow effectiveness for providers, nurses, and clinical support departments.

There are many ways to structure the pilot and the transition leading up to the main go-live. Some team members had advocated a more complex, sequential pilot leading up to the main go-live, whereas other members advocated a simplified pilot shortly followed by a "big bang" go-live implementation. Regardless, involving heavy users in the pilot is a sound strategy. It is also helpful to involve several special type workflows groups, such as hospitalists, surgeons, emergency department providers, and critical care. The length of the pilot may vary, but should be long enough to establish a credible proof of concept and allow for time to remediate any issues that arise. This typically requires a number of weeks up to several months, depending on the complexity of the go-live and the range of workflows that will require testing. If the pilot goes well initially, it is not unusual for other provider groups to request to join the pilot. This behavior is typically driven by anxiety over fear of being thrown in with the masses in the main go-live. In some cases, including additional specialist groups may prove helpful. In other cases, it may be prudent to ask them to wait, because of the challenges associated with supporting a very large number of pilot providers. The pilot may be limited not only to the number of providers, but also to specific geographic locations. This containment serves to localize the required support and to simplify the workflow analysis and issues tracking.

The Main Go-Live

The movement toward go-live will be afforded additional momentum as the physician pilots from a number of specialties find the EMR processes reasonably easy to navigate and use. The day of go-live should prove relatively uneventful with careful planning, education, expectation-setting, and robust, competent go-live support. For the go-live, excellent support staff that provides EMR transitional support in many hospitals may be recruited for this event. Interested individuals should be carefully screened and interviewed to ascertain their competency, experience, engagement qualities, and especially their interpersonal and communication skills. Go-live support staff should take positive action to engage providers in their workflow and not wait to be approached with questions. At least one or two individuals should be stationed on every clinical area. In addition, a small staff of "roaming" support personnel can be available to be deployed to any area where the other staff has trouble keeping up with the flow during peak hours. Nights and weekends should also be staffed, but at much lower levels, depending on the number of providers anticipated to be working on site. In general, the first three days should be fully staffed, followed by tapering support over a 10- to 14-day period, depending on the demand for assistance from the providers. An IT staffed command center for five to seven days as dictated by call volume and issues log, utilizing a rotating phone system to take calls requesting assistance. In general, the go-live support staff may be divided into teams. Team leads should be appointed to be responsible for ensuring proper performance of the team members, to triage and allocate staff as appropriate to the busiest locations and manage escalation of issues. Issues raised should be called to the team lead, who would determine if the issue can be managed directly or if a call to the command center is warranted. Typically the largest number of calls to the command center occur in the first 48 hours, followed by a rapid tapering. By the end of five days, the call volume should be very small. Most issues fielded can typically be dealt with through educational reinforcement. A smaller percentage will require more detailed analysis by the change control team, of which only a few percent should be expected to require some type of change in the build or escalation to the vendor for remediation. Within two weeks, in an absence of major issues or adverse events, and with rapid response to identified problems, the EMR implementation should be well on the way to cementing itself into the new culture of the electronic support of clinical patient care.

Change Control and Long-Term User Support: Final Polishing of the Product

Over the first three to four weeks following EMR implementation, a gradual decrease in need for assistance, but an increase in calls for improved computer access in specific locations and for improved functionality in terms of EMR build configuration and advanced decision support may be expected, particularly as the strain of new processes in downstream departments and services surface. The need for adequate ongoing maintenance, support, and education cannot be overemphasized. Postimplementation support by phone should be readily available 24/7 by an on-call team of trained users. Issues and concerns lodged should be registered, assigned to appropriate staff for remediation, and tracked to resolution. Solutions should be routed through a relatively small change control group consisting of IT staff and clinical participation from physician, nursing, and pharmacy representation, with others from specific departments as needed for dealing with problems relevant to their particular areas.

As a final note, decisions should be made up front regarding which data to collect to document the impact from the EMR transition on a variety of processes, including adoption, resistance, issues, safety, clinical outcomes, and financial outcomes. Time motion analysis of new EMR processes should also be evaluated for providers and other staff pre- and post- go-live.

Summary of Salient Recommendations

- Build a logical case for the necessity to move to a fully electronic medical record.
- The EMR journey ideally should be physician led.
- Involve the medical staff at the beginning of the process and have physicians champion innovations at each step along the continuum.
- Focus on and develop teams to support EMR prerequisites: performance, ease of use (functionality), provision of supporting results and documentation, access to computer workstations, adequate downtime procedures, communications, policies and regulations, education, and go-live support.
- Take whatever time is necessary to carefully document current processes in present state and then in the future state using process flow diagrams to properly integrate and positively leverage IT changes into clinical workflow.
- Provide features that save time, effort, and cost and that improve quality of care, drawing providers to engage and use the system. Measure and publish outcomes.
- Engage physician assistance in leadership, implementation strategy, design and build, demonstrations, piloting, and go-live support. A physician design team may be appointed to facilitate these goals.
- Create collaborative alignment among physicians, clinical support staff, administration, and board of directors.
- Develop an appropriate budget for CPOE. Treat the design and implementation as a formal project management initiative.
- Create evidence- and consensus-based order sets or Patient Care Pathways for all clinical specialties and departments.
- Communicate an honest, realistic expectation for the EMR transition in terms of workflow. Listen to and answer questions and concerns raised by the medical staff.
- Mandate participation in the use of the EMR.
- Mandate education for all users prior to go-live.

- Create educational support to make the process as efficient, yet comprehensive as possible, including computer-based training, classroom-based education, ad hoc targeted education, a train domain for users to practice, and support staff in physician lounges or other easy to access locations to answer questions.
- Enable and encourage the build of orders into favorites folders and documentation note formats and commands for users in the production domain prior to go-live. Establish and train users in the use of voice recognition software in advance of the go-live.
- Offer Category (I) CME for all users who go through the education and go-live process.
- Apply liberal usability testing to ensure that EMR processes and workflows perform smoothly and efficiently.
- Utilize an effective pilot strategy representative of important workflows, followed by a big bang go-live, assuming adequate support can be made available at go-live.
- Employ liberal, competent, and seasoned support for all users at go-live. Taper the support over two to three weeks.
- Employ the use of a command center, tapering to phone support, to provide rapid responses to questions that cannot easily be fielded by on site superuser support personnel.
- Develop a mechanism to capture all problems, issues, and requests for change.
- Issues should be triaged, analyzed, and referred for remediation as needed by a change control group that can provide prompt turnaround on requests for change.

Don't deviate too much from the preceding list if you want a successful implementation. The key is that physicians must use the system, so physicians must be involved in its development. Finally, remember the EMR processes are not completed until they are inclusive of those clinical support departments that provide front-line care to the patients: the nursing, pharmacy, and ancillary clinical support departments. After all, this is about patient care.

7

KNOWLEDGE TRANSLATION AND INFORMATICS IN HEALTHCARE

ANN McKIBBON

Contents

Introduction

Knowledge translation is the process whereby research findings, or any new and worthwhile knowledge and insights, are integrated into everyday practice. Louis Pasteur summed up this important aspect of research and development by saying: "To him who devotes his life to science, nothing can give more happiness than increasing the number of discoveries, but his cup of joy is full when the results of his studies immediately find practical applications."

Pasteur did not, however, include in this statement how important the movement of research into practice is for those of us who stand to benefit from the research findings—or how difficult it is. In the healthcare world, estimates of the size of the gap between what we know about the best possible care from research and what we receive from health professionals is significant. Estimates of the size of the gap translate into the fact that on average Americans receive only 55% of their recommended healthcare services.[1] This care gap comprises both care that is received that should not be given and care that should be administered and is not.

Woolf and Johnson make a strong statement about the magnitude of the effects of not using health research efficiently.[2] They provide substantial evidence that suggests we need to put more money and effort into determining the most effective methods of implementing existing knowledge rather than funding additional basic and clinical research and other projects designed to discover new knowledge. Their estimate of the relative amount of research investment between basic science and other research and implementation is likely 100:1, favoring the discovery of new knowledge. Until we can ensure that new and important knowledge is integrated into our healthcare system in a timely manner lives will be lost, care will be substandard, funding will not be optimized, and the healthcare system will continue to be inefficient and possibly even dangerous.

The gap between best possible care and actual care, or between evidence and practice, occurs because of many factors:

- Ever increasing growth of new knowledge that leads to information overload
- Growth in the complexity of healthcare and the need to document this carefully. The potential for litigation is also a factor here
- Increasing demands on the time clinicians have to interact with patients (For this chapter the term clinician refers to a health professional who helps make clinical decisions for and with patients—usually physicians, nurses, and pharmacists, although others are often included.)
- Structural issues related to disincentives to improve care (e.g., financial penalties to provide advice by email rather than clinical visits)
- Organizational issues related to matters such as an inappropriate skill mix to address patient needs, lack of facilities, inadequate staffing, or outdated equipment

- Peer group pressures (e.g., local standards that tend toward less than optimal care)
- Individual deficits in health professional knowledge, skills, and attitudes
- Individual deficits in patients' and families' knowledge, skills, and attitudes
- Patient expectations that are not aligned with best care (e.g., direct to consumer advertising or expectations related to antibiotics)
- Basic human nature and our inclination toward resistance to change

Many people across disciplines, domains, countries, and time periods are interested in optimizing knowledge translation to close the gap between evidence and practice. Consequently multiple terms referring to knowledge translation exist (see http://whatiskt.wiki spaces.com/) for a list of 100 terms related to the concepts of knowledge translation). For example, knowledge translation is a Canadian term. Other term examples include translational science/medicine in the United States, implementation science in the United Kingdom, research utilization in Australia, quality improvement/assurance in hospitals, and evidence-based practice/medicine/nursing in clinical care. For this chapter we use the term knowledge translation and we adhere to the term as defined by the Canadian Institutes of Health Research (CIHR):

> Knowledge translation is a dynamic and iterative process that includes synthesis, dissemination, exchange and ethically sound application of knowledge to improve the health of Canadians, provide more effective health services and products and strengthen the healthcare system.
>
> This process takes place within a complex system of interactions between researchers and knowledge users which may vary in intensity, complexity and level of engagement depending on the nature of the research and the findings as well as the needs of the particular knowledge user. (CIHR website: http://www.cihr-irsc.gc.ca/e/29418.html)

In its role to improve knowledge translation, CIHR has supported publication of a 2009 book on knowledge translation in the health sciences that can be used by those who want more information on the topic.[3]

Knowledge translation and its techniques are vitally important for researchers as well as developers and entrepreneurs in all knowledge domains. This chapter concentrates on knowledge translation and health information technology. Shekelle and colleagues summarized published evidence and showed that health information technology can be cost effective in improving the quality and efficiency of healthcare. These authors also present challenges to the health informatics community.[4] Their report is summarized as follows.

> Health information technology (HIT) has the potential to enable a dramatic transformation in the delivery of healthcare, making it safer, more effective, and more efficient. Some organizations have already realized major gains through the implementation of multifunctional, interoperable HIT systems built around an EHR. However, widespread implementation of HIT has been limited by a lack of generalizable knowledge about what types of HIT and implementation methods will improve care and manage costs for specific health organizations.

The following sections of this chapter describe the interventions and actions that are most likely to improve and speed the flow of research evidence into practice and how informatics applications can enhance the likelihood that patients and their families obtain the best care possible.

The informatics world needs to understand how to optimize knowledge translation for two reasons. First we need to produce tools and services that will best serve the needs of health professionals to optimize their care process. We need to produce systems that can ensure quick, efficient, and accurate implementation of appropriate new advances and promote or block discontinuation of outdated care. Once we produce these tools and services we must work to insure that they are adopted, implemented, and sustained by the intended users, utilizing the most effective change strategies. Without this knowledge translation by informatics practitioners our tools and projects will not be used to their fullest potential.

Strategies for Improving Knowledge Translation in Healthcare

Which tools and techniques are effective for behavior change of clinicians and their institutions and organizations? Knowledge translation in the domain of healthcare deals with changing the behavior of individual clinicians and how clinics, hospitals, cities, municipalities, states and provinces, and even countries respond to the challenge of making health decisions based on evidence in a cyclical, ongoing manner so that care provided is the best currently available. Once we know what changes behavior, we can determine if and how the informatics applications we implement can enhance these interventions. Bero and colleagues summarize the evidence on interventions or actions that close the gap between research and practice.[5] They summarize their findings of 18 separate review articles assessing interventions for health professionals into three categories: what works, what might work, and what does not work. Although the article by Bero et al. is somewhat dated, the general categories of what works and does not work remain applicable.

The first category is interventions that consistently change behavior: those that are supported by strong evidence that shows improved care across multiple studies and time periods.

- Educational outreach visits of an expert to discuss certain aspects of care, especially prescribing issues in North America. The drug companies use this technique quite effectively. Agnell cites data showing that 35% of the staff of pharmaceutical companies are employed in marketing departments, many of whom visit physicians, sponsor conferences, or provide educational sessions to emphasize drug adoption.[6]
- Computerized or manual reminders of care to be done or not done for a patient in a specific situation
- Multifaceted interventions (combinations of two or more of audit and feedback, reminders, local consensus processes, or marketing)
- Educational programs that are interactive—those that require discussion, role playing, or practice by health professionals in workshops or similar programs of active learning

The second group of interventions are those that show variable effectiveness. In some instances studies of these interventions have shown positive changes and some have been associated with no changes or detrimental outcomes.

- Audit and feedback of actual performance of the individual, often compared with group norms (e.g., surgical infection rates for a give individual that are 10% higher than those of the other surgeons in the hospital)
- Use of local opinion leaders (those in a group, such as a hospital or multiphysician clinic who are identified by their colleagues as being asked often for advice or guidance in care situations)
- Local consensus processes that involve practicing clinicians in a geographic area or group who work together to establish care norms or procedures for a specific situation or care issue. These documents have been called care maps or clinical practice guidelines. The can be for a small group such as a hospital ward or reflect the standard of care for national practice.
- Patient interventions whereby information is provided to patients, who in turn use the information to change clinician knowledge or behavior, for example, direct to consumer marketing

The third category is also important. These interventions have little or no effect on clinician behavior.

- Educational materials in paper or electronic format (not individualized)
- Didactic educational meetings, for example, lectures, and most standard conferences with featured speakers or researchers presenting papers to peers in lecture format

Areas of Health Professional Needs That Can Be Addressed by Health Informatics

The remainder of this chapter discusses challenges that clinicians face in improving their care of patients (ensuring the best possible care) and how various existing or new health information technologies can aid the knowledge translation process. The chapter ends with cautions for informaticians.

Information Overload

Information overload for clinicians is a real dilemma. The problem of too much information is evident on a number of fronts in the clinical world. Clinicians deal with approximately 11,000 different diseases and conditions, and most of these have multiple overlapping signs and symptoms. (For clinicians, symptoms are what patients report during a clinic visit and signs are what clinicians find when using their hands and tools such as thermometers, blood pressure cuffs, and stethoscopes.) Adding to this information that a clinician needs to synthesize and use for decision making is the information from the published literature. Medline, the major health database, contains approximately 17 million citations and publishes more than 12,000 articles per week. Of these, 300 are likely to have information relevant to clinical care.[7] In addition, the web contains an estimated 25 billion pages as of July 2009. All of these factors provide tremendous pressure and tax an individual's ability to cope. One way to alleviate this information overload is through the utilization of health informatics applications.

Point-of-care information systems are designed to address the flow of new information or can provide information backup when a clinician feels that he or she needs more information. These point-of-care systems provide access to e-resources using several communication means including hand-held devices. Prendiville et al. describe a study of Irish pediatricians using hand-held devices to answer questions that arose during hospital care.[8] The summarized conclusions that follow depict the importance of these point-of-care informatics resources for this group of physicians.

The study received 156 completed questionnaires, a 66.1% response. 67% of pediatricians utilized the internet as their first "port of call" when looking to answer a medical question. 85% believe that web-based resources have improved medical practice, with 88% reporting web-based resources are essential for medical practice today. 93.5% of pediatricians believe attempting to answer clinical questions as they arise is an important component in practicing evidence-based medicine. 54% of all pediatricians have recommended websites to parents or patients. 75.5% of pediatricians report finding it difficult to keep up-to-date with new information relevant to their practice.

Another study of question answering using health information technology was conducted in Ottawa, ON. Hand-held devices were given to hospital physicians and physicians in training to provide information support. These devices were programmed to provide electronic communication to an information service provided by librarians.[9] The librarian service was designed to provide fast and efficient answers and to determine if the twinning of the librarian with the mobile devices was more effective than with the devices with only access to online information resources. At the end of the study, more than 85% of the participants favored having direct access to a librarian to provide answers to clinical questions. Most of the physicians in the study felt that the service improved the care they provided. As another example of information support at the point of care, Cimino and colleagues have developed information systems embedded within electronic health records (EHR) systems. They provide strategically placed electronic "infobuttons" in systems in the EHR to indicate a probable information need. This might involve an issue such as an abnormal laboratory finding or some patient data suggesting a potential change in medication. The infobutton is actually a link to context specific information or another information resource that will likely address that abnormal finding or trend.[10]

EHRs also provide great value in helping clinicians with their information overload in other areas. A well-designed EHR will collect and integrate information from multiple sources such as hospitals, clinics, workplaces, and pharmacies for a given patient. A strong EHR will also enable important information to be collected just once and then make it available thereafter. For example, questions related to allergies, medications, home address, next of kin, and previous pregnancies are often asked and recorded multiple times during patient care encounters. This information should be collected once and then made available for all other recognized care providers. EHRs are also ideal tools for collecting and synthesizing sequential data and presenting it to depict time trends or abnormal patterns. Most chronic diseases such as heart disease, diabetes, and asthma rely on analyzing multiple data points and making decisions based on trends. The literature on EHRs is extensive: Häyrinen and colleagues have produced a systematic review of the definition, structure, content, use, and effects of EHRs.[11]

Clinical (or computerized) decision support systems (CDSSs) are also useful tools to help clinicians deal with information overload. CDSSs by definition are systems that integrate data from two separate sources. They store patient-specific information, entered either by the user or from EHRs. These patient-specific data are then integrated into a database of clinical knowledge rules or patterns (using an "inference engine"). This inference engine then produces suggestions for actions related to the diagnosis, treatment, or monitoring for that particular patient case—one of the main functions of CDSSs. The clinician can choose to act according to these recommendations or make other decisions. Open Clinical (an international organization that promotes the utilization of decision support and other knowledge-based technologies) provides a more detailed summary of the characteristics of CDSSs (http://www.openclinical.org/dss.html). Perreault and Metzger list the functions of CDSSs including the previously mentioned clinical support.[12]

> Four key functions of [C]DSSs are outlined: (i) Administrative: Supporting clinical coding and documentation, authorization of procedures, and referrals. (ii) Managing clinical complexity and details: Keeping patients on research and chemotherapy protocols; tracking orders, referrals follow-up, and preventive care. (iii) Cost control: Monitoring medication orders; avoiding duplicate or unnecessary tests. (iv) Decision support: Supporting clinical diagnosis and treatment plan processes; and promoting use of best practices, condition-specific guidelines, and population-based management.

Haynes and his group have updated their review of the evidence of the effectiveness of CDSSs.[13]

In addition to the point-of-care information systems and CDSS, almost all informatics applications have components that assist clinicians with information overload. Many of the systems are designed to collect and analyze large quantities of evolving data across systems and from research studies or patients in general and their functionality continues to evolve. Areas of ongoing development for enhanced functionality for informatics include interoperability, intelligent information retrieval, automated or manual (people centered) mechanisms to keep information resources current with the standards of best practice, and better integration of research findings into EHRs.

Clinician and Patient Deficits in Knowledge and Skills

Clinicians, patients, and caregivers can have deficits in knowledge and skills that can impede obtaining, providing, or acting on the best possible care. For the general public, an example of the magnitude of these deficits is a review of the literature on public knowledge of the risks for and signs and symptoms of stroke. Strokes are common, carry considerable disability, and fast access to care lessens the potential suffering. In a study that addressed levels of knowledge in select communities regarding the risks of strokes, Nicol and Thrif found that between 20% and 30% of the people surveyed did not know a single risk factor for stroke despite considerable distribution of this information.[14] Another example of clinician knowledge revealed that more than 75% of Australian family physicians felt that their knowledge of breastfeeding was inadequate.[15] Informatics applications can identify gaps in knowledge and provide learning based on these gaps. For example, at the University of Pittsburgh residents are taught how to identify pathology abnormalities and conditions, as well as report writing, using intelligent tutoring programs. The system uses natural language processing and other informatics tools to identify when the residents show they have mastered a given set of content or if a student needs more practice in identifying certain diseases or content areas.[16] Computer tutoring (individualized education) is on target to become even more highly used to educate undergraduate medical and nursing students and residents. Individualized educational programs that evaluate the learning achieved and direct further learning for patients have also been shown to be effective. For example, nursing researchers are building computer-medicated, Web-based, individualized, educational programs for women with ovarian cancer. Both format and content are based on the author's analyses of data in 40 studies of computer education for women with cancer and chronic diseases.[17]

Fordis and colleagues showed that online continuing professional education is as valuable for providing education as in-person continuing education. Continuing education is vital to health professionals for two major reasons.[18] First, because so much information is changing, health professionals must be lifelong learners to provide the best possible care. Second, health professionals must report formally on their learning to maintain their clinical certification. An added benefit of online courses and point-of-care learning systems over traditional learning is that the credential benefit (continuing education credits) of the course can be captured in a format suitable for submission to certifying bodies such as the American or Canadian Medical Associations. Some professional organizations are actively pursing automatic reporting of credit hours for certification via online systems. Keeping track of continuing education to support ongoing certification manually is time consuming and often inaccurate.

In addition to identifying knowledge gaps, health information technology can also detect errors. The U.S. Institute of Medicine has estimated that between 44,000 and 98,000 deaths occur in the United States annually because of errors in care.[19] One of the most important areas in healthcare where errors occur, especially in hospital and long-term settings, is with medications. Errors can occur during ordering (for patients in hospitals) or prescribing (for patients meeting health professionals outside hospitals). Because children are given doses based on weights and ages, some people estimate that pediatric patients have prescribing errors rates three times as high as for adult patients.[20] Ordering and prescribing can be improved using health information technology with technologies such as provider order entry systems (see later) to deal with poor handwriting and systems to block inappropriate dosing or prompt re-drug allergics. Dispensing can be improved by using bar code systems that notify the nurse giving the medicine that the bar code for the medication is not the same bar code that the patient has on his or her wrist. Monitoring of the patient to ensure that the drug is given in sufficient quantities to provide the proper effect and not cause adverse reactions is also available using information from EHRs. Agrawal provides more information on medication safety using health information technology.[21] Another more specific example is a review by Eberts and colleagues who discuss the benefits of physician order entry on prescribing in pediatrics intensive care units.[22] They found that the systems reduced prescribing errors but these errors did not reduce the rate of adverse drug reactions or mortality.

Time Pressures

Time is an important factor for current healthcare providers. Although clinicians perceive that EHRs, with or without personal health records (PHRs) components, consume more time than paper records they do offer some time-saving features.[23] Examples where EHR or PHR systems or other devices such as tablets in waiting rooms can save time is if they enable patients to book their own appointments and provide data on current issues before clinic visits. The patients and caregivers can state the reason for the scheduled visit plus signs and symptoms, provide detailed lists of prescribed and over-the-counter medications, and update information on addresses and insurance coverage. The time that is available for the appointment can then be spent analyzing the data and formulating decisions and care plans. EHRs that integrate data from multiple caregivers and settings (e.g., primary care clinics, nursing homes, specialists, and hospitals) also save time during patient visits. Complete records can also alleviate the need for duplicate diagnostic or evaluation studies if all the patient data are successfully aggregated in a timely manner and available for all caregivers and all locations of care.

Computerized Physician (or Provider) Order Entry

Another informatics application designed to save time as well as improve information flow and reduce errors is computerized physician (or provider) order entry (CPOE) systems (also mentioned previously in the error section). Using a CPOE system, healthcare professionals place their orders for components such as medications, diagnostic tests, appointments with specialists or generalists, or discharge instructions online rather than verbally or on paper. These online orders are then quickly distributed without transcription and its inherent errors to those who can ensure that the tests are booked, carried out, and the results reported back to all who are involved. CPOE systems can not only speed care but also check and verify that the data are accurate, actions are appropriate, their booking is efficient, and communication is facilitated and recorded. A study by Wietholter et al. illustrates the time savings potential made possible by CPOE systems. The study compared processing time for prescriptions (time from the initial order by the physician or nurse until it is prepared and delivered by the hospital pharmacists) with and without automated systems. Processing time for prescriptions showed a mean time of 115 minutes before automation compared with 3 minutes to process the same drug order after the introduction of CPOE for prescribing.[24]

Workflow Applications

Workflow is vitally important for clinicians in all care settings and has often been overlooked or underappreciated by system developers. Workflow refers to the processes and their time sequencing when patients, healthcare professionals, and their system interact. Often physicians have different ways of working than do nurses. New systems, either online or not, must respect and adapt to these differences. For example, in a teaching hospital, the physicians in charge "round" each morning, bringing along the care team of medical students, residents, and sometimes pharmacists, social workers, or librarians. They meet as a team with each patient assigned to their care, ascertain his or her progress and needs, and plan for next steps. Each patient is completed and orders are given to address all of the needs—a patient-centered workflow. Nurses in hospital units deal with patients differently. For example, one nurse provides all of the medications for patients several times per day. The nurse wants the information in an EHR to be focused only on the needed medications and presented in patient order—needed medications for the patient in room 1 bed 1, for the patient in room 1 bed 2, and so on. Those who schedule diagnostic testing or assign operating room time to physicians or teams need to see the clinical information in another format as do the administrative team who maintain supplies and equipment. Informatics professionals must ascertain the flow of people, tasks, and information: the workflow and how it differs for different groups of people before planning for new systems.

Zahra Niazkhani of the Institute of Health Policy and Management in the Netherlands provides a summary of what is known about the effects of CPOE on workflow.[25] Computerizing a system with existing poor workflow has been the downfall of many systems. Not recognizing and respecting the existing workflow as well as the culture of an organization has also proven costly and frustrating for system designers during implementation.

Computer Reminders

Manual or computerized reminder systems have been shown to be one of the most effective methods of improving clinical behavior, improving clinical practice or knowledge translation. Reminders originally were provided in the form of paper notes on paper charts for such things as missing childhood vaccinations, influenza shots, and mammographies. The next implementation came in the form of emails. These emails were often more general reminders such as notices of a new hand sanitizer solution system to be implemented into a hospital or to consider generic instead of brand name drugs. Paper and general email-based reminders are not as effective as those that are patient specific and delivered at the point of care from within an EHR. Shojania and colleagues produced a Cochrane Review of point-of-care reminders delivered by a computerized decision support system within an EHR. They reviewed 28 original studies that showed consistent increases in actions when the reminders were provided across a range of conditions, practitioners, and settings.[26]

Reminder systems within EHRs are important in many applications. The 28 studies in the Shojania review described the settings and content areas of the 32 comparisons in these studies:

> Of the 32 comparisons that provided analyzable results for improvements in process adherence, 21 reported outcomes involving prescribing practices, six specifically targeted adherence to recommended vaccinations, 13 reported outcomes related to test ordering, three captured documentation, and seven reported adherence to miscellaneous other processes (for example composite compliance with a guideline).

Reminder systems can work for patients also. For example, Puccio and colleagues studied whether reminders via cell phones would improve adherence (taking their medications) with HIV and AIDS medication in adolescents and young adults.[27]

Producing New Knowledge from Data

Another opportunity for increasing efficiencies in healthcare is that data stored and generated by powerful integrated EHRs and PHRs, hospital information systems, and insurance collections can be mined via quantitative analytic techniques to extract information and produce new knowledge. This new knowledge can, and will, direct an increasing number of patient-specific decisions. Currently our limited data collection and analysis capabilities could create knowledge only on groups of people (i.e., populations) rather than individuals. These new data will likely have an impact on being able to predict prognosis for an individual (the likely path that a person's disease or condition will take). This is very useful information for the patient, health professionals, and insurers. For example, data mining of information on 258 variables from 16,604 patients with heart–lung transplants showed associations between variables that could be used to predict survival in the patients where traditional statistical analyses of data sets with that many variables could not yield these results.[28]

In addition to data mining and knowledge discovery, advances in bioinformatics can link a person's health and family history data with his or her genomic data for decision making. This information will allow for better targeting of treatments: some drugs work well for some people and not for others. Strong data collection and analyses will be able to sort this puzzle out. Thervet and colleagues provide a summary of the promise of tailoring drugs based on genomic data.[29]

The production of new data is not really a classical knowledge translation task but it is one that will become more important over time as our data collection methods become stronger and more genomic data are available. Our systems will continue to play an increasing role in the application of new and proven knowledge to maintain optimal healthcare, especially in the production and integration of new patient-specific information.

Challenges

Challenges exist in producing systems and projects designed to improve patient care through knowledge application. These challenges relate to the complexities of care, its ever changing and advancing knowledge base, and the size of the healthcare enterprise. We also are held back by funding limitations. Despite the significant resource allocation by governments into health information technology, there is still not ample funding to produce ideal systems that integrate across the multitude of people and organizations. We also must deal with multiple players; conflicting local, national, and international standards and regulations; and the fact that patients differ in their preferences, resources, and attitudes. Whenever clinicians, patients, or both seek individualized and tailored care, complexity creeps into our design specifications. Another challenge is that although our systems often change care processes and improve some intermediate outcomes such as knowledge or skills improvement, many of our projects are like those of Egberts et al.: The process changes do not always improve clinically important outcomes such as reducing mortality.[22] Despite all of these challenges the opportunities are vast in the health informatics arena, where collaboration with our health professional peers will likely improve care.

Summary

Clinicians involved in healthcare struggle with changing practices, procedures, and the complexities of care in an ever changing world. Patients and their conditions, insurance providers, threats of litigation, and local organizational issues are factors that must be considered in managing resources in this dynamic environment. Clinicians need all the help that informatics have to offer in their quest to keep current with advances in care where effective implementation of new knowledge or knowledge translation is essential.

Enabling effective knowledge translation is an important and exciting challenge in the development in informatics. As we build and complete projects we need to think about the knowledge translation challenges our clinicians and other partners have in their quest to stay up to date and provide optimal care. We need to remember that some interventions such as timely, useful, and context-specific reminders; decision support systems and CPOE within EHRs; individualized and continuing audit and feedback; and combined interventions including patient training and educational interventions that allow interaction and reflection work well at improving care and bring care closer to the ideal.

This chapter was originally published in *Healthcare Informatics, Improving Efficiency and Productivity*, Taylor & Francis, New York, 2010.

References

1. McGlynn EA, Asch, J. Adams SM, Keesey J, Hicks J, DeCristofaro A, Kerr EA. 2003. The quality of health care delivered to adults in the United States. *N Engl J Med* 348(26):2635–45.
2. Woolf SH, Johnson RE. 2005. The break-even point: When medical advances are less important than improving the fidelity with which they are delivered. *Ann Fam Med* 3(6):545–52.
3. Straus SE, Graham ID, Tetroe J. 2009. *Knowledge translation in health care: Moving from evidence to practice.* Oxford: Wiley Blackwell and BMJ Publishing.
4. Shekelle PG, Morton SC, Keeler EB. 2006. Costs and benefits of health information technology. Evidence Report/Technology Assessment (Full Report). No 132 (pp. 1–71). Rockville, MD: Agency for Healthcare Research and Quality.
5. Bero LA, Grilli R, Grimshaw JM, Harvey E, Oxman AD, Thomson MA. 1998. Closing the gap between research and practice: An overview of systematic reviews of interventions to promote the implementation of research findings. The Cochrane Effective Practice and Organization of Care Review Group. *BMJ* 317(7156):4658.
6. Angell M. 2004. Excess in the pharmaceutical industry. *CMAJ* 171 (12):1451–53.
7. Glasziou PP. 2008. Information overload: What's behind it, what's beyond it? *Med J Aust* 189(2):84–85.
8. Prendiville TW, Saunders J, Fitzsimons J. 2009. The information-seeking behaviour of paediatricians accessing web-based resources. *Arch Dis Child* 94(8):633–35.
9. McGowan J, Hogg W, Campbell C, Rowan M. 2008. Just-in-time information improved decision-making in primary care: A randomized controlled trial. *PLoS ONE* 3(11e):e3785.
10. Del Fiol G, Haug PJ, Cimino JJ, Narus SP, Norlin C, Mitchell JA. 2008. Effectiveness of topic-specific infobuttons: A randomized controlled trial. *J Am Med Inform Assoc* 15(6):752–59.
11. Häyrinen K, Saranto K, Nykänen P. 2008. Definition, structure, content, use and impacts of electronic health records: A review of the research literature. *Int J Med Inform* 77(5):291–304.
12. Perreault L, Metzger J. 1999. A pragmatic framework for understanding clinical decision support. *J Healthcare Inform Manage* 13(2):5–21.
13. Implementation Science Series on Computerized Clinical Decision Support Systems. http://www.implementationscience.com/series/CCDSS (Accessed May 22, 2015).
14. Nicol MB, Thrift AG. 2005. Knowledge of risk factors and warning signs of stroke. *Vasc Health Risk Manage* 1(2):137–47.

15. Brodribb W, Fallon AB, Jackson C, Hegney D. 2009. Breastfeeding knowledge—The experiences of Australian general practice registrars. *Aust Fam Physician* 38(1–2):26–29.

16. El Saadawi GM, Tseytlin E, Legowski E, Jukic D, Castine M, Fine J, Gormley R, Crowley RS. 2007. A natural language intelligent tutoring system for training pathologists: Implementation and evaluation. *Adv Health Sci Educ Theory Pract* 13(5):709–22.

17. Dumrongpakapakorn P, Hopkins K, Sherwood P, Zorn K, Donovan H. 2009. Computer-mediated patient education: Opportunities and challenges for supporting women with ovarian cancer. *Nurs Clin North Am* 44(3):339–54.

18. Fordis M, King JE, Ballantyne CM, Jones PH, Schneider KH, Spann SJ, Greenberg SB, Greisinger AJ. 2005. Comparison of the instructional efficacy of Internet-based CME with live interactive CME workshops: A randomized controlled trial. *JAMA* 294(9):1043–51.

19. Kohn LT. 1999. *To err is human: Building a safer health system.* Washington, DC: National Academies Press.

20. Kaushal R, Bates DW, Landrigan C. 2001. Medication errors and adverse drug events in pediatric inpatients. *JAMA* 285(16):2114–20.

21. Agrawal A. 2009. Medication errors: Prevention using information technology systems. *Br J Clin Pharmacol* 67(6):681–86.

22. Egberts ACG, Bollen CW, van Rosse F, Maat B, Rademaker CMA, van Vught AJ. 2009. The effect of computerized physician order entry on medication prescription errors and clinical outcome in pediatric and intensive care: A systematic review. *Pediatrics* 123:1184–90.

23. Ash JS, Bates DW. 2005. Factors and forces affecting EHR system adoption: Report of a 2004 ACMI discussion. *J Am Med Inform Assoc* 12(1):8–12.

24. Wietholter J, Sitterson S, Allison S. 2009. Effects of computerized prescriber order entry on pharmacy order-processing time. *Am J Health Syst Pharm* 66(15):1394–98.

25. Niazkhani Z, Pirnejad H, Berg M, Aarts J. 2009. The impact of computerized provider order entry systems on inpatient clinical workflow: A literature review. *J Am Med Inform Assoc* 16(4):539–49.

26. Shojania KG, Jennings A, Mayhew A, Ramsay CR, Eccles MP, Grimshaw J. 2009. The effects of on-screen, point of care computer reminders on processes and outcomes of care. *Cochrane Database Syst Rev* (3):CD001096.

27. Puccio JA, Belzer M, Olson J, Martinez M, Salata C, Tucker D, Tanaka D. 2006. The use of cell phone reminder calls for assisting HIV-infected adolescents and young adults to adhere to highly active antiretroviral therapy: A pilot study. *AIDS Patient Care STDS* 20(6):438–44.

28. Oztekin Aa, Delen D, Kong ZJ. 2009. Predicting the graft survival for heart-lung transplantation patients: An integrated data mining methodology. *Int J Med Inform* 78(12):e84–96.

29. Thervet E, Anglicheau D, Legendre C, Beaune P. 2008. Role of pharmacogenetics of immunosuppressive drugs in organ transplantation. *Ther Drug Monit* 30(2):143–50.

8

APPLICATION OF HEALTHCARE INFORMATICS TO IMPROVING PATIENT SAFETY AND OUTCOMES

Learning from the Experiences of Trinity Health

RAJIV KOHLI, FRANK PIONTEK,
LARRY SELLERS, TOM MINER,
AND PAUL CONLON

Contents

Overview

Most healthcare information technology (IT) efficacy publications emerge from academic institutions that often develop their own proprietary information systems (IS). However, most patients in the United States are discharged from community hospitals. Community hospitals often implement advanced technology with a focus on global safety or quality, yet are faced with cost issues pertaining to large implementations and generally lack resources to measure the impact of such systems. This explains, in part, the limited research conducted among community hospitals to measure the economic and performance outcomes of healthcare IT. Therefore, it is important that experiences of community hospitals are documented and shared with hospital decision makers.

This chapter overviews the experiences of Trinity Health, a large multihospital community-based health system that initiated a systemwide information technology strategy to improve patient safety and clinical outcomes. Termed Project Genesis, the implementation of Trinity Health's strategy is represented through three case studies. Case Study 1 makes the argument that hospitals must involve physicians and effectively communicate with them to implement safety and cost containment initiatives. Case Study 2 presents Trinity Health's approach to developing an information systems tool, how physicians' access to information helped them identify changes to be made, and the resulting impact on patient safety and hospital outcomes. Finally, Case Study 3 presents an example of an IT-supported initiative that led to the reduction in adverse drug events (ADEs) among the hospitals of Trinity Health.

Introduction

Trinity Health is the fourth largest Catholic health system in the United States and employs 44,500 full-time equivalent employees with more than 8,000 active staff physicians. Its facilities include 44 hospitals, 379 outpatient clinics/facilities, numerous long-term care facilities, home health and hospice programs, and senior housing communities across seven U.S. states. For FY 2008, Trinity Health revenues were $6.3 billion, including $376 million that were returned to the communities in the form of healthcare for the poor and underserved.

Trinity Health gained nationwide exposure when it received the 2004 National Committee for Quality Health Care's annual award. The effective creation and implementation of the intranet-based information system called Integrated Information Shared Services (I2S2) played an important role in gathering, processing, and delivery of information. I2S2 delivered safety and quality outcome indicators for decision makers across the organization. The implementation of IT in Project Genesis employed an incremental step-by-step development approach in which the organizational and managerial issues were aligned with the IT.

Case Study 1: Physician-Led Informatics

This case study focuses on a continued initiative involving the tenets of customer relationship management (CRM) with the physicians.[1] Trinity Health learned from the CRM literature to build a service-oriented mechanism that consisted of delivering information and soliciting physician involvement. Trinity Health had previously deployed a web-based information system to deliver physician profiles of quality and costs. The Physician Profiling System (PPS) contained three fundamental hospital-based CRM characteristics: (1) administrative data-driven decision-making processes for healthcare problem identification, variation reduction, statistical process control, and other physician-driven performance pattern analyses; (2) identification of areas for improvement by benchmarking (either internal, external, or both) physician practices to desired patterns of quality and cost outcomes; and (3) involving the physicians as customers in improving operations using (1) and (2) by establishing critical success norms or other related evidence-based initiatives, particularly by using technology for rapid deployment, prompt feedback, and support for replication of best practices. The PPS deployment incurred an approximate cost of US$163,000 for the development and implementation in a single hospital. The return on investment (ROI) for that endeavor exhibited a mean decrease of 0.24 days of hospitalization, with an aggregate decrease of 845 total inpatient days along with multiple hospital department cost savings of US$1.42 million. For details of this initiative, please see Kohli et al.[1]

Approach

Although the one-off PPS was successful and provided the proof of concept, Trinity Health could not afford a multihospital implementation, one hospital at a time. So it extracted the learning from the PPS, enhanced the existing decision support system's (DSS) reporting capabilities, and delivered it through a web-based system for the entire organization (see Case study 2). The defining requirements emerging from the physician-led informatics initiative were as follows:

1. User-friendly design with common data structures for each ministry organization and a metadata level to speed query processing times
2. Enforced reconciliation of data with operational systems to ensure that all information systems provide consistent data
3. Seeking of value-added information such as cost accounting, expected reimbursement, and severity adjustment and assignment—processes that inform physicians about the impact of their decisions
4. Continuous improvement through cross-learning among ministry organizations and application development for quick deployment of best practices

Trinity Health created baseline assessments for disease categories (Table 8.1) to achieve the objectives of the physician-led informatics and to enhance ongoing physician alignment. These objectives were to share an innovative model for depicting individual physician resource utilization, the ability to identify physician variation in the clinical management, and to demonstrate the use of comparative benchmarking.

Results

The results from physicians' involvement were manifested as lower average length of stay (ALOS) and reduced patient charges. By contrast, among the hospitals where data were yet to be shared with

Table 8.1   Benchmarking Data to Support Physician Informatics

BENCHMARKING FOR CEREBROVASCULAR ACCIDENTS OR TIA				
	N	MEAN	MEDIAN	SUM
Quality	449			
Mortality	449	0.093	0	42
Expected mortality	449	0.114	0	51.186
Complications	449	0.167	0	74.983
Readmissions	449	0.081	0	36.369
Expected readmissions	449	0.109	0.106	48.941
LOS	449	4.55	4	2,042.95
Expected LOS	449	4.67	4.84	2,096.83
Costs	449			
FR	449	$247.40	$233.50	$111,082.60
ICU	449	$659.70	$0.00	$296,205.30
Lab	449	$217.50	$110.80	$97,657.50
Misc.	449	$574.60	$538.70	$257,995.40
Pharmacy	449	$370.40	$143.30	$166,309.60
Radiology	449	$404.60	$260.10	$181,665.40
Room	449	$1,290.70	$1,052.20	$579,524.30
Supply	449	$54.45	$8.41	$24,448.05
Surgery	449	$19.62	$0.00	$8,809.38
Therapies	449	$256.20	$179.10	$115,033.80
Total cost	449	$4,095.60	$3,209.40	$1,838,924.40
Expected cost	449	$4,307.60	$4,342.50	$1,934,112.40

physicians, the ALOS and charges began to increase. Trinity Health continued to monitor outcomes through the utilization collaborative team (UCT). Hospital- and physician-specific scorecards were developed by the UCT and distributed. Figure 8.1 presents a sample physician utilization report.

The utilization-based scorecards compared each physician's actual versus expected outcomes for ALOS, mortality, and patient charges for services. Comparable metrics for physicians within the specialty as well as other specialties are also reported. Finally, the scorecard presents a breakdown of charges by major categories such as lab, surgical, and pharmacy. Supported by the informatics, the physician and clinical staff practice changes resulted in lower than expected mortality rates as well as patient charges. With 2,932 patients, a drop in 0.32 day per patient in LOS equated to 938 fewer patient days and a reduction of $661.27 per patient in charges resulted in savings of nearly US$1.939 million.

Trinity St. Elsewhere Regional Medical Center	Physician Utilization Report
	by Physician Specialty and Attending Physician Number for Select MS DRGs

Selected MS DRGs: 234,236

Physician Specialty Code: 0004 CARDIOTHORACIC SURGERY

Physician Number and Name:

MS DRG code	MS DRG description		MS DRG geometric mean LOS	Patient count
236	CORONARY BYPASS WO CARD CATH WO MCC		6.08	16

(National-2005 V24)	Your Numbers	Ratio: observed/ expected	Same spec (excl. you)	Ratio: observed/ expected	All others (excl. spec)	Ratio: observed/ expected
Actual ALOS	6.00	1.00	5.13	0.85	9.50	1.11
Expected ALOS	6.03		6.03		8.54	
Actual Mortalities	0	0.00	0	0.00	0	0.00
Expected Mortalities	0.05		0.05		0.01	
Actual Average Charges	52,402.80	0.76	49,983.28	0.72	63,206.97	0.69
Expected Avg Charge	69,373.76		69,653.75		91,124.72	
Number of Patients	16		23		2	

Revenue code group	# of Pts	Avg charge	# of Pts	Avg charge	# of Pts	Avg charge
EMERGENCY	1	45.00	0	0.00	1	989.00
ICU	16	11,091.44	23	9,332.26	2	14,189.50
LAB	16	6,561.32	23	6,445.91	2	10,568.13
OTHER	16	1,509.63	23	1,588.04	2	2,138.50
PHARMACY	16	6,583.16	23	7,183.32	2	8,498.34
PROSTH	16	267.38	23	70.13	2	70.50
RADIOLOGY	16	1,132.75	23	1,043.22	2	969.00
ROOM	0	0.00	1	57.00	0	0.00
SUPPLY	16	12,123.00	23	11,936.71	2	12,567.00
SURGICAL	16	11,010.38	23	10,371.74	2	11,916.00
THERAPY	16	2,120.94	23	2,008.48	2	1,795.50

Figure 8.1   A sample physician scorecard.

The deployment of physician-led informatics prompted various feedback comments. Some admitted that they didn't realize the procedure costs that much, while others found the scorecards helpful and expressed eagerness for the next report. The outcomes in the report card prompted some physicians to review previous patients' charts and examine why they were in the hospital for that long, resulting in a retrospective learning and ideas about patient safety, improvement in ALOS, and how to contain costs.

Case Study 2: Integrated Information Shared Services (I2S2) Intranet

In the clinical arena, there is an expectation that quality must be measured on an ongoing basis. Healthcare organizations are monitored for quality and patient safety by the accrediting agencies and the U.S. government. Various agencies, public and private, publish

hospital and physician comparisons (see http://www.hospitalcompare
.hhs.gov, http://www.qualitynet.org/, and http://www.healthgrades
.com/). Prior to many of the public sources of comparisons, Trinity
Health desired transparency, so it published the quality performance
for each ministry organization (MO) on an intranet website called
Integrated Information Shared Services (I2S2). The transparency
of quality indicator performance enabled each hospital to identify
another hospital with better performance. Conversations about
higher performance led to performance improvement strategies and
action plans.

Approach

I2S2 was originally planned as an intranet web-based site. The development and maintenance was to be outsourced. However, owing to
the projected high costs of development, in-house resources completed the project. The I2S2 design uses content management software. Content management software is most often used for storing,
controlling, and publishing industry-specific documentation such as
articles, manuals, and guides. The content may include files, graphs,
images, databases, and documents with links to other websites (for
more information, see http://www.contentmanager.eu.com/history
.htm). Content management software integrated the interdependent
layers of data for managing Trinity Health's content as well as for
publishing the results to *any* individuals across the organization.

I2S2 recycles automatically every two hours. Costs include the
server hardware, the content management software, and the incremental labor from IT and clinical operations staff needed to input
content. The benefits clearly outweigh the costs. I2S2 is now a web
content management (WCM) system. This simplifies the publication
of the web content and allows the domain experts to focus on creating
content. The advantage of the WCM-based architecture is the ease of
use. Since the majority of contributions are from clinicians, content
submission does not require technical knowledge of HTML or file
uploads. As a result of the WCM, I2S2 is fully transparent to the
more than 50,000 Trinity Health employees who simply have to sign
on to the Trinity Health webpage for the vast information resources
available to them.

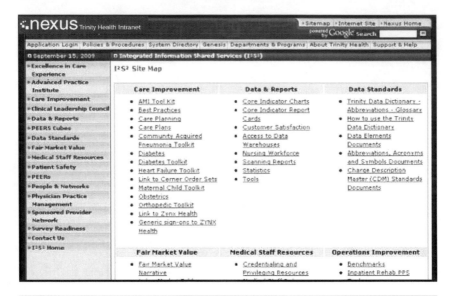

Figure 8.2   I2S2 user interface listing a site map with various categories of information and reports available.

The spectrum of I2S2 content, shown in Figure 8.2, can be logically organized in three primary areas: governance, data requirements, and guidelines and education. The following list provides descriptions of the salient topics for which I2S2 delivers support for decision makers. For each of the three areas, we discuss topics for which information is available.

1. Governance

Excellence in care experience. Patient satisfaction data, employee engagement, and physician satisfaction data are at the core and should be used to improve the overall experience of the patients and their families.

The Advance Practice Institute provides data to promote evidence-based best practices through advanced skills of nursing leaders, development of leadership skills to facilitate and complete projects, and the fostering of networks for creative thinking and issue resolution in the practice of evidence-based care.

Care improvement provides evidence-based tools, strategies, and resources to assist in providing excellence in care for specific clinical conditions such as acute myocardial infarction

(AMI), pneumonia, diabetes, heart failure, newborn and neonatal, obstetrics, orthopedics, and vaccine information.

The Clinical Leadership Council provides documentation for value and strategies of Trinity Health clinical services in accordance with the Trinity Health strategic plan. The goal is to develop high-quality and world-class service and to optimize value for the entire health system while maintaining organizational integrity and regulatory compliance. Minutes of monthly meetings and links to evidence-based practices and core clinical indicators are also provided.

2. Data requirements

Data standards connect decision makers to tools and resources related to Trinity Health's data standardization activities and include the data dictionary, approved abbreviations, dangerous abbreviations, supply chain links, glossary, data elements documents, and charge description master with standards. In addition, the charge description master file contains standardized detailed information on all services provided by the institution, including description, department codes, service code, and so forth.

The Data and Reports section provides views of clinical data, such as core indicator charts, report cards, customer and physician satisfaction data, medication/pharmacy scorecards, and scanning reports. For FY 2009, 28 core indicators are also available for each Trinity Health hospital, as well as other indicators for emergency room care, home care, and long-term care. Decision makers can also access data warehouses and download data for further analysis.

Patient Safety and Potential Error and Event Reporting (PEERs). This site links to best practices and related websites, patient safety tool kits, and numerous quality and safety reports for clinicians, as well as Trinity Health historical safety data. PEERs was designed by Trinity Health physicians, nurses, attorneys, and quality and risk management professionals to capture near-miss and errors/events data. Modeled after NASA's voluntary reporting system, PEERs is rated very high in the ease of use and ensuring anonymity.

3. Guidelines and education

Medical Staff Resources delivers policies, procedures, links, articles, and more on current issues affecting medical staffs. Links and related topics include credentialing and privileging resources, medical staff by-laws, rules and regulations, medical staff development plans, hospital–physician partnerships, peer review, and physician recruitment and satisfaction development forums.

Fair Market Value. This site provides information to find competitive national survey data and the fair market value narrative that provides a methodology on how to complete a fair market value assessment. The links are in compliance with the Stark II regulations that established a new safe harbor for determining the fair market value of physician compensation.

People and Networks is a resource to find a person who has the information decision makers need to move forward with an idea or project. The clinical operations department provides additional assistance in connecting people. Other items include information pertaining to the Pharmacy Council, the Health Information Management Council, the Educator Network, and related links.

The Physician Practice Management site provides a variety of practice management tools to assist the physician networks in best practice management from a broad spectrum of business disciplines, including finance, operations improvement, compliance, legal, human resource management, planning and marketing, clinical quality, insurance and risk management, and payor contract negotiations.

Sponsored Provider Network provides networking opportunities for executives, controllers, and physician leaders to share best practices in revenue management and expense reduction to drive improved financial and operational performance of the employed primary care physician networks. The meetings are rooted in the application of correct business principles and sharing of management philosophy to develop and achieve performance targets.

The Survey Readiness link connects administrators and clinicians to resources and useful tools for The Joint Commission preparation and continual readiness. It also contains Trinity Health hospitals' Joint Commission survey highlights, news flashes, and hot topics.

Results

I2S2 has emerged as the go-to online resource for decision makers at Trinity Health. The users span the spectrum of functions across the hospitals. Usage statistics for August 2009 tracked 2,972 average daily hits. More than 901 pages were viewed by Trinity Health users, who viewed an average of 12.69 pages per visit. These metrics indicate that I2S2 had indeed been helpful in delivering pertinent information to decision makers. It can be hypothesized that availability of data and the expanse of use contributed to an informed decision maker and resulted in improved performance outcomes.

Trinity Health received the 2004 National Committee for Quality Health Care's Annual Award. At that time it was only the 12th healthcare system in the United States to be so designated. In 2009, Trinity Health was named as one of the top 10 health systems in the *Thomson Reuters 100 Top Hospitals®: Health System Quality/Efficiency Study*, which identifies the top U.S. health systems by objectively measuring the clinical quality and efficiency of member hospitals.* Therefore, it is reasonable to assume that I2S2 contributed to Trinity Health hospitals' above national average performance and top decile ranking on many critical measures. This information delivery tool is dynamic and must be updated regularly. To ensure that the information in I2S2 remains current, relevant, and appeals to a wider user base, Trinity Health has instituted a process for reviewing the topical

---

* http://www.reuters.com/article/pressRelease/idUS87944+10-Aug-2009 +PRN20090810. The study evaluated 252 health systems—with a total of 1,720 hospitals—on measures of clinical quality and efficiency. The top ten represent the top 2.5% of the systems studied. Five measures of performance were used to evaluate systems: mortality, complications, patient safety, length of stay, and use of evidence-based practices. All of these are available in I2S2. I2S2 allows decision makers in all Trinity Health hospitals to leverage the collective clinical knowledge and best care practices and for rapid replication and improving the quality, safety, and satisfaction of patients throughout the course of their delivery of care.

areas and the content available to decision makers, as well as a forum where innovative uses of data are shared.

Each year Trinity Health reviews its quality indicators and targets areas for improvement. Changes in the scientific evidence, data definitions, and public awareness are a few of the several reasons for the periodic review of the I2S2 clinical indicators. Other reasons include improvements in performance and the board's oversight. Trinity Health has established the following internal criteria for choosing indicators to monitor and disseminate through I2S2.

1. Applicable to multiple reporting organizations (e.g., The Joint Commission/Centers for Medicare & Medicaid Services)
2. Sufficient patient volume to demonstrate change in performance
3. Emerging opportunities for improvement (includes variation in performance)
4. Evidence of improved process that influences the indicator
5. National norms for indicator are available
6. Alignment of metrics with the Trinity Health strategic plan
7. Burden of data capture does not exceed the value of the indicator

The process of selecting quality indicators involves representatives from each of the MOs, and is subsequently approved by senior management and the board.

In order to assist in this sharing of ideas, the I2S2 People and Networks section enables individuals to identify who to call for assistance. I2S2 has become a virtual library resource for standardized content. Any employee or physician can access the website and view a current or historical document that shows a six-month rolling average performance. A link for each indicator for a particular MO allows the user to drill down and view a 24-month trend graph.

Case Study 3: Clinical Adverse Drug Event (ADE) Alert System

Background

In the 1990s the pressure of managed care challenged U.S. hospitals to ask the following questions: How does a healthcare organization link patient care quality with investment in clinical IT? What part of healthcare is in need for urgent technological support? At about the same time, the issue of adverse drug events or medical errors had gained attention through various publications.[2,3] Subsequent studies examined hospitals' responses and established that ADEs could be prevented.[4]

Previous research indicates that implementation of computerized ADE systems involves at least three steps: (1) capturing patient data electronically; (2) applying algorithms, rules, and queries to find cases that might be consistent with ADEs; and (3) determining the accuracy of the systems.[5] Many hospitals have information systems that contain integrated patient encounter data that include demographics, pharmacy orders, and laboratory results.[6] Some hospitals create their own systems, while others integrate off-the-shelf commercial products. There are two forms of ADE systems. *Basic systems* perform functions such as drug-allergy checking, dosage guidance, formulary decision support, duplicate therapy checking, and drug-to-drug interaction evaluations. *Advanced systems* perform more complex functions, including dose adjustment, guidance for medication-related laboratory testing, and drug–disease contraindication flags.[7]

Approach

Trinity Health led the effort to build an advanced ADE alert system with support from a commercial provider, Discern Expert, Cerner Corp., as part of Project Genesis. A rules engine with 17 ADE alert rules was installed. These alerts were triggered using a computerized algorithm after examining demographics, clinical lab values, and medications.

A key assumption to construct an ADE model is that as much as possible, all data about the events and actions taken must be derived and analyzed to develop the model. For instance, the ADE information must include the drugs administered, mode of administering the drug, patient demographics, actions taken, and the result. For an ADE system to be successful, it is imperative that data standards must be developed and followed. The scope of data standardization for the first phase included general laboratory results, pharmacy descriptions/Charge Description Master (CDM), and a partial list of ADT (Patient admitting/discharge/transfer systems)/registration data elements required to support the ADE functionality and patient chart capabilities. However, achieving data standardization is also a political exercise in building consensus.

Trinity Health entrusted its Functional and Clinical Councils and Standards Leadership Team with approval from the COO/CFO and Clinical Leadership Council (CLC) oversight groups. The Standards Leadership Council directed the implementation of policies and procedures for change management, audit and reporting mechanisms, and outcome measurement. Data standards have met the requirements and are adjusted to meet the changing business environment.

After literature reviews for medication safety and quality from the pharmacoepidemiological and pharmacoecomonical literature, rules were generated using computerized algorithms to examine demographics with clinical lab values and medications. An example of a rule is presented in the following paragraphs.

Trinity Health ADE Alerts   An alert is triggered based on a number of grouped events. A rules engine with 17 of these alerts is generated by computerized algorithms examining patient demographics, clinical lab values, and medications. The ADE alerts are triggered in real time so that any change in medication or lab result will be evaluated as soon as reported. This allows pharmacy intervention immediately and eliminates the possible 12- to 24-hour delay seen before implementation of the system. The pharmacists rely on the system to screen new lab results as they are reported, and this allows the pharmacists to prioritize their workflow to address the most critical issues and patients in a timely manner. The following is an example of this alert process. A pharmacist inputs a physician order for a potassium-containing or potassium-sparing drug. Yet the patient has a lab result for serum potassium > 6.0 mEq/L. Consequently, the potassium medication dose or medication itself needs to be adjusted for these patients because the alert is evoked when a high potassium level is evidenced. Current orders are checked for any of the specified drugs that may cause hyperkalemia.

Trinity Health's experience suggests that to implement an ADE system successfully, the following conditions must be met.

1. This project must have executive support for the adoption of defined data standards.
2. The data standards must be approved by the senior leadership and implemented organization-wide.

3. All hospitals and entities must actively participate in the Functional and Clinical Councils.

4. Project participants must provide a timely response to data requests and data review to ensure timely implementation.

5. Following the implementation of data standards, the organization must provide ongoing support of the change management process and commitment to the standards developed.

6. The implementation should be stratified and should be deployed in areas where quick results can be achieved. Learning from such projects can be applied to more complex applications.

7. The recommended model must be accurate, consistent, user-friendly, and compliant with existing computer applications and all governing bodies.

8. Although data standards do not cause any operational changes, redesign efforts must be accommodated in the clinical and patient administration projects.

9. A change management process will be defined and followed to add to the standards. Conformance to standardization will be monitored and reported.

Results

Once buy-in from the stakeholders was achieved, work planning and milestone schedules for the laboratory and pharmacy were established. Trinity Health's philosophy is to design once, implement many times. The ADE application followed this guiding principle to implement the ADE system across several hospitals. For ease of maintenance and updates, the computing hardware was standardized and the ADE application software was centrally developed. In using the ADE system, Trinity Health focused on evaluating the effects and derived benefits from usage and expected to achieve cost savings and reductions in patient mortality in line with the published literature that decreases in the harmful events save both human lives and money.

The ADE project implementation assigned a project manager, a data manager, a systems technical analyst, a systems business analyst, and an administrative support staff. There were 4.5 FTEs (full-time equivalent employees) at start-up and implementation, and now 2.5 FTEs are assigned for maintenance and reporting. The following are additional activities required by the hospitals to support the ADE project.

Lab kickoff meeting	2 hours/site	Laboratory Council
Lab phone interview	1–2 hours/site	Med Tech
Lab Standards Review	8 hours/site	Med Tech × 3 sites
Lab standards approval	3 hours	Laboratory Council
Pharmacy kickoff meeting	2 hours	Pharmacy Council
Pharmacy phone interview	1–2 hours/site	Pharmacists
Pharmacy standards review	24 hours	Pharmacy subgroup
Pharmacy approval	3 hours	Pharmacy Council
Pharmacy mapping review	8 hours/site	Pharmacist
Reg./HIM/pt. acct. kickoff meeting	2 hours/site	Directors
UB92 review	8 hours	Pt. admin./reg./HIM managers
UB92 mapping review	8 hours	Pt. admin./reg./HIM managers

In deploying the ADE system among the hospitals, the senior leadership declared that a financial impact analysis was not required. The urgency and the impact on patient mortality outweighed the need for economic justification. As seen in the preceding text, labor was the cost driver for implementing the ADE system. The question then is: How much cost has to be absorbed when the financial benefits are not assessed? For ADEs there are significant financial costs affixed to each event. Yet there are clinical "costs" as well in human pain and suffering, not to mention litigation. Previous literature has cited that each ADE costs about $6,685,[8] and that computer systems play a decisive role in preventing ADEs.[9] Thus, there is significant evidence in the literature to support that preventing ADEs can reduce hospital costs in addition to increasing patient care quality.

At Trinity Health the impact of implementing the ADE system was evident principally in the reduction in pharmacy costs, a savings of 5%. These pharmacy cost savings in the targeted hospitals exceeded US$3.5 million. Internal and external control groups demonstrated no such cost savings. There was also evidence of decreases in severity-adjusted LOS and mortality rates.[10]

Conclusion

This chapter chronicled three case studies as milestones in the journey of Trinity Health to gather, process, and disseminate data to improve patient safety and outcomes. We established that for hospitals to be effective in using information for improved decision making, physicians' leadership and involvement is necessary. Once metrics are agreed on, an effective data delivery mechanism must be put in place. Through rich descriptions and examples we presented Trinity Health's intranet-based information system, I2S2. Descriptions of categories of information content provide an overview of range of data available to the decision makers. Finally, we presented an example of a value-added application that emerged from the leadership by physicians and the development effort of the information systems professionals to implement an ADE alert system. Lessons learned from building the ADE system will assist readers in avoiding pitfalls and preparing for their own value-added applications.

This chapter was originally published in *Healthcare Informatics, Improving Efficiency and Productivity*, Taylor & Francis, New York, 2010.

References

1. Kohli R, Piontek F, Ellington T, VanOsdol T, Shepard M, Brazel G. 2001. Managing customer relationships through an e-business decision support application: A case of hospital physician collaboration. *Decis Support Syst* 32:171–87.
2. Bates DW, Leape LL, Petrycki S. 1993. Incidence and preventability of adverse drug events in hospitalized adults. *J Gen Intern Med* 8:289–94.
3. Grasela TH, Walawander CA, Kennedy DL, Jolson HM. 1993. Capability of hospital computer-systems in performing drug-use evaluations and adverse drug event monitoring. *Am J Hosp Pharm* 50: 1889–95.
4. Bates DW, Leape LL, Cullen DJ et al. 1998. Effect of computerized physician order entry and a team intervention on prevention of serious medication errors. *JAMA* 280:1311–16.
5. Evans RS, Pestotnik SL, Classen DC, Horn SD, Bass SB, Burke JP. 1994. Preventing adverse drug events in hospitalized patients. *Ann Pharmacother* 28:523–27.

6. Raschke RA, Gollihare B, Wunderlich TA et al. 1998. A computer alert system to prevent injury from adverse drug events—Development and evaluation in a community teaching hospital. *JAMA* 280:1317–20.
7. Wolfstadt JI, Gurwitz JH, Field TS et al. 2008. The effect of computerized physician order entry with clinical decision support on the rates of adverse drug events: A systematic review. *J Gen Intern Med* 23:451–58.
8. Senst BL, Achusim LE, Genest RP et al. 2001. Practical approach to determining costs and frequency of adverse drug events in a health care network. *Am J Health Syst Pharmacy* 58:1126–32.
9. Yan Q, Hunt CA. 2000. Preventing adverse drug events (ADEs): The role of computer information systems. *Drug Inf J* 34:1247–60.
10. Piontek F, Kohli R, Conlon P, Ellis J, Jablonski J, Kini N. 2010. Effects of an adverse-drug-event alert system on cost and quality outcomes in community hospitals. *Am J Health Syst Pharmacy* 67:613–20.

9

THE NEW MEDICAL FRONTIER: REAL-TIME WIRELESS MEDICAL DATA ACQUISITION FOR 21ST-CENTURY HEALTHCARE AND DATA MINING CHALLENGES

DAVID LUBLINER AND STEPHAN P. KUDYBA

Contents

Introduction

Medical sensors, fixed, wireless, and implanted, are growing at an exponential rate. This trend is amplified by the growth of smartphones and tablets that provide the potential to provide real-time monitoring and proactive prevention. Cisco has estimated[1] that by 2015 mobile cellular traffic will reach an annual run rate of 75 exabytes, 10^{18} bytes or 1 billion gigabytes. This enormous amount of data doesn't even factor into the growth of this new emerging field of real-time wireless medical devices, where studies have shown them to be a significant benefit to early detection and reduced acute emergency room visits. In 2012 the Federal Communications Commission allocated part of the spectrum for medical body area networks (MBANs), which will accelerate adoption of these technologies. Add to that genomic sequencing and the need to categorize, evaluate trends, mine data sets spanning large populations, and compress and store data that will potentially dwarf current storage architectures. The challenge is enormous but so too are the potential benefits. Kryder's law for data storage,[2] an offshoot of Moore's law for microprocessors, shows similar patterns of growth of data storage systems, but may still not be enough to satisfy projections. New storage technologies utilizing molecular storage[3] may come to our rescue. We are at a critical inflection point where data, communications, processing power, and medical technologies have the potential to transform our ways of life. The real challenge is extracting meaning out of this torrent of information.

This chapter is a primer for those interested in exploring mining of medical data, in particular the challenges of extracting meaning from the new breed of wireless medical monitoring devices. The "Evolution of Modern Medicine: Background" section begins with a brief history of the quantification of medical practices and the advances that have led to the doubling of life expectancy in the past 100 years. The "Medical Data Standards" section introduces medical terminology that is crucial to developing a standard lexis of medical terms for data sharing. The "Data Acquisition: Medical Sensors and Body Scanners" section introduces medical data acquisition and the theory behind many popular sensors and medical scanners. The "Wireless Medical Devices" section introduces the communications and integration of these wireless sensor networks. The "Expert Systems Utilized to Evaluate Medical Data" section discusses expert systems, which is the first step in extracting meaning from medical data and provides techniques to make these data available to medical professionals and the public. The "Data Mining and Big Data" section discusses medical data mining and the new initiatives by the National Science Foundation (NSF), National Institutes of Health (NIH), and Department of Defense (DOD) to extract meaning from these big data sets in the petabyte ranges of 10^{15} to 2^{50}.

We are entering into a brave new world of medical data acquisition. The potential benefits may transform healthcare from reactive to proactive treatment, reducing the burden of emergency rooms but increasing that on a new breed of medical informatics professionals. The challenge is to develop guidelines to ensure that privacy and support systems are constructed to provide preventive care to maximize the benefits and ensure equal access to these technologies.

Evolution of Modern Medicine: Background

Medical knowledge has paralleled our perceptions of our place in the universe. When superstition dominated our discourse, illness and disease were predominantly attributed to forces beyond our control. Ancient Egyptian and Babylonians around 3300 BC began to quantify a system of medicine that included diagnosis and medical examination, but still included aspects of external forces as part of the equation. One of the first rational medical documents, the Edwin

Smith Papyrus[4] on trauma and surgery, Egypt ca. 1500 BC, details 48 cases of injury with a detailed diagnosis, examination, and treatment strategies. Treatment includes both suggested medication and spells to treat the condition. The text appears to be a transcribed copy attributed to Imhotep, a physician and high priest ca. 3000 BC. The first hospitals, "Houses of Life," were also mentioned in this same era.

Babylonians, 1067–1046 BC, wrote a medical text *The Diagnostic Handbook*,[5] by Esagil-kin-apli; it included patient symptoms and treatment through creams, pills, and bandages. In India, 600 BC, the "Complete Knowledge for Long Life" described herbal remedies and appears to be linked to Buddhist practices. In China, 500 BC, "Yellow Emperors Inner Cannon" drew a parallel between the physical world and the spiritual aspects of disease. Another milestone in our quantification of medical practice was the Hippocratic Oath, Greece, ca. 500 BC, in which physicians were given guidelines on ethical practice and treatment. This oath incorporated treatises to external forces: "Apollo Physician and Asclepius and Hygeia and Panacea and All the Gods and Goddesses, Making Them My Witnesses, That I Will Fulfill according to My Ability and Judgment This Oath and This Covenant." Around this period the first Greek medical school in Cnidus, now part of Turkey, was established. The guiding philosophy was to restore the balance of humors in the body.

In the Middle Ages, 1200 AD, Islamic medical science advanced medicine in pharmacology, surgery, and ophthalmology guided by a systematic approach to medical practice. In the Renaissance, 1500 AD, experimental science in anatomy, neurology, and the circulatory system began our movement away from folklore. The first pharmaceutical text, *Antidotarium Florentine*, in 1542, was published by the Florence College of Medicine. By the early 1600s medicines were in common use in London. The College of Physicians issued guidelines for the preparation of drugs by authorized apothecaries. By 1750 an official pharmacological guide was published where only treatments sanctioned by a pharmacopeia committee were included.

Modern medicine truly began in the 1800s with anesthesia, the "germ theory of disease,"[6] use of antiseptics, *Introduction to the Study of Experimental Medicine* by Claude Bernard in 1865 describing a scientific method of medical inquiry, bacteriology (Robert Koch), and many other developments. Nursing practice and education were quantified by Florence Nightingale with her book *Notes on Nursing* (1859). Her statistical analysis of infection and sanitation was influential in creating the public health service in India.

In the early part of the 20th century new diagnostic techniques, antimicrobial therapy, and evidence-based medicine such as triple-blind randomized trials accelerated medical knowledge and effectiveness. In the later part of the 20th century the exponential growth of medicine began: genomics, medical imaging, stem cell therapy, and modern surgery. The explosion of new microtechnology, gene therapies, transplants, and the World Wide Web of integrated knowledge sharing have put us on the threshold of this next great leap forward. As shown in Figure 9.1, there has been a direct correlation with evidence-based medicine and the doubling of life expectancy over the last 100 years.

With this exponential growth in medical knowledge come enormous stores of data. The technology for genomic sequencing data has been reduced from a year to hours. This storehouse will continue to accelerate. The National Institutes of Health in 2012 released a genomic data store of 200 terabytes, soon to enter the petabyte range, 10^{15}. With the advent of real-time wireless medical sensors, millions will be transmitting data. It's difficult to estimate the data volume, but in the first decade the terabyte–petabyte range is not unreasonable (see p. 241). Data mining of medical data will present enormous challenges and benefits.

Medical Data Standards

A critical consideration in the analysis of medical data is to ensure all parties are using the same nomenclature. How can we extract usable information unless all parties adhere to international standards for data classification?

There are a number of national and international data standards that provide ubiquitous communications between doctors, health insurance companies, labs, and pharmacies, and for interoperability between electronic health records (EHRs).

The U.S. government in 1996 created a series of standards and specifications for electronic health records and data security. The National Institute of Standards is responsible for standards for federal agencies. The department responsible for health services is the U.S. Health and

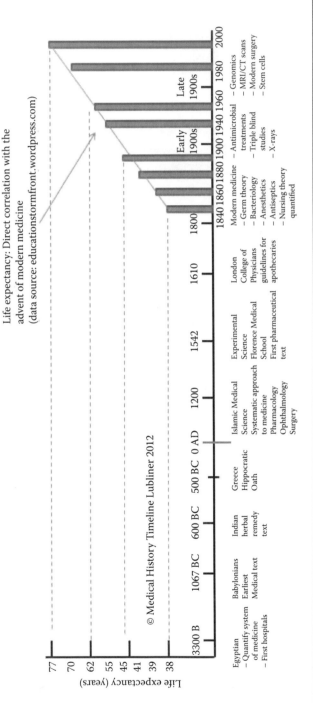

Figure 9.1   Evolution of medical science overlaid with life expectancy improvements.

Human Services Department (HHS). In 1996 the Health Insurance Portability and Accountability Act of 1996 (HIPAA, Public Law 104-191) established guidelines for medical data and security of that information (Figure 9.2). These have been periodically updated, and a recent update to HIPAA Title II on data security[7] provides confidentiality, integrity, and availability (CIA) for medical information.

- Health Level Seven (www.HL.org), an organization started in 1987, has become the most popular international standard for data interoperability for medical practitioners (Table 9.1). Collectively, it develops standards designed to increase the effectiveness, efficiency, and quality of healthcare delivery. HL7's primary mission is to create flexible, low-cost standards, guidelines, and methodologies to enable the exchange and interoperability of electronic health records. Such guidelines or data standards are an agreed on set of rules that allow information to be shared and processed in a uniform and consistent manner. Without data standards, healthcare organizations could not readily share clinical information.

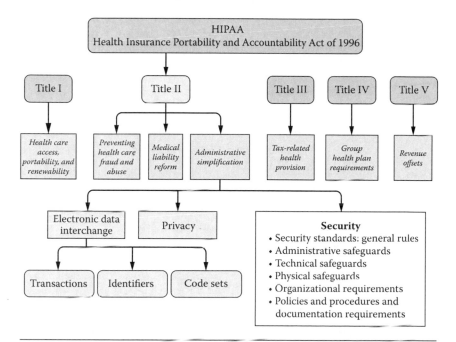

Figure 9.2 HIPAA standards created by the U.S. government in 1996. (From HHS, http://www.hhs.gov/ocr/privacy/hipaa/administrative/securityrule/nist80066.pdf.)

Table 9.1   Data Interoperability Standards

United States	Health Level 7 (HL7) and Healthcare Information and Management Systems Society (HIMSS) are involved in the standardization process for HER in the U.S.
	The Certification Commission for Healthcare Information Technology (CCHIT) is a private not-for-profit organization founded to develop and evaluate the certification for EHRs and interoperable health informatics networks.
	The American Society for Testing and Materials (ASTM)
INTERNATIONAL	
Europe	CEN's TC/251 is responsible for EHR standards
	ISO TC215 produces standards for EHR requirements as well as accepting certain standards from other standards organizations.
	The openEHR Foundation develops and publishes EHR specifications and open source EHR implementations, which are currently being used in Australia and parts of Europe.
Canada	Canada Health Infoway (a private not-for-profit organization started with federal government seed money) is mandated to accelerate the development and adoption of electronic health information systems.

- HL7 is an all-volunteer, not-for-profit organization involved in the development of international healthcare standards.
- Headquartered in Ann Arbor, Michigan, Health Level Seven is a standards developing organization (SDO) that is accredited by the American National Standards Institute (ANSI).
- Founded in 1987 to produce a standard for hospital information systems, HL7 is currently the selected standard for the interfacing of clinical data in most institutions.
- HL7 and its members provide a comprehensive framework (and related standards) for the exchange, integration, sharing, and retrieval of electronic health information.
- The standards, which support clinical practice and the management, delivery, and evaluation of health services, are the most commonly used in the world.

There are numerous other standards for data interoperability. The International Statistical Classification of Diseases (ICD-10) is a standard created by the World Health Organization (WHO) that contains more than 14,000 names, codes, and descriptions of diseases so international medical practitioners can share findings using the same terminology. Another important standard is Systemized Nomenclature of Medicine (SNOMED) that provides a consistent way to describe medical diseases, diagnoses, and symptoms. Communicating and transmitting x-ray images and magnetic resonance imaging (MRI), computed tomography (CT), and positron emission tomography (PET) scans utilizes the Digital Imaging and Communications in Medicine (DICOM) standard. The Institute of Electrical and Electronic Engineers (IEEE) standards association publishes approximately 200 standards. Examples are 802.11 for wireless medical device transmissions and 11073 for plug-and-play interoperability of medical devices.[8]

Data Acquisition: Medical Sensors and Body Scanners

Medical data acquisition falls into a number of categories: electrical (EEG, EKG), electromagnetic, imaging (MRI, PET), chemical, biological (cultures), and genomic data sequencing. This section describes the theory behind some of those data acquisition technologies and also describes various medical sensors and scanners. A prerequisite for mining data and extracting meaning is a basic understanding of those technologies that generate this information.

Sensors

Electrical: Current in nerve cells. At the highest level of abstraction current flows (electrons—valence electron [ve]) toward a positive potential; that is, one side of a wire or nerve is positive. In a battery you have two chemical solutions initially both neutral; let's say for argument's sake that the atoms on each side of the battery have 10 protons and 10 electrons. When charging a battery you move electrons from one side to the other; that is, one side has 9 electrons and the other 11 (Figure 9.3a). This provides a positive potential difference between the two sides of the battery; that is, one side is more positive than the other. When connecting a wire between terminals of the battery the electrons, negative, move to the positive side. Once both sides are neutral, both have 10 protons, positive, and 10 electrons; the potential difference disappears and no current flows.

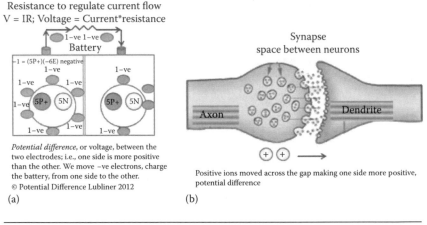

Resistance to regulate current flow
V = IR; Voltage = Current*resistance

Synapse
space between neurons

Battery

−1 = (5P+)(−6E) negative

Potential difference, or voltage, between the
two electrodes; i.e., one side is more positive
than the other. We move −ve electrons, charge
the battery, from one side to the other.
© Potential Difference Lubliner 2012

(a)

Positive ions moved across the gap making one side more positive,
potential difference

(b)

Figure 9.3   (a) Potential difference in a battery. (b) Potential generated in a synapse.

The same is true for electron flow in the body. For current to flow, a potential difference must be created from one synapse, the space between neurons, to the next. This is achieved by pumping positive ions across that gap between nerves. This is a sodium (NA^+)-potassium (K^+) pump (Figure 9.3b).

Electrical (EKG, EEG)

An electrocardiogram (EKG) measures the electrical activity of the cardiac muscle of the heart. When the sinoatrial (SA) node, the pacemaker of the heart located in the right atrium, initiates signals, it sends signals to the atrial-ventricular node, then to the Purkinje fibers that propagate the signals to the rest of the heart.

In the SA node/pacemaker step 1, a large number of sodium ions (Na^+) and a small number of potassium ions (K^+) are migrating through the cell. Then in step 2, calcium (Ca^{2+}) channels open up, creating an (action) potential, that is, cell more positive generating a current (flow of electrons) in millivolts, a thousand volts (Figure 9.4). In step 3, a potassium channel opens up so more potassium ions flow out and the potential difference returns to negative, stopping the flow of current.

The action potential in cardiac muscle cells is initiated by a sodium spike that generates a calcium spike, which then produces muscle contraction (Figure 9.4). The voltage of a cell is usually measured in millivolts (mV), a thousand volts.

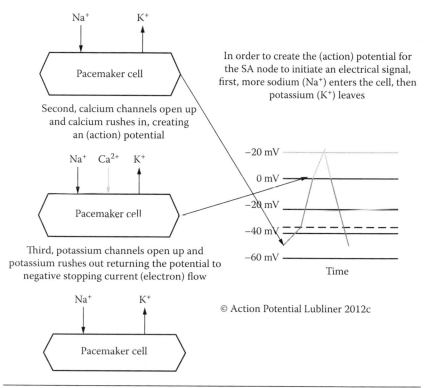

Figure 9.4   Action potential in cardiac nerves.

Pulse Oximetry

Pulse oximetry is a method of monitoring oxygen saturation of a patient's hemoglobin. The process uses a pair of light-emitting diodes (LEDs) on one side of a finger and a photoreceptor on the other. There are two LEDs, one red at 660 nm wavelength and a second at 905–940 nm in the infrared range. The absorption at these wavelengths differs between their oxygenated (ox) hemoglobin and deoxygenated state. The ratio of the two can be calculated using the two frequencies. The absorption is calculated from the minimum versus peak values, which makes simultaneously monitoring the pulse critical.

Medical Scanners

MRI is a noninvasive method used to render images of the inside of an object. It is primarily used in medical imaging to demonstrate pathological or other physiological alterations of living tissues.

Magnetic Resonance Imaging (MRI) vs. Computed Tomography (CT)   A CT, originally known as computed axial tomography (CAT), scanner, uses a type of ionizing radiation to acquire its images, making it a good tool for examining tissue composed of elements of a relatively higher atomic number than the tissue surrounding them (e.g., bone and calcifications [calcium based] within the body [carbon-based flesh] or structures [vessels, bowel] than the surrounding flesh[iodine, barium]). MRI, on the other hand, uses nonionizing radio frequency (RF) signals to acquire its images and is best suited for noncalcified tissue (Figure 9.5).

- The magnet is the largest and most expensive component of the scanner, and the remainder of the scanner is built around the magnet. Just as important as the strength of the main magnet is its precision. The straightness of flux lines within the center or, as it is known, the isocenter of the magnet, needs to be almost perfect. Magnetic gradients are generated by three orthogonal coils, oriented in the x, y, and z directions of the scanner. These are usually resistive electromagnets powered by sophisticated amplifiers that permit rapid and precise adjustments to their field strength and direction.

- In 1983 Ljunggren[9] and Twieg[10] independently introduced the k-space formalism, a technique that proved invaluable in unifying different MRI techniques. They showed that the demodulated MR signal $S(t)$ generated by freely precise nuclear spins in the presence of a linear magnetic field

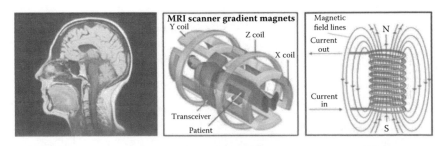

Figure 9.5   MRI scan, schematic of scanner gradient magnets, and magnetic fields generated. (From the Magnetic High Magnetic Field Magnetic Laboratory, University of Florida, http://www .magnet.fsu.edu/education/tutorials/magnetacademy/mri/fullarticle.html.)

gradient G equals the Fourier transform of the effective spin density, that is,

$$S(t) = \tilde{\rho}_{\text{effective}}\left(\vec{k}(t)\right) \equiv \int d^3x \rho(\vec{x}) \cdot e^{2\pi_2 \vec{k}(t) \cdot \vec{x}}$$

- MRI is essentially the manipulation of spins within a strong magnetic field, which then return to an equilibrium state. That a particle has spin is actually a mathematical description of the quantum mechanical nature of the particle—that happens to behave mathematically like spin—rather than a conceptual one (a sphere spinning on an axis). It is easy to imagine a positively charged sphere (e.g., the proton) of finite size (radius ~10^{-14} m), finite mass (~10^{-27} kg), and a net electric charge (~10^{-19} C) spinning, and therefore possessing a magnetic dipole moment.

Positron Emission Tomography (PET) PET is a nuclear medicine medical imaging technique that produces a three-dimensional image or map of functional processes or metabolic activities in the body. To conduct the scan, a short-lived radioactive tracer isotope, which decays by emitting a positron, which also has been chemically incorporated into a metabolically active molecule, is injected into the living subject (usually into blood circulation) (Figure 9.6).

The data set collected in PET is much poorer than that in CT, so reconstruction techniques are more difficult (see section on image reconstruction of PET).

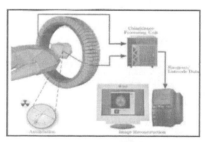 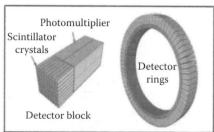

Figure 9.6 Positron emission tomography (PET) scan. (From the Max Planck Institute for Neurological Research, http://www.nf.mpg.de/index.php?id=78&L=1.)

Computed Tomography (CT)   CT is a medical imaging method employing tomography where digital geometry processing is used to generate a three-dimensional image of the internals of an object from a large series of two-dimensional x-ray images taken around a single axis of rotation. Cranial CT scans are shown in Figure 9.7. The bones are whiter than the surrounding area. Whiter means higher radio-density bones are whiter than the surrounding area. Whiter means higher radio density (i.e., the CT scan is designed to show higher-density structures).

DICOM: Digital Imaging   Digital Imaging and Communications in Medicine (DICOM) is a format used for storing and sharing information between systems in medical imaging (also referred to as ISO 12052:2006) (Figure 9.8). It was developed in 1993 and is designed to ensure the interoperability of system sharing of medical images. The National Electrical Manufacturers Association (NEMA) holds the copyright to the standard (http://dicom.nema.org/).

Imaging Informatics

Imaging informatics is the discipline associated with the acquisition, storage, knowledge base, mathematical modeling, and expert systems involved with the medical imaging field. A generic imaging system is described as a picture archiving and communication system (PACS), which communicates, stores, and analyzes data from multiple data formats and scanning technologies (e.g., DICOM, ultrasound, endoscopy, and CT and MRI scanners). There are standard DICOM query protocols to transmit and retrieve images, C-MOVE protocols, and a PACS[11] database using CQUERY. PACS links hospitals, imaging centers, and radiological groups to multiple hospitals. Hospitals access

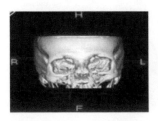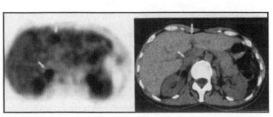

Figure 9.7   PET scan vs. CT scan. (From RadioGraphics, http://radiographics.rsna.org/content/30/4/939/F37.expansion.html.)

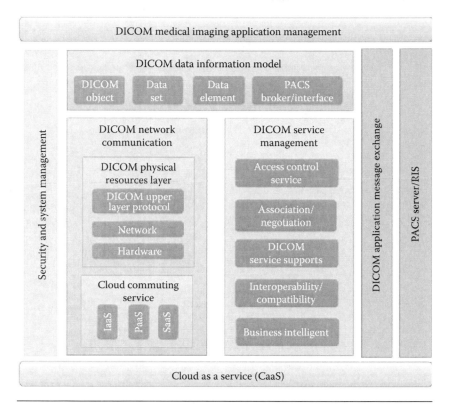

Figure 9.8 DICOM storage architecture and typical multiview DICOM storage. (From *Oracle® Multimedia DICOM Developer's Guide*, http://docs.oracle.com/cd/B28359_01/appdev.111/b28416 /ch_cncpt.htm.)

larger PACS systems through an internal radiological information system that includes patient tracking, patient scheduling, and workflow management.

As an example of an expert system used for the analysis and detection of cancer, it has been shown that the fractal dimension of 2D microvascular networks (Figure 9.9) can discriminate between normal versus tumor tissue.[12,13] Research is continuing into fractal characteristics of 3D microvascular networks to determine if there is a correlation between the computed fractal characteristics and the nature of the tissue of origin. Automated assist and diagnosis software is approaching the quality of human experts that evaluate images. During the last decade (2000–2010), the reliability of expert system software, blue line, approached that of their human counterparts, that is, radiologists.

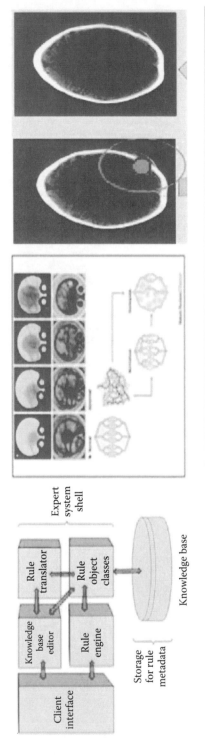

Figure 9.9 Expert system architecture, fractal capillary formation, and enhancement of tumors. (From *Physiological Reviews*, http://physrev.physiology.org/content /91/3/1071.full.)

The creation of a continuum from data collection, diagnosis, and treatment incorporated into electronic health records is transforming healthcare delivery and improving the overall quality of care in the healthcare system.

Wireless Medical Devices

Wireless medical devices can contain local data storage for subsequent download or transmit data in real time via various wireless technologies such as Bluetooth or protected wireless spectrums designated by the Federal Communications Commission (FCC), as indicated by 802.11b specifications.

These sensors are classified as either stand-alone devices or integrated in a sensor network where all devices share a common microprocessor controller that sends information as an integrated package. Both hospitals and individuals now currently utilize these devices. Research has indicated that this real-time data has reduced follow-up admissions. A new field is emerging where body sensor networks, an integrated suite of mobile medical monitors, are often integrated into clothing, which can be a significant aid to prevention of more serious conditions.

As wireless medical devices or body sensor webs become common, large real-time data streams are creating a new challenge in real-time data mining and big data, defined as extremely large data sets, to respond to possible life-threatening conditions in a timely matter. Some of these can be alleviated by locally intelligent processing; other issues will require a new breed of medical informatics professionals to analyze and develop protocols. As indicated in Figure 9.1, life expectancy has doubled in the last 100 years; the potential to match this rate of improvement using real-time wireless sensors integrated with smart devices/phones could be transformational.

Bluetooth Wireless Communications

Bluetooth is one of the most accepted international wireless standards for wireless medical devices. It is characterized at short range, and recently in low-power variants with well-defined security protocols. It also contains specifications for personal area networks, piconets, of up to eight integrated devices.

There is an international organization/special interest working group (SIG) (https://www.bluetooth.org/apps/content/) that includes representatives from most medical equipment manufactures and publishes standards and holds regular seminars. The group also certifies testing laboratories to ensure Bluetooth standards meet local regulations. HL7, another international working group (www.HL7.org) that establishes Electronic medical record (EMR) standards, closely works with this and other standards organizations, such as Healthcare Information and Management Systems Society (HIMSS), which is "focused on providing global leadership for the optimal use of information technology (IT) and management systems for the betterment of healthcare" (http://www.HIMSS.org).

Body Sensor Networks

A body sensor network (BNS; Figure 9.10) is a series of medical devices, either external or implanted, worn by patients. The concept involves linking series of devices, using Bluetooth short-range communications, with a computer or smart device into an integrated packaged signal. Up to this point Bluetooth standard IEEE 802.15.4 has been a relatively inefficient system with higher transmission power

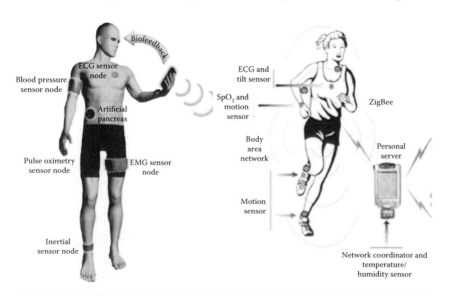

Figure 9.10   Body sensor networks. (From Robust Low Power VLSI Group, http://rlpvlsi.ece.virginia.edu/category/projects/body-sensor-networks.)

required for communications. A new low-power Bluetooth called Wibree may provide longer battery life for these BSNs.[14]

There are a number of standards for this evolving field to standardize these integrated systems.

- ISO/IEEE 11073: Low-level data standards for plug-and-play devices integrated into these BSNs that can contain a maximum of 10 connected devices.
- Integrating the Healthcare Enterprise (IHE) patient care domain (PDE): A joint effort by multiple medical sensor vendors to standardize interoperability between sensors and device interfaces. They are associated with Healthcare Information and Management Systems Society (HIMSS) and the American College of Clinical Engineering (ACCE).

Wireless Medical Device Protected Spectrum

In May 2012 the Federal Communications Commission (FCC) set aside part of the spectrum, 2360 to 2400 MHz, for use by low-power medical devices. The term for these low-power medical networks, typically used in hospital environments, is medical body area networks (MBANs). This spectrum was selected to prevent interference from Wi-Fi devices. Initially, this spectrum will be used by medical device manufacturers in relatively structured environments, but will evolve for all wireless medical devices.

Integrated Data Capture Modeling for Wireless Medical Devices

There are several changes evolving in various areas of data generation. This includes more structured environments in fixed medical facilities, and less structured platforms (e.g., nonstructured private emergency care delivery and loosely structured technology-mediated monitoring); see Figure 9.11. This new model involves integrating multiple data sources into EMRs, personal data records (PDRs), and continuity of care records (CCRs) and providing intelligent software to correlate data.[15]

In structured environments the need to correlate patient data, common physiological monitoring parameters (CPMPs), blood pressure,

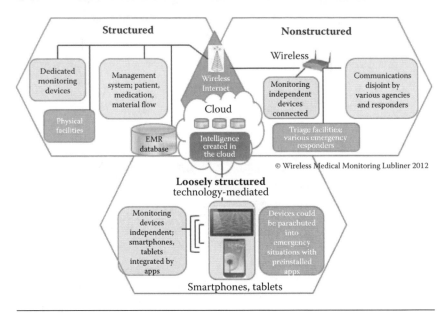

Figure 9.11   Structured, nonstructured, and loosely structured medical monitoring.

heart rate, pulse oximetry, blood gases, and so forth, requires integration into a larger data repository, EMRs, which includes medications, lab tests, MRI/CT scans, and feedback from medical practitioners. Expert systems are evolving to manage and report on potential adverse scenarios.

In nonstructured environments, a disaster scenario involves N number of patients with various levels of acuity and the need to coordinate response and transport based on acuity triage models. This can be divided into several subcategories.

- Professional: Trained personnel entering the environment. FEMA, Red Cross city or federal services.
- Volunteers: Local respondents responding to assist family or neighbors.
- Possible automated devices: Dropped in methods to utilize the large base of wireless smart cell devices.

This typically involves personnel finding and deploying monitoring equipment. Because wireless devices are relatively short range, some temporary wireless network/monitoring structures need to be established that are linked into longer-range systems for coordination, point-to-point vs. wide area response. GPS and establishing patient ID also augment these systems.

Expert Systems Utilized to Evaluate Medical Data

Expert systems can be referred to as computer-based systems that provide decision support to users by incorporating hardware and software components and domain-specific information to emulate human reasoning. The core components of an expert system are a *knowledge base*, composed of rules and facts, and an *inference engine*, supplied with data from a user, that selects the appropriate rules based on the data and calculates probabilities that the rules apply to a particular situation. An additional component is feedback from clinical data that cross-checks the validity of the rule/diagnosis, which then adds to the refinement of the expert system knowledge base (see Figure 9.12).

Once a basis framework has been selected, the inference engine asks a series of targeted questions proposed by the expert system to refine matches to the existing knowledge base. A list of probabilities are then generated; that is, an example of a system used for determining heart arrhythmias states to the medical professional that 62% of arrhythmias are due to hypokalemia, a low potassium level, and 75% to hypomagnesemia, low magnesium, which might be making the patient more prone to arrhythmias. The system asks the individual to enter potassium and magnesium results from blood tests to validate or refute the hypothesis. This type of feedback mechanism provides a more accurate diagnosis where additional data increases the probability of accuracy. This is an example of a rule-based (RB) expert system.

Other paradigms for medical expert systems are case-based reasoning (CBR), cognitive systems, and crowd-based expert systems. CBR utilizes an evolving library of cases where matches are made to

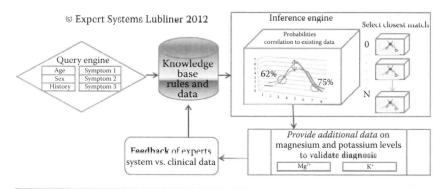

Figure 9.12 Expert system architecture.

the current case, rather than utilizing a standard rules-based engine; this is similar to the process of how doctors make a diagnosis. The process involves four steps: retrieve similar cases, reuse the case to solve similar problems, revise and modify the case, and retain the new case with updates for the case library (4Rs).

Cognitive systems[16,17] are a series of artificial intelligence paradigms with "the ability to engage in abstract thought that goes beyond immediate perceptions and actions." Originally comprehensive artificial intelligence (AI) systems attempted to model human consciousness, but due to their lack of success were modified for a more narrow expertise in specific domains of knowledge. An example is chess programs that are the equal of the best master-level chess players. Cognitive systems utilize structured representations and probabilistic models to support problem solving utilizing concepts from psychology, logic, and linguistics.

Crowd-based systems, wisdom of the crowds, provide a new method to extract large amounts of relevant data from the web on the assumption that large data sets may be more accurate than limited clinical data from the web. So far this approach has yet to be validated in the medical arena. This crowd-based approach has shown some success on social networking sites, where specific diseases are targeted and individuals supply anecdotal data.

Data Mining and Big Data

Data mining can be defined as the process of finding previously unknown patterns and trends in databases and using that information to build predictive models.[18] In healthcare data mining focuses on detailed questions and outcomes. What symptoms, quantitative data, and clinical outcomes in combination lead to specific diagnoses and treatments? As discussed in the previous section, a combination of probabilistic and human-directed diagnoses evolves into a knowledge base. This works well with a finite data set, but with big data it can become difficult to process. Imagine millions of individuals with real-time wearable or implanted medical sensors sending data through smartphones. The data stream would certainly be in the terabyte range, but as these devices became ubiquitous, petabytes levels of data would not be unreasonable. Information can be summarized and evaluated locally on ever-evolving smartphones, but additional analysis and correlation, on a regional or global level, would require new stochastic techniques, that is, algorithms to analyze random events. This seems like a contradiction in terms. Markov chains, random events, quantified as time series events or limited by a field space, or a finite geographical area or subpopulation can provide a deterministic function used to correlate or classify seemingly random events. Examples are plumes of breast cancer patients that appear to be random but with large enough data sets can create correlations, that is, the butterfly effect, the concept that a butterfly flapping its wings in one area can create small finite effects over larger distances. Tracking the cause back to that original butterfly or a random mutation of flu virus anywhere in the world could predict and prevent epidemics.

Genomic Mapping of Large Data Sets

Current genomic, genetic mapping, research has generated terabytes of data and is the focus of NSF and NIH research grants. The NIH in 2012 released its first genomic 200-terabyte data sets (equivalent to the size of the entire Library of Congress). This data set will grow exponentially as routine genetic mapping is a predictive medical diagnostic tool. If, for example, you have a 50% likelihood of developing breast cancer, proactive medical treatments will be prescribed decades before the first symptoms might arise. It may be possible to provide treatment in the womb to inhibit the activation of these epigenetic factors entirely. There is a new field of epigenetics that suggests either environmental or inherited factors are responsible for activating these genetic traits (i.e., the gene for breast cancer will remain dormant if the trigger that prevents the underlying inherited gene is not present). If removed, there is a low likelihood that these genetic traits will be expressed. In that case, genetic mapping, as technology reduces time and cost, most likely will become commonplace. The cost to map a single genetic sequence has gone down from $100 million in 2001 to $5000 in 2013, and from a year to a few hours (see Figure 9.13).

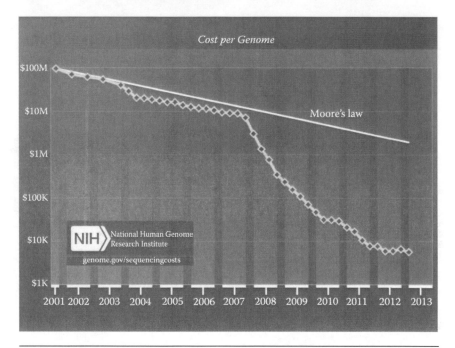

Figure 9.13   Reduction in costs of mapping a single genetic sequence. (From the NIH Human Genome Project.)

Future Directions: Mining Large Data Sets: NSF and NIH Research Initiatives

This section describes initiatives underway to analyze the growing field of big data and provide significant research funds to enhance analysis of medical data and new methodologies that potentially may be utilized by other disciplines. NSF and NIH research is often a predictive indicator for future medical innovations, similar to previous Defense Advanced Research Projects Agency (DARPA) investments that were responsible for many of today's computer advancements.

This field, big data, ca. 2012, is the focus of support by several U.S. research agencies: the National Science Foundation (NSF), Department of Defense (DOD), and National Institutes of Health (NIH), committing $200 million to this big data initiative.[19–22]

The following was a solicitation on an NSF page to researchers to submit grants.

The Obama Administration announced a "Big Data Research and Development Initiative." By improving our ability to extract knowledge and insights from large and complex collections of digital data, the initiative promises to help solve some of the nation's most pressing challenges.

To launch the initiative, six federal departments and agencies announced on March 29, 2012 announced more than $200 million in new commitments that, together, promise to greatly improve the tools and techniques needed to access, organize, and glean discoveries from huge volumes of digital data.

NIH also has dedicated significant funds to the analysis of larger data sets, specifically focused on genomic research. NIH announced in 2012 that the world's largest set of data on human genetic variation, produced by the international 1000 Genomes Project, was available on the Amazon Web Services (AWS) cloud at 200 terabytes, the equivalent of 16 million file cabinets filled with text. The source of the data, the 1000 Genomes Project data set is a prime example of big data, where data sets become so massive that few researchers have the computing power to make the best use of them. AWS is storing the 1000 Genomes Project as a publically available data set for free, and researchers only will pay for the computing services that they use.

Large data sets are also currently being generated by researchers in other fields. Some of those research initiatives are:

- Earth Cube: A system that will allow geoscientists to access, analyze, and share information about our planet.
- DARPA: An XDATA program to develop computational techniques and software tools for analyzing large volumes of data, both semistructured (e.g., tabular, relational, categorical, metadata) and unstructured (e.g., text documents, message traffic). Harness and utilize massive data in new ways and bring together sensing, perception, and decision support to make truly autonomous systems that can maneuver and make decisions on their own.
- The Smart Health and Wellbeing (SHB) program: By the NSF,[9] the SHB's goal is the "transformation of healthcare from reactive and hospital-centered to preventive, proactive, evidence based, person-centered and focused on wellbeing rather than disease." The categories of this effort include

wireless medical sensors, networking, machine learning, and integrating social and economic issues that affect medical outcomes.

The following is a representative funded research grant in the field of wireless medical device.

NSF award to utilize wireless medical sensors for chronic illnesses

Telemedicine technologies offer the opportunity to frequently monitor patients' health and optimize management of chronic illnesses. Given the diversity of home telemedicine technologies, it is essential to compose heterogeneous telemedicine components and systems for a much larger patient population through systems of systems. The objective of this research is to thoroughly investigate the heterogeneity in large-scale telemedicine systems for cardiology patients. To accomplish this task, this research seeks to develop (1) a novel open source platform medical device interface adapter that can seamlessly interconnect medical devices that conform to interoperability standards, such as IEEE 11703, to smartphones for real-time data processing and delivery; (2) a set of novel supporting technologies for wireless networking, data storage, and data integrity checking; and (3) a learning-based early warning system that adaptively changes patient and disease models based on medical device readings and context.

The challenge of the aforementioned grant is not just to collect data, but also to build in sociological components, stress, economic conditions, and so forth, that might generate transient results. Results from previous studies have shown that filtering out unusual readings may result in more reliable data. Also, integrating smoking, drinking, and so forth, helps quantify the results. So apps that allow users to input data regarding their frame of mind or habits while the data are being monitored on the wireless medical devices can provide invaluable information for analysis of causal effects to physiological readings.

Assuming wireless mobile medical devices become common, estimates of data generated daily, with only a million users, range from 1 terabyte (TB) to 1 petabyte per/day (Figure 9.14). To put this in perspective, the digital storage for the Library of Congress is 200

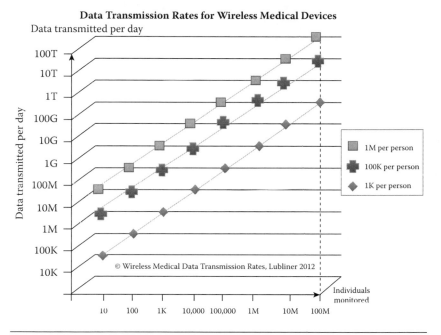

Figure 9.14 Smart Health data transmission projections as wireless medical sensors become commonplace.

terabytes. The population in 2012 is 300 million in the United States and 7 billion worldwide, and 50% of Americans have some type of smartphone or tablet. Over the next few decades, 20% of the U.S. population will be older than 65, making either wearable smart medical devices or those abilities directly embedded in smart devices likely to expand rapidly. This flood of potential data dwarfs all other applications. Data mining of this treasure trove of medical data will be the challenge of the decades to come.

Other Evolving Mining and Analytics Applications in Healthcare

Additional analytic applications that involve more basic business intelligence approaches of reporting and online analytical processing (OLAP), optimization techniques to the more complex mining methods address three major areas that include workflow activities of healthcare service provider organizations, risk stratification of a patient population, and enhancing patient treatment and outcomes with electronic health records data.

Workflow Analytics of Provider Organizations

Large healthcare service providers (e.g., hospitals, healthcare systems, accountable care organizations [ACOs]) are generating greater varieties of data resources that include metrics that measure the performance of numerous activities. Processes within these large service providers are continuously monitored to achieve greater efficiencies that ultimately can reduce costs and enhance patient outcomes. Some prominent performance measures which care providers seek to manage include the following:

- Patient length of stay at a provider facility
- Patient satisfaction
- Capacity utilization (e.g., bed utilization rates)
- Staffing (e.g., nurses to patient optimization)
- Patient episode cost estimation
- ER throughput
- Estimating patient demand for services

These high-level metrics measure the performance of a diverse set of healthcare processes and require analysts to identify and manage a great variety of data variables to better understand the factors that impact or drive these measures. Provider organizations generate and record vast data resources in measuring activities at the patient level. One source of data is generated through the establishment and recording of time for activities. Time stamps that record the initiation and ending of corresponding subcomponents of workflow processes enable analysts to create duration variables according to various attributes of the process. For example, time stamps can facilitate the generation of the time that is required from initiating a lab test for a patient and receiving the results of that test (duration of patient test), which can play an important factor in affecting the length of stay of a patient. Other variables that help provide descriptive power to analytic, decision support models involve the utilization of data according to standardization codes such as Diagnostic Related Group (DRG), Physician Specialty, Treatment Area, and so forth, along with patient descriptive information.[23]

- DRG of patient
- Attending physician specialty

- Patient descriptors (demographic, physiological)
- Treatment descriptors (frequency of visits by nurses and doctors)
- Duration of workflow activities (time to receive lab results)

All of these variables provide the building blocks to better understanding higher level performance metrics of care providers.

More basic analytic approaches (e.g., reporting, dashboards, cubes) can yield timely, actionable informative results, however these are more retrospective in nature (e.g., what has happened with a particular workflow). More sophisticated quantitative, multivariate based approaches in the mining spectrum can identify patterns that depict relationships between descriptive and performance metrics and can provide more robust decision support capabilities.

Analytic approaches can be used to better understand additional performance metrics such as patient satisfaction rates, staffing optimization, and so forth. However, differences lie in the relevant data resources and availability of those resources that describe process activities. Some of these data resources may require additional administrative actions to be initiated to generate essential descriptive data, hence a greater variety of data. For example, patient surveys must be introduced to extract data variables to provide explanatory information as to what drives a patient's experience, not to mention the performance metric of how that experience is measured.

Risk Stratification

Perhaps one of the most noteworthy concepts that addresses true success in healthcare, namely, achieving a healthier population with optimal resource management, is the idea of better identifying illnesses that are evolving in patients or identifying individuals at risk of developing serious, chronic illnesses and applying pre-emptive treatment to mitigate or avoid those illnesses. Risk stratifying patient populations has been a standard analytic application in the healthcare sector for years. Much analytic work has utilized financial, insurance claims based data as it involves patient based descriptors, diagnosis and treatment descriptors along with the important data of costs involved with corresponding service activities. Stratification techniques can include mathematic equations and weighting of corresponding variables, multivariate statistically based methods, and mining based approaches to determine the risk level of a patient developing a chronic illness.

The term "hot spotting" has received great attention recently when considering the identification of high cost drivers in resource utilization of healthcare services.[24] Some enlightening information around this topic is the inclusion of such patient descriptors as geography and economic status when attempting to identify individuals that are high resource users of healthcare services, or more simply put, individuals that may become sicker than they otherwise would be because of the location of their residence, inability to pay, and lack of access to care providers. All these new variables or "variety of data" play an essential role in better understanding an individual's likelihood to develop serious illness and be high resource users of healthcare services. The ultimate result of robust analytic models that can more accurately identify those factors that lead to higher risk is the ability to mitigate those factors that lead to higher illness and cost driver rates. These factors may apply not only to diet and behavioral attributes, but also to simple logistics such as lack of access to transportation to reach a healthcare facility.

Combining Structured and Unstructured Data
for Patient Diagnosis and Treatment Outcomes

Electronic health records provide an essential data resource that provide descriptive information of a patient and various treatment activities they undergo. Some of these data are structured (e.g., demographics, physiological attributes), however, there is an unstructured portion to an EHR and this includes added notes or comments by attending physicians relevant to treatment activities. This latter information comes under the variety of big data and offers potential insights into how a patient may have reacted to certain procedures or why drug prescriptions had been changed, to name a few. This unstructured element introduces the potential for greater decision support information as to better treatment and outcomes or diagnosis.

An essential analytic method that can be utilized to unlock the potential value to the verbiage that is included in an EHR involves text mining that incorporates semantic rules. As was illustrated in Chapter 14 of this book, text mining can add structure to unstructured data that can then be analyzed with other mining methods to extract actionable information.

Some examples of the value of incorporating both structured and unstructured data in the case of EHRs can include insights such as the following:

- Avoiding possible adverse drug events as comments from attending physicians describe a patient's reaction to particular drugs or dosage of drugs.
- Optimizing diet or rehabilitation activities according to patient reactions to prescribed plans
- Considering psychological effects to applied treatments

Creating value from unstructured data is a difficult task, however, the benefits may warrant the effort. This provides a good segue to the following issue. A perplexing decision for many organizations in the evolving big data era is whether the value of pursuing big data initiatives warrants the costs involved. In the case of healthcare, the topic may be less of a conundrum given that many data attributes are already being recorded and the value can be substantial when considering the increase in quality to human life.

Summary

Homo sapiens, modern man, arrived on the scene, as indicated by the fossil record,[25] around 200,000 years ago. Quantification of medical practices began around 5000 years ago in Egypt and soon after in China. But the true emergence of medical science arose only 200 years ago. Due to these advances, life expectancy has doubled from 38 to 77 in the past 100 years. We have reached a new milestone where science, technology, and communications have truly created one unified planet, at least scientifically. If we harness these recourses properly, this nexus of science and technological advances can lead to another doubling of life expectancy and reduce human suffering. The real challenge lies in extracting meaning, that is, data mining this flood of information and making it readily available. I hope you are up to the challenge.

This chapter was originally published in *Big Data, Mining, and Analytics: Components of Strategic Decision Making*, Taylor & Francis, New York, 2014.

References

1. Dignan L. 2011. Cisco predicts mobile data traffic explosion. Retrieved from http://seekingalpha.com/article/250005-cisco-predicts-mobile-data -traffic-explosion.
2. Walter C. 2005. Kryder's law. *Scientific American* July 25.
3. Gopakumar TG. 2012. Switchable nano magnets may revolutionize data storage: Magnetism of individual molecules switched. Retrieved from http://www.sciencedaily.com/releases/2012/06/120614131049.htm.
4. Ritner RK. 2001. Magic. *The Oxford encyclopedia of ancient Egypt.* Oxford reference online, October 2011. Retrieved from http://www .oxfordreference.com/search?q=Ritner+magic&searchBtn=Search&is QuickSearch=true.
5. Geller MJ. 2010. *Ancient Babylonian medicine: Theory and practice.* Oxford: Wiley-Blackwell.
6. Crookshank E. 1888. The history of the germ theory. *BMJ* 1(1415):312.
7. HHS.gov. HIPPA Title II regulations. Retrieved from http://www.hhs .gov/ocr/privacy/hipaa/administrative/securityrule/nist80066.pdf.
8. IEEE. 2012. Medical interoperability standards. Retrieved from http:// www.IEEE.org/standards.
9. Ljunggren S. 1983. A simple graphical representation of Fourier-based imaging methods. *J Magnet Reson* 54(2):338–48.
10. Twieg D. 1983. The k-trajectory formulation of the NMR imaging process with applications in analysis and synthesis of imaging methods. *Med Phys* 10(5):610–12.
11. Oosterwijk H. 2004. *PACS fundamentals.* Aubrey, TX: OTech.
12. Gazit Y, Berk DA, Leuning M, Baxter LT, Jain RK. 1995. Scale-invariant behavior and vascular network formation in normal and tumor tissue. *Phys Rev Lett* 75(12):2428–31.
13. Gazit Y, Baish J, Safabakhsh N, Leunig M, Baxter LT, Jain RK. 1997. Fractal characteristics of tumor vascular architecture during tumor growth and regression. *Microcirculation* 4(4):395–402.
14. Ross PE. 2004. Managing care through the air. *IEEE Spectrum* December:14–19.
15. Mahn T. 2010. Wireless medical technologies: Navigating government regulation in the new medical age. Retrieved from http://www.fr .com/files/uploads/attachments/FinalRegulatoryWhitePaperWireless MedicalTechnologies.pdf.
16. Langley P. 2012. The cognitive systems paradigm. CogSys.org.
17. Brachman R, Lemnios Z. 2002. DARPA's cognitive systems vision. *Comput Res News* 14:1.

18. Kincade K. 1998. Data mining: Digging for healthcare gold. *Insur Technol* 23(2):IM2–IM7.
19. House.gov. 2012, March 29. Obama administration unveils "big data" initiative: Announces $200 million in new R&D investments. Retrieved from http://www.google.com/#hl=en&tbo=d&sclient=psy-ab&q=data ±mining±healthcare±definition&oq=data±mining±healthcare±definition &gs_l=hp.3..33i29l4.1468.8265.0.8387.33.28.0.5.5.1.195.2325.26j2.28 .0.les%3B..0.0...1c.1.JgQWyqlEaFc&pbx=1&bav=on.2,or.r_gc.r_pw.r_qf .&fp=775112e853595b1e&bpcl=38897761&biw=908&bih=549.
20. NSF. 2012. Big data NSF funding. Retrieved from http://www.nsf.gov /funding/pgm_summ.jsp?pims_id=504739.
21. NSF. 2011. Utilizing wireless medical sensors for chronic heart disease. Retrieved from http://www.nsf.gov/awardsearch/showAward?AWD _ID=1231680&HistoricalAwards=false.
22. NSF. Links to U.S. federal big data initiative 2010:
    a. NSF: http://www.nsf.gov/news/news_summ.jsp?cntn_id = 123607.
    b. HHS/NIH: http://www.nih.gov/news/health/mar2012/nhgri-29.htm.
    c. DOE: http://science.energy.gov/news/.
    d. DOD: http://www.DefenseInnovationMarketplace.mil.
    e. DARPA: http://www.darpa.mil/NewsEvents/Releases/2012/03/29 .aspx.
    f. USGS: http://powellcenter.usgs.gov.
23. Kudyba S, Gregorio T. 2010. Identifying factors that impact patient length of stay metrics for healthcare providers with advanced analytics. *Health Inform J* 16(4):235–45.
24. Gawande A. 2011. The hot spotters. *The New Yorker* January 24.
25. McHenry HM. 2009. Human evolution. In M. Ruse and J. Travis (eds.), *Evolution: The first four billion years*, p. 265. Cambridge, MA: Belknap Press of Harvard University Press.

10

THE WORLD OF HEALTH ANALYTICS

JASON BURKE

Contents

Introduction

Evidence-based medicine. Personal electronic health records. Disease management. Personalized medicine. These terms, among many others, reflect a rapidly growing change within the health sciences ecosystem—a transformative shift toward more information-based decision making related to patient care and healthcare cost management. For decades, the efficiencies and improvements attained in other industries through the adoption of information technology (IT) have largely been missing in healthcare, an ecosystem mired in paper records, administrative overhead, and labor-intensive business processes.

But that is all changing. The sustained rise in healthcare costs, consistent problems in patient safety, highly expensive prescription drugs, and inconsistent treatment outcomes have all contributed to a new drive toward making better use of the tremendous volumes of information flowing through the ecosystem. Whereas historically hospitals have looked to expansions in service lines and facilities to drive top-line revenue growth, analytics that provide business opportunities in utilization, cost containment, and quality control are now seen as critical enablers of bottom-line financial performance. Health plans that have relied on relatively simple business rules to determine the appropriateness of reimbursements are now looking to advanced analytical models to identify previously undetected fraudulent claims activities and patterns. Drug researchers, struggling to find ways to bring innovative and safe therapies to market faster and cheaper, are aggregating tremendous volumes of data covering many years of research to look for biomarkers that can accurately predict drug safety and efficacy in named patient populations. Across the board, electronic data, whether business based or science based, are now seen as the fuel to power the engines of business and clinical analytics driving the evolution of patient outcomes and wellness.

But those growing volumes of data contain a hidden burden: How can we efficiently and effectively manage such large and disparate volumes of information? How do we make it useful? With information flowing from every corner of the healthcare ecosystem, how do we prioritize which data are most important, and how can we simplify the inherent complexity down to something with which educated human beings can make rational decisions? Anyone seeking an easy answer to this dilemma will be disappointed.

Modern IT, especially in the areas of data integration, data quality, data management, and advanced analytics, holds the key to unlocking the power of this information and the corresponding business and scientific transformation contained within. Advanced analytics and information management sit at the center of the new health enterprise—an information-driven business and science-informed medical practice that can dramatically reduce healthcare costs and improve health outcomes for all patients. But only if organizations embrace them.

Analysis Paralysis

The healthcare industry is no stranger to technology—hospitals have invested millions in medical devices for decades, for example. But

capabilities with respect to IT—electronic data collection, management, quality, analysis, and reporting—are reasonably new. Extensive
paper-based forms, change-averse physicians, tightly controlled business processes, overtaxed nurses, and business demands on self-funding
investments have conspired to inhibit the proliferation of IT in much
of the healthcare sector. But as the industry has sought to better
understand its deep-rooted problems in cost, quality, safety, and outcomes, a growing recognition has emerged that IT must be a priority
for every health enterprise.

Yet, when we speak of advanced analytics in healthcare, it is not
uncommon to hear a list of excuses why the industry is not ready for
them.

- More technology. Many people argue that until the industry
  has had more time to implement more technology that col-
  lects information electronically, there is little use in investing
  in advanced analytics.
- More integration and standards. Some people argue that,
  because the industry has historically lacked data standards
  that facilitate information aggregation and sharing, any insights
  that might be derived from their existing data would be of
  questionable value.
- Data privacy. Inevitably, some people will question the appropriateness of using personal medical information outside the
  context of care for that particular patient; the Health Insurance
  Portability and Accountability Act of 1996 (HIPAA) is usually cited.

As organizations consider analytics-oriented projects and hear
these concerns, it is quite easy to fall into "analysis paralysis"—
continuously trying to find ways to overcome issues that cannot be
overcome without doing the projects that elicited the issues in the first
place. Organizations will always need more technology, but we have a
lot today. We will always need better integration and deeper support
in standards, but we have standards and integration models that are
proven today. We should always be holding patient data privacy at the
forefront of our minds, but we have many ways of protecting patient
privacy while also allowing us to pursue improvements that will inevitably benefit those patients.

The question should not be whether to take on analytics as a corporate priority; the question should be how. And the answer is surprisingly simple, residing in the neonatal and pediatric units of every hospital in the world. Newborn babies, infants, and toddlers physiologically develop along a predefined biological path, one that serves to gradually bring new biological systems online and grow the systems already online until the person reaches adulthood. It is a long-term process, but one with clearly defined steps and associated personal abilities. Such is this case with analytics as they are born and grow inside companies.

Analytical Maturity and Objectives

The term *analytics* may be one of the most overused and misunderstood terms in the business community today, with the possible exception of *business intelligence*. Every software application that has the ability to run reports with numbers in them suddenly provides analytics. Any person who has taken a statistics course is suddenly capable of performing whatever analytics are needed for an organization. Even the definition of the term *analytics* is used in one context to describe web reporting, while in another context it describes the most obscure statistical methodology imaginable.

When we use the term *analytics* in healthcare, we are using it to mean something very specific:

> *Analytics* are the complete series of integrated capabilities needed to provide progressively deeper statistical insights into health-related information.

We are describing capabilities—a capacity that can be found or learned within organizations and individuals. Those capabilities should be complete, meaning they cover all of the needed areas of information access, integration, quality, storage, management, interpretation, and governance. Those capabilities are also progressive, meaning that the simpler capabilities need to be in place to enable the more sophisticated capabilities to operate. They are statistical in nature, not merely mathematical. And they are progressively deeper, meaning the insights derived from higher-order analytical capabilities offer greater value than those of lower-order capabilities.

The Eight Levels of Analytics

So what are these capabilities that organizations and individuals need to have? There are eight levels of analytical capabilities that any organization or person needs to fully address the challenges in healthcare (see following figure).

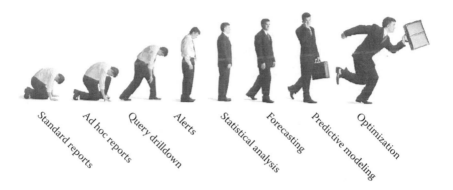

1. **Standard reports.** Answer the questions: What happened? When did it happen?
2. **Ad hoc reports.** Answer the questions: How many? How often? Where?
3. **Query drilldown.** Answer the questions: Where exactly is the problem? How do I find the answers?
4. **Alerts.** Answer the questions: When should I react? What actions are needed now?
5. **Statistical analysis.** Answer the questions: Why is it happening? What opportunities am I missing?
6. **Forecasting.** Answer the questions: What if these trends continue? How much is needed? When will it be needed?
7. **Predictive modeling.** Answer the questions: What will happen next? How will it affect my business?
8. **Optimization.** Answer the questions: How do we do things better? What is the best decision for a complex problem?

Let's use a hypothetical example to illustrate how these various capabilities are developed and used. Christopher Regional Hospital is struggling to understand why its operating margins are decreasing. In particular, the cardiac service line, typically associated with a good contribution margin, has seen a decline over the last six months.

Hospital administrators decide to undertake an analytics initiative to understand what is causing the decline in contribution margin.

1. **Standard reports.** The problem was identified when the administrators consulted a series of standard reports that the hospital uses on a monthly basis. They realized the cardiac service line's contribution margin was down from the same period last year.

2. **Ad hoc reports.** These standard reports did not currently show all of the performance indicators the administrators needed to understand the issues, so they asked for a few specific reports related to the inpatient and outpatient volumes as well as statistics trending by fiscal period over the previous year. These reports showed that patient visits were not down and the service line was fairly busy, and so the problems were not simply a matter of getting more patients. The administrators asked that these ad hoc reports become a part of the hospital's standard reporting environment.

3. **Query drilldown.** To explore the problem further, hospital administrators asked the head of the cardiac service line to investigate the problem and report back at the next service line committee meeting. He formed a series of hypotheses about potential causes, and then explored a number of other factors related to contribution margin, such as length of stay, payor, and service utilization. The reporting environment allowed him to use a web browser to dynamically divide, subset, and report on these business metrics. During his query drilldown work, the administrator noticed something peculiar—there were a lot of reimbursement denials for patients having a "rule out myocardial infarction" code. The director checked with the billing department and was told that they are being denied because the hospital will not receive payment for "rule out MI" patients unless they are coded in an observation status and not as an inpatient.

4. **Alerting.** To understand what was happening with these patients, the director set up an alert that was sent each time a patient received the "rule out MI" code and had a status of an inpatient. Those alerts were sent to the case manager and the nurse manager of the cardiac unit so that they could monitor the care to understand what was happening.

5. **Statistical analysis.** The director then decided to analyze the data for this particular diagnostic code. Running a series of statistical analyses on this patient population, he found a correlation between inpatient status, longer lengths of stay, and days of the week the patient arrived in the emergency room. In particular, he noticed that patients who were admitted in an inpatient status, with lengths of stay between three and four days, who had come to the emergency room with chest pain on a Friday or a Saturday were most of the denials. This finding was reaffirmed when following up on the alerting procedure: the nurse manager of the cardiac unit knew that these patients required a stress test, and stress tests were not performed in the hospital on Saturdays or Sundays. Patients were admitted to stay through the weekend to receive their stress tests on Monday; standard procedure was to schedule the stress test within 24 hours, allowing the patients to be placed in a cardiac ICU bed and not be admitted. The director also realized when speaking with the nurse manager that more and more "rule out MIs" were taking up beds in the cardiac ICU.

6. **Forecasting.** After hearing the findings in the service line committee meeting, the administrators wanted to know what the impact of this trend would be over a longer time horizon. They constructed a forecast of patient admission, diagnosis, length of stay, and payments over the next 24 months based on the past four years of hospital data, census data for their region, and projections from several medical institutions. The forecast showed that their hospital's patient admissions around this condition were expected to grow 56% each year for the next two years due to the recent closing of area hospitals. It also showed that their relatively small drop in contribution margin today could easily grow into a bigger problem in the next 18 months unless they found a way to address both the availability of stress testing on weekends and the problem this condition presents on utilization of beds in the cardiac ICU. This analysis highlighted the patient throughput issues that were just starting to develop, affecting the quality of care for the cardiac patients.

7. **Predictive modeling**. The hospital leaders now wanted to understand the value of more timely treatments and care focused on acuity. The administrators wanted to know whether receiving stress tests within 24 hours and removing cardiac rule-outs from the emergency room to an observation unit were beneficial from a quality, safety, and financial perspective. They had staff construct a statistical model that could predict patient outcomes. By using historical patient information, the statistical model could predict the likelihood of death, readmission, disease progression, and long-term costs based on the timing and the treatment that was administered. This model showed opening an observation unit and staffing stress testing on weekends could decrease this condition's returns to the emergency room visits; reduce medical errors and negative outcomes, including death; and create more cardiac ICU beds, increasing throughput for critical cardiac patients and reducing expenses by staffing by acuity. They also found out something else.

8. **Optimization**. During the predictive modeling exercise, the hospital analysts used data mining software to look for trends in the electronic medical records that might have an impact on outcomes. They uncovered a previously unknown trend: patients under the care of one physician in the hospital were 32% less likely to be readmitted after a cardiac catheterization. The administrators contacted the clinical chief of cardiology and informed him of the analysis. When the clinical chief questioned the physician about her treatment strategies, she indicated that she required her patients to follow up with a cardiovascular exercise and diet program. She had her staff follow up on her patients to make sure they completed program. Predictive modeling showed that patients that participated in that program, as well as received timely treatment, had 61% fewer admissions in the following two-year period.

The preceding example illustrates how health insights are derived through a successive series of steps. Each step provides vital information needed to make the next step feasible and effective. It would have been quite difficult, for example, to know what statistical analyses needed to be run if the organization did not already have some direction from the query drilldown. Each step is also more complex than the former, requiring deeper analytical skills, better data, and more coordinated engagement within the organization.

Business versus Clinical Analytics

The numbers and types of analytics that can be applied to healthcare are practically endless, constrained only by the creativity of the human mind to ask intelligent questions and define mathematical inferences. When comparing health and life sciences to other industries' use of analytics, one characteristic stands out as somewhat unique: the questions, data, and decisions involved include traditional types of business information—sales, operations, and so forth—but also include scientific information and interpretation. This distinction brings an additional level of complexity to looking at analytics as a transformative engine for healthcare. Whereas many software tools and people skills applicable to other businesses can be applied equally to health and life sciences, there are a variety of science-oriented capabilities that are not as broadly available. And for many business insights in healthcare, it is the combined view of both business and scientific information that enables more educated decisions.

Any analytical solution in health and life sciences exists on a continuum of business-focused to clinically focused analytics (see following figure). Some types of insights—assessing profitability of a

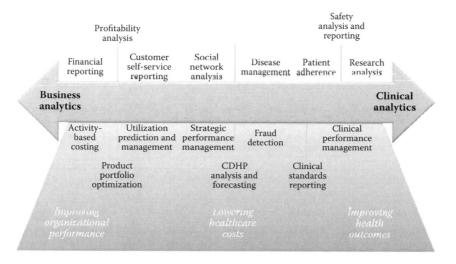

business unit or providing a standardized financial reporting environment—mainly involve the use of information from business units, systems, and knowledge workers. Other insights, such as the safety dimensions of a drug therapy or the outcomes of a clinical research study, reside more clearly in the realm of patient information and scientific interpretation. Between these two extremes lies an entire continuum of analytical applications that provide a unique view into the operations of a health enterprise, the management of patient populations and diseases, and the primary determinants of costs, quality, and outcomes.

With such diversity and breadth of scope, it is difficult to develop any taxonomy of analytical capabilities that adequately conveys all of the various analytical dimensions of the ecosystem. However, at the highest level, any healthcare-related analytical application can be said to target at least one of three main business imperatives.

1. **Improving organizational performance.** These analytics focus on the financial and commercial performance of the organization. Profitability and performance management are commonly cited issues in this area.

2. **Lowering healthcare costs.** These analytics focus on cost avoidance, active cost management, cost reduction through improvements in efficiency, and other aspects of operational improvement. Detection and prevention of healthcare fraud, as well as activity-based costing initiatives, often fall into this area.

3. **Improving health outcomes.** These analytics focus on improved patient outcomes, including areas of patient safety and treatment efficacy. Clinical research of novel drugs and therapies can be considered a component of this area.

Obviously, there is a close interdependency between these three business imperatives, and it is not uncommon for improvements in one area to impact the other areas. But for an organization considering a new analytics project, these imperatives represent a critical aspect of project scoping. For an analytics program to be successful, absolute clarity needs to exist in the program's intended objectives. Programs with scopes intending to cover all three imperatives are unlikely to be successful; the data, objective measures, people, and impacted business processes are dramatically different. But for targeted analytical programs, the impact to each of these imperatives can be equally dramatic.

With these imperatives and the business–clinical continuum as context, let us look more deeply into some representative programs.

Improving Organizational Performance

At its core, healthcare is a business just like any other industry. Profitability is linked to efficiency and competitive differentiation. Innovation breeds opportunity. Quality can command premium pricing. Customer relationships determine long-term revenue potential. These and many other business principles serve as the underpinning for a portfolio of analytical capabilities that can have a tremendous impact on the quality, safety, and cost of healthcare delivery.

Aside from issues related to clinical outcomes (considered separately in a subsequent section), there are three general categories of organizational performance analytics:

- Financial: Analytical capabilities related to revenue, operating costs, and investments. Typical topics include financial management, revenue cycle optimization, and profitability analysis.
- Operational: Analytical capabilities related to the way an organization operates internally. Typical topics include utilization management, human resources, and other enterprise-wide competencies.
- Commercial: Analytical capabilities related to the way an organization sells, markets, and interacts with its customer and partner base. Typical topics include customer targeting, retention, and sales and marketing effectiveness.

Table 10.1 highlights some of the more common performance-oriented analytical scenarios found across the healthcare ecosystem today.

Let us look at one real-world example of an organization using analytics in this way. A large, nonprofit teaching hospital cares for more than 40,000 inpatients and 750,000 outpatients every year. Like any large hospital, its databases and reports are incredibly diverse, covering financial, quality, and patient satisfaction information. But it

Table 10.1   Common Performance-Oriented Analytical Scenarios

Financial	Financial management	Expense management
	Revenue management and cycle optimization	Contribution margin analysis
		Provider profitability analysis
Operational	Human resource performance management and optimization	Strategic performance management
	Reporting standards and requirements	Operational performance management and monitoring
	Utilization prediction, management, and analysis	Inventory management
Commercial	Cross-selling	Customer satisfaction
	Member/customer campaign management	Health plan reporting
		Customer/group defection
	Multichannel relationship marketing	Customer experience analytics
	Physician targeting	Provider/customer self-service reporting and explanation of benefits
	Provider/customer selection, retention, and acquisition	Risk stratification
	Sales force and territory optimization	
	Sales force effectiveness	

was quite difficult for executives to see the information in a way that would facilitate better decision making. For example, what was the relationship between patient-related services and productivity in the different care units?

The hospital developed a performance management system utilizing balanced scorecard concepts to draw correlations between measurements from the different areas of their organization. By combining data relating to 50,000 patient encounters a year from 29 different sources, the system analyzes and distributes operational metrics to executive management, physicians, and front-line employees throughout the hospital. Whether in a patient care setting or in the business office, about 900 employees at all levels can see how their actions, individually and as a whole, affect the organization and its patients. More than 30 metrics detail key financial information, length of stay, and patient satisfaction measures. Select physicians and nurses even have their own scorecards, enabling them to share information relating to finance, productivity, workload, and quality indicators with their colleagues.

Some department heads now routinely use the system to gauge hospital performance and spot anomalies relating to length of stay, spikes in certain diagnosis-related groups, and procedural delays. As an example, operating room efficiency and productivity are impacted significantly by start times. If more cases start on time in the morning, then efficiency and productivity increase. So by identifying patterns relating to delays in operating room start times, physicians can have a better understanding of the impact of specific test orders and procedures. Using this approach, the hospital can also identify best practices.

The key to unlocking the value of performance solutions is in the identification and measurement of key performance indicators (KPIs). In this area, healthcare actually has a fair amount of information already available from which to draw. Organizations such as The Joint Commission (http://www.jointcommission.org), the Agency for Healthcare Research and Quality (http://www.ahrq.gov), and the National Quality Forum (http://www.qualityforum.org) have completed extensive work in identifying critical healthcare KPIs that every healthcare enterprise should monitor. These measures cover the gamut of business and clinical analytics, and are themselves the subjects of entire books. Table 10.2 gives a small sample of these types of KPIs.

When considering a performance management program and its associated KPIs, it is important to keep several things in mind.

1. KPIs should be empirically measurable. The idea in performance management is to make better decisions based on real data.
2. KPIs should be linked directly to a business objective. Simply measuring performance with no intended action based on the measurement is a waste of effort.
3. KPIs are the indicator, not the problem or the solution. The goal in performance management is to use KPIs as a detection tool for the business; the root cause analysis of a failing indicator is a separate process often involving different analytical techniques.
4. Measuring and reporting are not the end goal. The reason to use analytics in performance management is not to create easy-to-read dashboards (though good reporting is required). Rather, the end goal is to be able to *predict* and *optimize* performance along those specific performance dimensions.

As you might imagine, one of the more significant areas to predict and optimize is costs.

Table 10.2 Types of Healthcare Key Performance Indicators

FINANCIAL	OPERATIONAL
Net revenue, profit/loss, and contribution margin per health system, facility, service line, condition, and physician	Nurse-to-bed ratio overall and per nursing unit
	Attrition overall, per role, and per department
Actual and overtime expenses to budgeted per health system, facility, service line, and department	Throughput red alerts per health system and facility
	Length of stay per health system, facility, service line, condition, and physician
Cost per service line, condition, physician	Percentage of 11 a.m. discharges per health system, facility, service line, nursing unit, and physician
Nursing travelers' expense per health system, facility, service line, and department	
Ambulatory surgeries per health system, facility, and surgeon	Number of tests performed by test, health system, facility, service line, condition, and physician
Clinic and ER visits per health system, facility, and clinic	Door to bed time
	Registration to triage time
	Days to appointment
	Physician order entry compliance
	Registration to triage time
	Days to appointment
	Physician order entry compliance

QUALITY AND SAFETY	NURSING CARE
Percent of patients who received recommended care, and percent of process measures met for specific conditions by health system, facility, service line, nursing unit, physician, etc.	Percent of inpatients with a hospital-acquired pressure ulcer
	Rate of urinary tract infections with catheters
	Rate of bloodstream infections with catheters
	Ventilator-associated pneumonia
Percent of patients who received recommended surgical infection prevention, and percent of process measures met by health system, facility, service line, nursing unit, physician, etc.	Smoking cessation counseling for acute myocardial infarction, heart failure, and pneumonia
	Number of registered nurses per patient day and number of nursing staff hours (registered nurse, licensed vocational/practical nurse, and unlicensed assistive personnel) per patient day
Infection rates for specific conditions by health system, facility, service line, nursing unit, physician, etc.	
Medication errors per 1000 orders	Nursing work life scores related to participation in hospital affairs, foundations for quality of care, manager ability, staffing and resource adequacy, and collegiality of nurse–physician relations
Pediatric IV infiltration rates	
Psychiatric patient assault rate	
Percent of major surgical inpatients with a hospital-acquired complication and death	
Inpatient falls per inpatient days with and without injuries	

Lowering Healthcare Costs

Many people would argue that the concept of lowering healthcare costs is a measure and benefit as opposed to a business imperative. In some sense, this is probably true. Many analytics initiatives related to organizational performance or healthcare outcomes are justified by illustrating the impact on health-related expenditures in R&D, marketing, reimbursements, and other sources. But considering the central role that rising costs are playing in healthcare market dynamics, it is also useful to consider cost reduction programs as a separate topic in its own right. In fact, many organizations place a greater emphasis on cost management initiatives than performance or outcomes, as the organizational "pain" is so acute.

One example of analytics applied in this way pertains to healthcare fraud. Historically, an organization's ability to detect abusive or fraudulent activity has been limited to solutions that are called rules engines. Rules engines—a simplification of the "alerting" tier in our taxonomy—maintain an inventory of known fraud and abuse schemes, and can draw a sample from the collection of all healthcare transactions to look for situations that violate the rules. There are problems here, though.

1. The rules engine is usually only collecting a sample of records; it is not looking at every transaction. So low-volume fraud transactions are likely to slip through undetected.
2. When a rules engine detects a deviation, it is detecting only a violation of a rule. There are countless reasons why that rule violation might occur that are perfectly legitimate. There is little ability to understand the actual likelihood a given incident is indeed fraudulent, or what the real financial impact of that violation might mean for the organization. As such, fraud investigators spend time investigating a large number of incidents that waste time and money.
3. The volume of false positives (transactions that are identified as fraudulent but actually are not) creates a situation where investigators have very limited bandwidth to investigate fraudulent activities. As such, they tend to focus their efforts on high-dollar transactions. Fraud and abuse schemes

consisting of low-dollar transactions are unlikely to trigger an investigation.

4. For a rules engine to know about a fraudulent activity, the activity must have been previously detected and codified into a rule. So rules engines always suffer from a delay between someone finding a fraud scheme, someone else coding into a rules system, and then organizations implementing the updated rules. These delays can span from months to years. And even a slight modification to an existing fraud scheme can render its existing rule useless.

5. Generally speaking, there is a complexity ceiling for rules engines. Abuse patterns that do not easily lend themselves to the relatively simple structure of a codified rule—for example, a complex matrix of collusion—are not easily detectable by rules engines.

So the smart fraudster is one that generates low-dollar transactions at a relatively low and distributed volume so as to not show up in the rules engine sampling. Of course, there will always be a pattern to the activity, but as long as the volume doesn't look suspicious and the dollar value is low, the likelihood of detection remains small. Even if the fraudulent scheme is detected, by the time it becomes a rule deployed within health-care institutions, the fraudster can be already working the next scheme.

The use of analytics for fraud detection is not encumbered by these shortcomings. An analytical model looks for patterns, not rule deviations. As opposed to sampling a small group of transactions, an analytical model can be applied to every single transaction flowing through a healthcare system, even in real time. It is less likely to produce false positives because the detection is not based on somewhat arbitrary comparison criteria, but rather on a model. Indeed, an analytical model can even be applied to the targets identified by rules engines to help separate the real signals from the noise. Note also that the delay between fraud identification and deployment of a detection process is much lower because the analytical model can be "tuned" in real time based on real-world experience.

Analytical fraud models also offer the ability to detect fraudulent or abusive patterns whose complexity is larger than what can easily be understood by the human mind. For example, a collusion scheme might actually involve three people working in four different organizations and generating six different types of claims. It is quite difficult for an investigator to ascertain a pattern across so many variables and permutations. But by applying data mining algorithms that examine each of the variables, relationships, and interdependencies, a pattern of social "connectedness" between these three people can emerge that is markedly different from those of their cohorts.

Fraud is only one example of the potential contribution of analytics to cost management and reduction. Other examples include:

- Portfolio optimization—Ensuring that high-value products and services are progressed, and stopping investments in products and services predicted to be unviable or unprofitable
- Product development and pricing—Balancing market opportunity to pricing strategy to maximize profit (not necessarily price), minimize leakage, and ensure competitiveness
- Case management/readmission prediction—Identifying and targeting patient cost factors and proactively introducing interventions to avoid the costs
- Activity-based costing and management—Understanding where an enterprise is actually incurring costs in specific activities, as well as identifying and predicting the outcome of potential changes

Regardless of the specific focus area, all of these analytical opportunities revolve around a common concept of using prediction to maximize investments in the right areas of the business, and minimize exposure to areas that extend costs without sufficient upside.

Let's look at another real-world example. One of the Blue Cross and Blue Shield insurance providers in the United States sought to gain a better understanding of costs and cost overruns within its organization. Traditional accounting systems provide departmental budgets, but beyond budget line items, those systems typically lack the analytical sophistication needed to look at financial information along different cost dimensions: corporate versus departmental processes, predicted versus accrued costs, and so forth. In this particular case, the company's finance managers could perform basic budget variance at the corporate and department levels, but they could not break out costs by product or individual lines of business, or even scrutinize contributions to activity costs at the program level.

The lack of process-oriented insights, which is far from unique to this particular insurer, has several ramifications. First, there is no way of ensuring that a given customer contract would be profitable. In one case, executives believed the company was losing money on a particular contract, but had no comprehensive way to evaluate all of the costs that supported this agreement. Profitability calculations can be very complex, as the way that costs are accrued (i.e., by individuals) differs significantly from the way that pricing is structured (e.g., by family, employee, child, etc.). Second, this lack of visibility at the contract level is further complicated by the fact that the administrative costs of plans differ between large group plans, small group plans, individual products, and government plans. Third, even if a single contract is unprofitable, unless there is a mechanism to ensure cost management on an ongoing basis, future contracts will suffer similar problems.

To address these concerns, the insurer adopted a particular analytical framework focused on activity-based costing and management. This solution pulls data from its corporate and departmental account systems, enabling planners to explore and predict cost data at all different levels of the business. For many programs, budgets need to actually be set at the individual business activity level. As opposed to simply watching budget reports for cost deviations, the analytical solution allows them to actively monitor projected costs and compare actual costs with the allowable rates for each activity. It becomes much easier to recognize potential cost overruns and institute changes to the company's activities to fall within acceptable cost parameters.

Moving from reactive to proactive, this same approach is also used to help managers decide when to modify the pricing plans for contracts, or when to restructure expenses by outsourcing or consolidating tasks. This concept provides real value when considered at the enterprise level. Departmental budgets often mask the costs associated with cross-functional business activities such as corporate sustaining activities, sales and marketing, and product service and support. Using this approach, an organization can even establish and measure corporate benchmarks as part of a broader transformational strategy.

Ultimately, the solution allows the company to evaluate costs for every business process and to identify areas for implementing cost-saving measures and companywide process improvements. Marketing and underwriting can see how product costs vary depending on the size and type of the group plan; department managers can see what activities performed truly at cost; and executives can look at administrative costs for specific lines of business as a ratio to revenue, claims paid, or other financial metrics.

In this scenario, notice the many different levels of costs being impacted.

- Budget management—Ensuring programs and business units stay to budget
- Activity management—Ensuring efficiency and consistency in execution
- Work reduction—Spending less time manipulating data, improving decision speed
- Profitability—Ensuring that contracts and pricing are actually profitable
- Cost arbitrage—Facilitating outsourcing to lower-cost fulfillment options

The breadth of scope and impact is one reason why reducing healthcare costs can stand on its own as a business imperative, and not simply reflect the outcome of other improvement programs.

Improving Healthcare Outcomes

Beyond any of the organizational productivity or cost issues presented so far, the Holy Grail in healthcare analytics is all about improving the health of patients. Though providers, payers, researchers, manufacturers, and policymakers can disagree on most other aspects of the healthcare ecosystem, everyone can agree that we need more health in healthcare. Analytics provide the means of finding that health, and bringing it to scale.

Health-oriented analytics are not new. Every prescription drug discovered and marketed in the past two decades was required to demonstrate safety and efficacy via statistical models before being approved for use. Epidemiologists rely on computational methods in studying the progression of diseases in populations. Analytical models and methods are used to explore the estimated 3 billion chemical base pairs and 20,000 genes in the human genome. In truth, advanced analytics have been a long-standing tool in understanding the scientific bases of biology and medicine.

Despite this analytical heritage, the hardest health-related questions—the ones that will likely have the biggest impact toward the lives of patients—are just now rising to the surface. Why? There are several reasons.

1. Scientific advancement. Our understanding of the fundamental nature of human physiology, genetics, and disease is reaching a point where we can more directly apply the learnings toward making patients better.
2. Convergence. The health-related improvements needed in any one health market—providers, payers, researchers—require access to information in the other markets. As greater transparency and openness to collaboration unfold, new opportunities to apply advanced analytics arise as well.
3. Cost. The dramatically rising costs of healthcare around the world have brought a new level of discrimination in treatment efficiency and effectiveness. Rather than continuing to fund expensive treatments with unclear outcomes, a better fiscal policy would focus on funding the best treatments with the best cost structures.

So what types of opportunities exist now? The following table highlights some of the main categories of outcomes-oriented analytics. It is important to note that this list is just a sampling. The ability to impact the treatment programs and corresponding patient outcomes positively is limited only by the creativity of the human mind to develop novel ideas and test them. As you will see in the examples in the table below, there are many different ways to look at health outcomes.

PROSPECTIVE PERFORMANCE AND INTERVENTION	OPTIMIZED AND TARGETED TREATMENTS	ADVERSE EVENT AVOIDANCE
Disease and population management	Biomedical informatics	Adverse event detection and prediction
Expedited research	Clinical and patient decision support	Biosurveillance
Member and patient programs	Clinical program compliance	Clinical alerting
Pay for performance	Clinical research analysis	Clinical quality performance analysis and reporting
Provider performance	Evidence-based clinical decision support	
Provider/physician profiling	Clinical performance management	
	Patient adherence	

Consider the following real-world example. A professor of epidemiology at a large Canadian university is studying the risk factors and relationships between cardiovascular disease and cholesterol levels, lifestyle, diet, childhood experiences, and environmental factors. The research includes studying the incidence and distribution of diseases by combining massive amounts of data from many disparate sources: nutrition databases, healthcare delivery data, community demographic information, national patient surveys, and information supplied by Health Canada and the U.S. Centers for Disease Control and Prevention. By bringing these large, disparate information resources together, the professor has been able to develop statistical models that establish the relationship between high cholesterol intake at an early age and chronic diseases later in life. For example, the evidence indicates that cardiovascular disease has a long latency time, and that problems begin in early childhood. By looking at a variety of factors such as cholesterol intake, height, weight, and level of physical activity, the professor can predict childhood risks of adult cardiovascular illness and death.

So how can analytics like that be put into action? In one case, a large U.S. health services company uses data mining to help identify people who would benefit from preventive care services. The data mining software predicts hidden relationships in millions of member records to (1) determine patient risk levels and (2) develop more targeted intervention and prevention plans. Large volumes of clinical and operational data are applied in statistical models that can predict the members in greatest need of support programs. In addition, by identifying high-risk patients and implementing preventative actions against future conditions, health problems and treatments can actually be avoided.

In another case, a western European health research institute sought a way for doctors and patients to predict the effects of drugs, other treatments, and lifestyle factors on patients with rheumatoid arthritis. To do this, they developed two analytics-based solutions: one enables rheumatism patients to examine the factors that affect their health, and the other helps rheumatologists select the best treatment for each patient. A statistical methodology called factor analysis is used to test various treatment hypotheses with the support of randomized trials. The goal is to find the scientifically best combination of various lifestyle factors for each individual case. Patients choose what they would prefer to improve, such as pain, and up to four independent lifestyle factors, such as exercise, diet, and sleeping habits, which might conceivably reduce pain. The system then generates a test plan that the patient prints out as a diary of what should be tested each day. At the end of the period, the program calculates which combination of factors provided the best lifestyle impact.

More than 50 clinics have been involved in the collection of these data from patients and physicians: more than 26,500 patients and 144,000 consultations have been collected and analyzed. The predictive model uses patient data as the basis for predicting the results of various treatments such as different drugs and drug combinations. In other words, instead of a physician relying on a generic treatment plan that may or may not be the best option for a particular patient, the system assists doctors in choosing the best treatment for each patient based on that patient's profile. This approach has the added benefit of avoiding the costs associated with expensive treatments or drugs that are unlikely to be a good fit for a given patient.

Unfortunately, in many cases, humankind has yet to find cures or even strong treatments for diseases. It is in these areas where analytics can have a dramatic impact. For pharmaceutical and biotechnology companies, the development of a new medicine can take more than a decade—a decade of great expense for the developer and of prolonged anxiety for patients in need of new treatments. Meanwhile, the escalating cost of research and development, accompanied by the increasing complexity and expense of human clinical trials, threatens pharmaceutical innovation and drives up healthcare costs.

Using analytics, it is possible to develop simulations of human clinical research (clinical trials simulations) that can considerably expedite the development of novel therapies and save millions of development dollars. Simulated clinical trials are virtual replicas of actual clinical trials. The simulations take data models developed from actual clinical trials and develop clinical scenarios and putative trial results that take into account variability caused by treatment effects, survival times, adverse events such as the occurrence of headaches or nausea, and other events that occur during trials. Researchers might perform 10,000 simulations of a single scenario, which means an entire trial can generate millions of observations. Using this approach, a U.S. biotechnology company is actively exploring new treatments for HIV infection, hepatitis, various forms of cancer, inflammatory diseases such as rheumatoid arthritis, and many others. Its solution, which also takes advantage of grid computing technology, can produce as many as one million patients for two terabytes of data in a single simulation. The company has the ability to do more than 10,000 replicates in an hour, and that rate is growing.

Summary

With all of the different dimensions of analytics covered so far, it is logical to ask where an organization begins in its journey toward deeper insights. As you might expect, there is no single correct answer—the journey depends on the traveler and the desired destination. In watching many organizations move through their analytical maturity process, one key theme emerges among successful companies: start where you are. As mentioned earlier, it is easy to fall prey to analysis paralysis, constantly evaluating abilities instead of instituting programs to change those abilities. You will never have enough electronic data, it will never be clean enough, there will always be conflicting priorities, and you will never have enough of the right resources to focus on the project. But in all likelihood, you have enough of all of the above to get started.

Another trap some organizations fall into is "boiling the ocean." It is impossible to take on all of these analytical challenges and opportunities at the same time. And even if you could, it would not be advisable. Organizations and their knowledge workers need time to learn, determine what makes sense for their company, find the pitfalls and build bridges over them, and institutionalize those learnings for future projects. The intelligent enterprise identifies a significant, clearly defined business challenge and puts an agile team together to demonstrate success. With a successful project completed, the ability to launch the next initiative is much easier, and the people involved in the first project are now tour guides on the journey.

Using this approach, leading organizations often create an analytical center of excellence (ACE) within their enterprise. An ACE consists of a small, cross-functional group of people who help the many different parts of the company successfully leverage analytics. ACEs provide several benefits.

- Provide internal consulting and training on how to apply analytics to business problems
- Serve as business sponsors in the identification and management of data integration, quality, and management activities that support analytics
- Establish clear accountability for the advancement of analytical competencies within the enterprise
- Ensure consistency in the selection and use of enterprise architecture, analytical tools, and solutions to support analytics across the enterprise

Whether you are starting your first analytics initiative or finishing your hundredth project, you hopefully are getting a sense of the curiosity and excitement many people feel about analytics: there is always another question to ask with hidden gems in the answers. In healthcare, we are just at the beginning of seeing how analytics—whether biased toward the business or clinical sides of the spectrum—can transform our ecosystem. Analytics will give us better guidance on how to control costs—not just line items, but also the hidden and true costs of healthcare. Analytics will help us identify and dismantle old assumptions about the way healthcare is delivered—not relying on gut instincts and hearsay, but real evidence. Analytics will allow us to determine not only the treatments that produce the best outcomes, but the real factors that determine optimum treatment efficacy and cost. The hidden gems in healthcare will surface, and with them will come better lives for patients everywhere.

Acknowledgments

I am grateful for the contributions of Cindy Berry and Rick Pro, both from SAS's Health and Life Sciences organization, to the content and review of this chapter.

This chapter was originally published in *Healthcare Informatics, Improving Efficiency and Productivity*, Taylor & Francis, New York, 2010.

11

INFORMATION CREATION THROUGH ANALYTICS

A Healthcare Focus

STEPHAN P. KUDYBA

Contents

The primary initiative in leveraging the value of data resources lies in the realm of analytics. This term, however, encompasses a wide variety of methodologies that can provide descriptive, comparative, and predictive information for the end user. This chapter provides a brief background and description of some noteworthy analytic approaches as applied to more historical, structured data and includes references to big data issues along the way.

Analytic methods can range from simple reports, tables, and graphics to more statistically based endeavors to quantitative-based methods. We provided some analytic approaches according to some commonly referred to categories below. Regardless of the techniques deployed, the end result of an analytic endeavor is to extract/generate information to provide a resource to enhance the decision-making process.

1. Spreadsheet applications (also facilitated by vendor software packages)
   a. Data/variable calculations, sorting, formatting, organizing, transforming
   b. Distribution analysis and statistics (max, min, average, median, percentages, etc.)
   c. Correlation calculation between variables
   d. Linear and goal programming (optimization)
   e. Pivot tables (an intro to online analytic processing [OLAP] and business intelligence)
2. Business intelligence
   a. Query and report creating
   b. Online analytic processing
   c. Dashboards
3. Multivariate analysis (also part of business intelligence)
   a. Regression (hypothesis approach)
   b. Data mining applications (data-driven information creation)
      Neural networks
      Clustering
      Segmentation classification
      Real-time mining

4. Analysis of unstructured data
   a. Text mining
5. Six Sigma
6. Visualization

The type of analytic approach is generally dictated by the objective of what the user of the analysis requires, and where the objective and overall initiative needs to be clearly defined to achieve the most effective and informative results. This problem definition process generally involves the selection of a performance metric and identification of variables that impact that metric. Once the scope of the analytic endeavor (problem definition) has been established, then corresponding data resources must be managed (variables selected at a particular level of detail) and analysis can begin. The remainder of this chapter provides an overview of some of the aforementioned business intelligence–based analytic methods and includes some basic examples pertaining to healthcare.

Introduction to the Concept of Analytics

One of the initial stages of any analytic endeavor is the incorporation of an investigative study of a data resource. In other words, before a report is generated or quantitative modeling is conducted, an analyst needs to better understand what's in a data file. This investigative process involves conducting a distribution analysis of various data variables, perhaps calculating maximum, minimum, and variance metrics such as standard deviations. This provides a descriptive character of what the data variables comprise and renders additional analysis more robust, as it identifies the presence of such issues as data bias or skew, outliers, and even errors in data resources.

Business Intelligence

Reports

The focus of this book revolves around informatics, which largely involves the utilization of business intelligence applications (e.g., OLAP, dashboards, mining) to extract actionable information from all types of data to enhance the decision-making process. One of the most basic levels of this approach is the creation of business reports that incorporate sequel-related queries of data resources to extract variables that describe a business scenario. The introduction of big data involves additional requirements for this process; namely, when devising the parameters of the report to be created, the decision maker now must consider new variables that impact that conceptual report. The volume of data that must be processed must also be considered, and finally, the currency of the report (e.g., how often a report must be updated to provide adequate information for the decision maker). However, as simple as the process of generating a report may be, creating one that provides essential information to those that receive it may be a quite complex task.

Consider a request by a hospital's administrative area to produce an analytic report that provides some information on patient volume and hospital capacity along with patient satisfaction. Although this initiative appears to be straightforward and simplistic in nature, one must consider all the variables that comprise the area to be analyzed, along with the needs of the user of the report.

Some dimensions and variables that could be included in this analysis would involve the following.

TIME	PERFORMANCE METRIC	CARE AREA	DETAILED DESCRIBERS
Day	Bed utilization	Cardio	DRG
Week	Patient volume	Pediatrics	Physician
Month	Satisfaction rate	Med/surg oncology	Staffing

When conducting customized analytics (tailored analytics to a specific company's activities) data experts and analysts must apply due diligence to acquire that information that provides a strategic advantage in the marketplace. This involves the storage, processing, management, and ultimate analysis of data resources that describe a particular process.

Well-designed reports that incorporate the pertinent and available variables that describe a business activity can be an important source of information to decision makers (see Figure 11.1). However, the limitation of information creation at the report level is that the user often scans a report, assimilates the information, and quickly thinks of alternative business scenarios that are essential to providing more

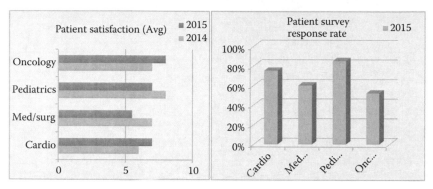

In-patient care area	# Patients daily (Avg)	% Change prev. year	Beds	Capacity rate	Days over capacity
Cardio	50	(2%)	60	83%	5
Med/surg	120	35%	125	96%	20
Pediatrics	42	20%	60	70%	10
Oncology	35	3%	45	78%	8
Total	247		290		43

Figure 11.1 **(See color insert.)** Hospital patient volume and satisfaction.

robust information regarding a process or activity. The report is limited to its current level of data aggregation and variables depicted. The next step to analysis or business intelligence involves the application of OLAP, which gives users the flexibility to view and analyze multiple scenarios of a business process. Before we describe the application of OLAP functionality that leverages large data resources and addresses currency of data, consider the more simplistic spreadsheet application of pivot tables.

Pivot Tables

A simplistic version of OLAP that many users can quickly relate to includes the use of pivot tables in a spreadsheet environment. Pivot tables leverage data in a flat, spreadsheet file to present alternative scenarios that describe a business activity. Through basic spreadsheet functionality, users can quickly generate a table view of relevant variables at a particular level of aggregation. For example, a spreadsheet of data that describes a software company's sales activities can include numerous rows according to corresponding variables. Hypothetical data recording national sales activities of branches across the country are illustrated in Table 11.1.

Table 11.1 Hypothetical Data Recording National Sales Activities

SALESPERSON	PRODUCT CATEGORY	CITY/AREA	CUSTOMER INDUSTRY	UNITS	SALES
KDE	ETL	NY	Finance	90	$45,000
SEF	Reporting	NY	Insurance	80	$24,000
CHT	Analytics	Boston	Finance	10	$20,000
HHT	Database	Philadelphia	Retail	55	$41,250
GGN	Database	Atlanta	Manufacturing	65	$48,750
THT	ETL	DC	Retail	18	$9,000
TTW	ETL	Philadelphia	Retail	42	$21,000
AHY	Analytics	Chicago	Healthcare	30	$60,000
FDO	Reporting	San Francisco	Manufacturing	39	$11,700
JJT	Reporting	Chicago	Finance	42	$12,600
GHI	ETL	NYC	Transportation	32	$16,000
BDE	Analytics	DC	Transportation	71	$142,000
PEC	Reporting	NYC	Finance	26	$57,045
LYJ	Database	Chicago	Insurance	52	$39,000
KIP	Analytics	San Francisco	Insurance	75	$150,000
OBN	Database	NYC	Retail	53	$39,750
ERB	Database	San Francisco	Manufacturing	93	$69,750
SEN	Reporting	LA	Healthcare	17	$5,100
JJR	ETL	NYC	Retail	96	$48,000
WNS	ETL	Philadelphia	Manufacturing	32	$16,000
DHK	Reporting	Boston	Finance	26	$7,000
TRN	Reporting	Boston	Transportation	30	$9,000
RGH	Database	Philadelphia	Retail	54	$40,500
MMR	Database	Atlanta	Retail	46	$34,500
SJP	ETL	Atlanta	Healthcare	80	$40,000

With a simple pivot function, Table 11.2 could be calculated with ease.

Dynamic Reporting through OLAP

Pivot tables are similar to OLAP in that they provide a multidimensional view of an activity. Enterprise OLAP provides greater scale to the analytic process, as it provides the platform to address multiple levels of aggregation of data resources, can depict updated views as source data are updated, and can process extremely large volumes of data. With this flexibility OLAP can help decision makers investigate information addressing multiple descriptive scenarios regarding

Table 11.2   Sales by Product Category by City

ETL (Extract Transfer and Load)

New York	$61,000
DC	$9,000
Philadelphia	$37,000
Atlanta	$40,000
Total	$195,000

Reporting

New York	$81,045
San Francisco	$11,700
Chicago	$12,600
Boston	$16,800
Los Angeles	$5,100
Total	$127,245

an operation's activity, therefore enhancing the knowledge generation process and overall ability to generate effective strategic conclusions. The diversity of information views involves various dimensions of time, performance metrics, and descriptive variables.

GENERAL CUBE INPUTS		
TIME	DESCRIPTIVE VARIABLES	PERFORMANCE METRICS
Daily	Demographics	Sales
Weekly	Behavioral	Response rate
Monthly	Strategic	Operational performance
Quarterly	Process related	Units

These inputs must be organized to provide information (variables at levels of detail) that describes a business scenario to facilitate decision support for the end user. Consider the graphical view of a cube in Figure 11.2.

Figure 11.2 depicts an illustration of an OLAP cube that facilitates analytics of patient satisfaction rates at a cardio area in a hospital. The cube presents a multidimensional view of a few variables that could potentially affect patient satisfaction. The platform gives the analyst the ability to query data variables from different levels of detail and in different combinations, through both numeric data and visualization. The tabs at the top of the graphic depict the variables that are available to be analyzed. The scenario depicted illustrates the number of daily

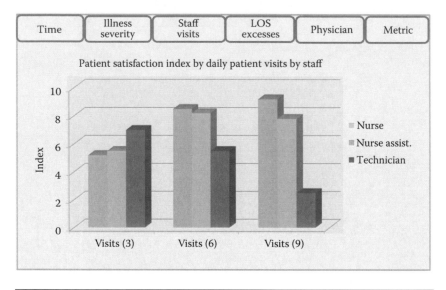

Figure 11.2 **(See color insert.)** Multidimensional cube.

visits to a patient by hospital staff (nurses, nurse assistants, technicians) and the corresponding patient satisfaction rates.

Users also have the ability to change variable views regarding patient satisfaction from different perspectives, including:

- Time (weekly, monthly, quarterly)
- Illness severity (critical, observation: according to cardio Diagnosis-Related Group [DRG])
- Length of stay (LOS; duration of excess of LOS beyond expected)
- Physician (primary physician, specialty)

By navigating the different dimensions of the cube, the analyst can quickly identify strengths and weaknesses of different operational and patient descriptive variables on the performance metric. OLAP enhances the decision makers' ability to understand more fully some of the attributes that drive patient satisfaction. Other variables can be introduced with the deliberation of stakeholders (e.g., staff training in patient communication tactics, etc.).

So what about big data you say? Remember, big data entails not only volume of data but also the new variables (sources of data). Both of these factors are considered when conducting analytics. In other words, a conceptual model must be generated that best describes the attributes of a desired process (entity to be better understood), and then data corresponding to those variables must be applied to that analytic framework. Big data adds complexity to the generation of the conceptual model as it introduces new descriptive variables that may not have been available or incorporated in the traditional structure of the particular process (e.g., categorizing physician comments on electronic health records [EHRs] during patient visits). The value of big data follows the basic concepts just mentioned; however, it can provide even greater value to the user by providing more robust models that provide greater descriptions and understanding of what affects process performance. In the patient satisfaction scenario depicted in the preceding text, perhaps a new variable that leverages social media (e.g., hospital Facebook likes) can be incorporated for another frame of reference. When considering big volumes and velocities of data in an OLAP environment, methods such as parallel processing and map reduction of data resources must be considered.

OLAP provides a robust source of business intelligence to decision makers, as it can leverage data resources including big data volumes and also provides a platform that offers a flexible, accurate, and user-friendly mechanism to understand quickly what has happened and what is happening to a business process. The multidimensional framework will give users the power to view multiple scenarios of a given process, such as the following:

- Are there associations between DRGs and excesses in patient LOS?
- What association do nurse-to-patient ratios have with readmit rates?
- How does patient demand for healthcare change during different months of the year?

The key to a valuable OLAP cube involves the combination of a few factors. One of these relates to the concept mentioned earlier, namely, that a cube must effectively describe a business scenario. The conceptual model that is used to build the cube must include noteworthy variables (relevant) with an appropriate detailed format that give users true business intelligence. The next major factor is filling the cube with accurate, current, and consistent data. Deficiencies in either of these areas can quickly render the analytic method useless for decision making. It should be noted that using OLAP for certain healthcare applications (e.g., outcomes associated with processes) introduces greater complexity than standard industry environments (e.g., sales by product by region) and requires more complex dimension modeling.[1]

Analytics at a Glance through Dashboards

In today's ultrafast, ultracompetitive information-based economy, it seems that the more senior a manager you may be, the less time that is available for investigation and drilling around multidimensional cubes. Often the level of analytics is filtered down to a few insightful reports, ongoing insights absorbed in the marketplace, and the access to real-time dashboards that display key performance indicators relevant to a particular process. These dashboards are designed to provide decision makers with a feedback mechanism as to how an organization is performing closer to real time. In the healthcare industry, streaming data from a medical sensor depicting real-time vital information of a patient takes the importance of a dashboard to a new level (just consider the traditional EKG or heart monitor). The key elements of dashboards are the delineation of relevant key performance indicators (KPIs) to a particular process, timeliness of their readings (currency of information), and finally, a user-friendly visual that provides the decision maker with a clear way of determining whether a process is operating successfully or not. The more traditional visual platform resembles that of an odometer in an automobile, where color schemes of performance reflect that of traffic lights (e.g., green, all is well; yellow, caution; and red, something is wrong and needs to be investigated). However, dashboard technology is quickly evolving where styles can include combinations of a variety of visuals (bar, line, pie charts) according to designated scales and are being utilized by decision makers at all levels in an organization.

The key to the effectiveness of a dashboard design involves its connection to the process at hand and use for decision making. Displays must be simple to understand and interpret. Just as a simple graphic display must adhere to design conventions (e.g., coherent color scheme, axis labeling, scale), so too must dashboard design, which adds complexity to the process as it combines various visual elements. The true key to a successful dashboard is evident by its effectiveness in providing timely, easy-to-understand decision support of a corresponding process. Dashboards that are too busy (include too many visuals), that are difficult to interpret, can quickly become omitted from an analyst's arsenal of decision support information.

Consider the dashboard example in Figure 11.3. The various graphic displays are clearly delineated from one another (separate sections) and are clearly labeled. Also, the design includes different visual displays, so the information presentation does not appear to overlap or include a blended view. Finally, complementary but distinctly different KPIs give the decision maker a well-rounded view of a human capital management application in this case.

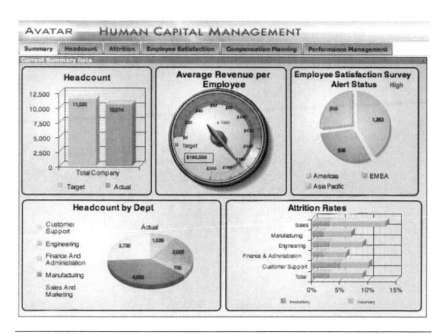

Figure 11.3   (See color insert.) Clearly designed employee analytic dashboard. (From http://www.dashboards-for-business.com/dashboards-templates/business-intelligence/business-intelligence-executive-dashboard; Domo, Inc., http://www.domo.com.)

Robust Business Intelligence and Drill-Down behind Dashboard Views

Dashboards provide an instantaneous mechanism to analyze the performance status of a process. Organizations with extensive analytic capabilities through business intelligence applications can have OLAP cubes that can be quickly drilled into from a dashboard KPI that provides descriptive analytics of underlying variables that underpin the KPI. A prime example of an e-commerce-based KPI is the bounce rate on a landing page for an organization, especially when a new marketing initiative has been launched. Perhaps an organization has initiated an Internet marketing campaign with banners listed on various complementary referral sites. A red signal indicating a higher than acceptable bounce rate would provide decision makers with a timely analytic alert mechanism to investigate the source of the problem. A real-time cube or report could quickly depict which referral site may be the greatest source of misdirected traffic.

Not all dashboard displays need to be real time, where a simple refresh of data on an interim basis provides decision makers with an accurate indication of whether a process's performance is adequate. However, the big data era involving high velocity of streaming data resources often requires a real-time dashboard visual of a given process to provide users with a quick view of variable impacts on KPIs.

Data Mining and the Value of Data

As we've illustrated in the business intelligence section (e.g., reporting, OLAP, dashboards), a primary approach to generating value from data resources is to manage it into useful information assets (e.g., building conceptual models and viewing data according to level of details according to variables that describe a process). The next step in the valuation process is to generate a higher level of knowledge through the information created from data. Data mining involves the application of quantitative methods (equations and algorithms), along with forms of statistical testing that process data resources, which can identify reliable patterns, trends, and associations among variables that describe a particular process. Techniques such as segmentation classification, neural networks, logistic regression, and clustering, to name a few, incorporate the use of algorithms and code or mathematical equations to extract actionable information from data resources. Chapter 14 provides more information on applications of major mining methods.

Why Things Are Happening

Data mining can provide decision makers with two major sources of valuable information. The first refers to descriptive information, or the identification of why things may be occurring in a business process. This is done through the identification of recurring patterns between variables. Cross-sectional graphic displays can add significant information to decision makers to illustrate patterns between variables. Figure 11.4 provides a simple graphical view that illustrates an advertising spend versus dollar revenue elasticity curve as identified in the mining process. The figure depicts that a recurring pattern exists between the two variables, and that a direct relationship is prominent, where an increase in ad spend yields an increase in product revenue. Many non-mining-centric analysts would quickly raise the point that this information is not noteworthy, given the natural relationship between the two variables (e.g., the more spent on advertising, the more sales that are generated); however, this criticism is quickly dispelled when posing the question: If ad spend is increased

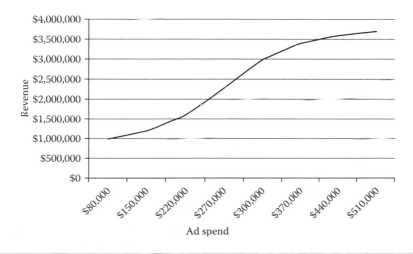

Figure 11.4 Advertising spend versus revenue curve.

by 5% from \$200,000, what is the expected increase in revenue? That question is difficult to answer without the use of mining.

Mining methods can yield insightful patterns as to demographic and behavioral attributes of consumer response to marketing initiatives, the impacts of process components on performance metrics, and many more. The following are a few prominent applications where mining is often utilized:

Healthcare-related areas (outcomes measurement, treatment effectiveness, operational performance)
Consumer propensities
Marketing and advertising effectiveness
E-commerce initiatives
Fraud detection
Worker and team performance
Pricing policies
Process-related applications (throughput, workflow, traffic analysis)
Risk assessment

What Is Likely to Happen

The other main source of information where mining provides value to decision makers is in the deployment of mining results. The patterns that have been identified are often embedded in an equation or algorithmic function, which are often referred to as the model, can be used to perform a "what if" analysis or estimate future expected results based on inputs. In other words, if I market my product to a particular market segment defined by demographics, what is my expected response rate? Or, is a particular activity (e.g., credit card use) likely to be fraudulent? If the analysis is based on a time series approach, mining models can provide forecasts for product sales. The analyst in this case needs to make assumptions as to future input values.

The healthcare industry involves a number of diverse areas for which analytics are required for knowledge generation. These scenarios often involve a number of diverse variables that encompass the descriptive drivers of performance metrics. Consider all the variables that follow and the corresponding level of detail that may provide descriptive information in better understanding performance metrics.

DRGs
Physician related
Nurse and staff related
Service entity (primary care physician, hospital, accountable care
   organization)
Patient descriptive and behavioral
Treatment related
Prescription related
Area of care
Time related

The incorporation of data mining methods that enable analysts to discover recurring patterns in an array of variables is often an essential technique to generate vital information.

Real-Time Mining and Big Data

The evolution of the big data era has increased the utilization of the concept of real-time or streaming mining approaches. More traditional streaming mining involves the creation of models through analyzing a data sample or historical data of a given process. The resulting model then becomes a function that can be used to process streaming or real-time incoming data, and corresponding actionable outputs are generated in real time as well. Streaming mining addresses the big data concept of velocity and volume of data and is incorporated in processes in which timely results are needed to improve strategies. Streaming mining applications are commonly applied in

Website traffic analysis for real-time online marketing
Fraud detection for online transactions
Financial market risk and trading

However, with the more prominent use of medical sensors that monitor patient metrics in the healthcare industry, the future may incorporate these real-time advanced analytic techniques to identify "trouble in the pipeline" for patients given the streaming data of vital signs.

Some big data sources (e.g., sensor- and satellite-producing entities) with extreme velocity and volume sometimes render the ability to extract a sample that represents the entire data source difficult, to say the least. In these instances, the ability to create optimized quantitative models to process this streaming data is limited. Techniques such as multisampling[2] and the implementation of self-optimizing quantitative techniques that learn as data are encountered have evolved to address this issue.

Analysis of Unstructured Data and Combining Structured and Unstructured Sources

Up to this point, this chapter has dealt with analytics of structured data. The big data era, however, largely involves the incorporation of unstructured data resources that need to be analyzed to identify actionable information that enhances strategic initiatives. Text mining addresses the analytics of textual data (words, phrases, messages, emails, etc.). At a high level of description, text analytics seeks to create structure from unstructured sources. It does this by processing various unstructured forms and classifies them into particular categories. Processing is generally based in mathematics or linguistics.

In the realm of the vastly growing utilization of electronic communication, which includes texting, tweeting, leaving content on social media, emailing, and so forth, one can quickly see the possible value that exists in deploying analytic techniques to extract information that describes responses to marketing initiatives and product and service offerings, reactions to news and events, and general consumer behavior and sentiment.

An example involving the analysis of both structured and unstructured data for informative decision support is evident when examining patients' EHRs to better understand treatment outcomes and patient diagnosis. More structured physiological data (e.g., blood sugar levels) can be combined with unstructured data (e.g., physician comments on treatment) to better understand a patient's status. Analytic techniques such as semantic mining can be applied in this situation to extract actionable information.

Six Sigma Analytics

Still many other analytic approaches exist outside the realm of business intelligence applications. More intensive, user-generated analytics include Six Sigma–based initiatives. The core of Six Sigma is a philosophy and focus for reducing variability in process operations. It involves process definition and the incorporation of an array of statistical analytic methods to measure the performance of various attributes.[3] Classic Six Sigma is underpinned by the DMAIC methodology, which is an acronym for

Define: Process attributes and project objectives.

Measure: Identify relevant data variables and measure performance of the process.

Analyze: Identification of sources of unacceptable variances.

Improve: Initiate strategic tactics to address causes of variance.

Control: Establish metrics to measure performance for ongoing feedback and take appropriate actions to address shortcomings of the process.

The initial three steps to the methodology clearly depict classic analytics as they involve the definition of the problem objective and corresponding use of statistics and techniques to analyze the performance of the process. Consider the recent evolution of the healthcare industry that has involved an aggressive adoption of information technologies to underpin the vast processes that exist in a healthcare provider's operations in treating patients. Workflow processes (e.g., the stages that a patient must go through when visiting the emergency room, or on a more detailed basis, the activities that are entailed from when a physician orders an exam to when the results are available) are often time stamped, which enables the estimation of time duration of activities. This provides a prime example for Six Sigma analysis. Chapter 12 illustrates the use of Six Sigma for better understanding the efficiency of treating patients at the emergency room.

Analytics of Episodes of Care and Episode Treatment Groups

Episodes of Care (EOCs) measure a more complete set of activities when considering the treatment of an individual's ailment or illness instead of considering a single outcome to an isolated procedure (e.g., surgery). EOCs consider the entire set of activities that encompass a patient's treatment. In the case of an acute situation, an EOC begins or takes its anchor with an initial diagnosis or identification of an ailment and includes all activities (prescriptions, procedures, etc.) and ends when the ailment subsides. Measuring the cost of the entire episode captures a more complete picture of the healthcare process.

To analyze EOCs in the aggregate to determine more or less effective treatment procedures, episodes need to be categorized into similar groupings to perform a comparative analysis. Categories can include DRG-related ailments that must be adjusted for any comorbidities, complications or treatments that dramatically change a patient's clinical profile, care utilization, and costs. The ultimate result is an Episode Treatment Group® (ETG®) or a grouping of individuals with similar EOCs. ETGs become a homogenized group of episodes that can be compared and analyzed to identify those activities that depict or drive high cost variances or outliers in relation to the expected cost of a given EOC in an ETG.[4]

When analyzing a high-cost EOC, one should keep in mind what the episode really depicts. An EOC can be comparable to a workflow process or even a supply chain of events. In a traditional business workflow, a project requirement is received and a series of activities must be carried out to complete the task. In a supply chain, orders for products are received and parts must be acquired, assembly takes place, and shipping to the final destination occurs. A breakdown in any of the chain of events in workflows or supply chains can have adverse effects on the final performance metric.

Analyzing episodes of care is no simple task, given the chain of activities that are involved. A good starting point is the identification of the outliers of episodes within the homogeneous categories or ETG. ETGs should be assigned an expected performance outcome, similar to LOS estimates according to DRGs. The outlier provides an identification mechanism that a particular episode of care has weak links. Perhaps prescription medications were not adhered to; a procedure was not appropriately administered; error in instructions or recording of information took place, and so forth.

However, even when a disruptive activity within an EOC has been identified, this may not be actionable information because it pertains to an individual instance of an individual case. High-value information comes in the form of identifying recurring patterns of events that result in high cost or suboptimal care. This gives the analyst and ultimately service provider the ability to identify noteworthy, repeated breakdowns in care and also provides focus for a solution (e.g., implement a prescription alerting system). The result should be a better functioning episode, where future recurring breakdowns are mitigated, which is high-value analytics. Data mining techniques provide effective analytic methodologies for the aforementioned case. The algorithmic processing of data with statistical techniques is well suited to identify patterns that enable a solution provider to pinpoint the areas of concern within an EOC.

Cognitive Systems in Healthcare*

One of the most ambitious approaches to decision support in healthcare involves the use of cognitive systems—those technologies that seek to emulate or improve upon human decision-making capabilities, and have some degree of autonomous intelligence. These systems typically involve a combination of analytics, machine learning, natural language processing, and event processing or workflow functions. The most well known example is IBM's Watson, but there are systems from a variety of companies that are being used in healthcare.

Healthcare is well suited for the use of cognitive systems because it is increasingly difficult for humans to master all the health and wellness information necessary for effective decision making. In oncology, for example, physicians now believe that there are more than 400 kinds of cancer, with hundreds of potential oncogenes and tumor suppressor genes that can govern the growth of cancers. There are more than 75 alternative drugs to treat breast cancer alone, and new cancer treatments emerge almost daily. In short, the amount of complex and rapidly changing information an oncologist would need to master is well beyond most human capacities.

Even in situations in which human clinicians can keep up with the information complexity, there are economic and wellness benefits to cognitive systems. They can provide "second opinions" to clinicians, and can advise patients on treatment and wellness issues when they are not in a doctor's office or hospital. In some cases they may allow nurses to dispense medical advice that would otherwise require a

---

* Section contributed by Thomas H. Davenport.

physician. They can provide a level of detail and personalization in recommendations that goes far beyond any existing medical website. And in that remote care context they can be easily updated to accommodate advancing medical knowledge.

There are three primary applications of cognitive systems in healthcare thus far. One is the diagnosis and treatment of complex diseases, with physicians as the primary users. Memorial Sloan Kettering and M.D. Anderson Cancer Centers both have cancer treatment projects underway with IBM Watson. Such projects tend to be large, expensive, and time consuming; they are the "moon shots" of cognitive systems in healthcare. When fully implemented they are unlikely to replace human physicians, but it is possible that they could affect physician employment on the margins. Rural hospitals, for example, might be able to get by without certain types of specialists if the knowledge for that specialty was contained in a cognitive system and could augment the work of an internist or hospitalist.

Somewhat less ambitious cognitive projects involve treatment and care recommendations for patients. M.D. Anderson and Intermountain Healthcare, for example, are in the process of implementing systems to provide care and wellness recommendations for patients with cancer and type 1 diabetes, respectively. These systems can incorporate data from patients' electronic medical records as well as home monitoring and activity tracking devices. Both are employing technology from startup vendor Cognitive Scale. Welltok, a startup in the wellness space, employs IBM's Watson for similar patient care recommendation purposes.

Finally, there are a variety of administrative activities in healthcare that can also benefit from cognitive tools. They include billing, IT support, admitting, and other financial and operational processes. M.D. Anderson, for example, is using a Cognitive Scale system to score patient bills that are the least likely to be collected. That institution's chief information officer, Chris Belmont, has identified more than 50 use cases for cognitive technology, and has already implemented several.

Given the complexity of healthcare and the need for performance improvement, it seems very likely that cognitive systems—which might be called "decision support on steroids"—are likely to become much more common in the field. They may not significantly reduce employment levels for clinicians, but they do present opportunities for more efficient and effective care, and they are likely to have significant impacts on care delivery, both within and outside of medical institutions.

An Often Overlooked Sector of Analytics (Power of the Simple Graphic)

Although many think of analytics as crunching numbers through an array of techniques and interpreting metrics to support decision making, analytics are greatly enhanced by the incorporation of an often taken for granted application of visual displays. Just think of having to analyze tables and columns of pure numbers when reviewing analytic reports. The process can quickly become mundane and even painful. In the host of analytic applications we described in the preceding text and for numerous additional analytic methods, there is a common denominator to a successful endeavor, and that is the use of graphics to disseminate information. A simple view of a well-designed graphic can provide the decision maker with a clear presentation of extensive analytic results in a comprehendible manner.

To leverage graphics successfully, a few key points need to be considered. Before you become intrigued with robust colors and images that quickly draw you to generate dramatic conclusions about a particular process, take a step back and increase your understanding of what the information is actually portraying. In other words

1. Analyze the titles and legends.
2. Take notice of the scale of the axis.
3. Understand the graphic/chart method used.

When the analyst fully understands the variables that are depicted in the graphic, what the type of graphic focuses on, and the scale of the axis, only then can he or she begin to generate effective interpretations. In the following section, a variety of graphical styles are listed with some simple descriptions of when they should be used. Keep in mind that when considering graphics in a big data era, the most significant elements are real-time graphics that provide analysts with a streaming view of processes. The real-time streaming visualization of data actually becomes a dashboard that analysts can monitor to observe variances in KPIs in relation to some event.

Graphic Types

Figure 11.5 illustrates the classic pie chart that depicts how a whole unit is divided among some subcomponents (pieces of an established pie). Market share is a prime example for pie charts, where share can be delineated by product lines, regions, industry competitors, etc. Pie charts have limitations when considering negative values.

Despite the seemingly simplistic bar chart depicted in Figure 11.6, the visual actually incorporates a number of important elements in the realm of analytics. The graphic depicts a comparative view of a multicomponent process (call centers in this case) in a time series setting (quarterly views). With a quick glance, the analyst can make

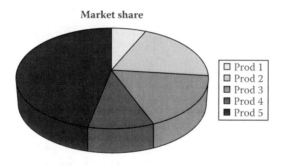

Figure 11.5   Pie chart depicting market share.

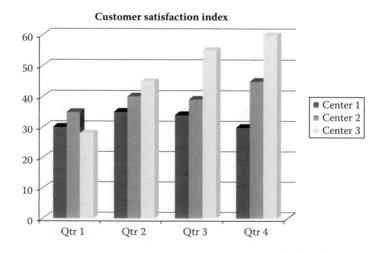

Figure 11.6   Bar chart (comparative view of multicomponent process).

inferences regarding relative performance (customer satisfaction) of three different call centers over time. Bar charts are more appropriate in depicting quantities or amounts of select variables.

Bar charts are also often used to illustrate variable distributions (percentages of ranges or categories of a given variable). Figure 11.7 depicts a categorical age variable and the amount of data that exists in selected ranges. This gives analysts a better understanding of the dimensions of a given data variable, and in this case enables them to determine if there is any age skew or bias (high percentage of one age range relative to the population). In conducting market research, a variable distribution view enables the researcher to determine if a target market is included in a data resource.

Variable distribution analysis can often include visuals via line graphs that are useful in illustrating scenarios involving continuous variables. Figure 11.8 illustrates the continuous data variable of mall foot traffic for a given day according to retailers.

Time series line charts provide users with a visual of potential seasonality in processes. Figure 11.9 depicts the classic holiday effect in retail as is seen in the repetitive bump in sales in Q4.

Another type of chart involves the scatterplot that is commonly used to illustrate correlations between variables, where simple plots of individual data points are depicted. Figure 11.10 depicts data points illustrating correlations between employee performance and training received.

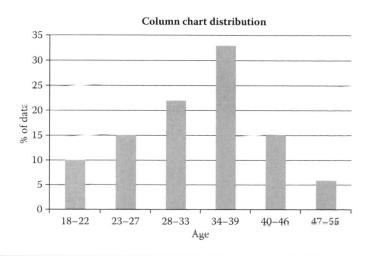

Figure 11.7   Age distribution chart.

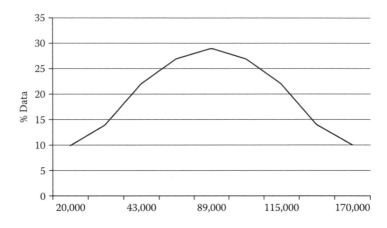

Figure 11.8 Line chart of continuous variable distribution of mall traffic.

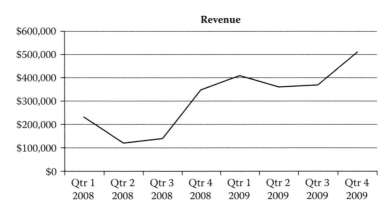

Figure 11.9 Time series line charts for seasonality.

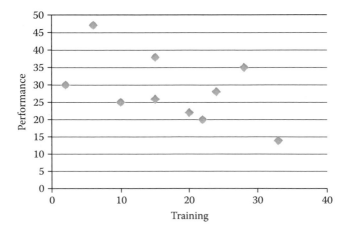

Figure 11.10 Scatterplot for correlations.

A rather insightful chart style is the bubble chart. The bubble graphic enables analysts to depict three-dimensional scenarios in a coherent fashion by incorporating bubble size to illustrate variable attributes. Figure 11.11 depicts the multidimensional scenario of organizational team performance according to workload and team size.

Yet another graphic style that has increased in importance over the evolution of the big data era is the use of maps. Map visuals are generally utilized when an analysis involving location is emphasized; however, location can also refer to a process location. Applications such as traffic analysis or population analytics are common examples. Traffic can refer to website activities, vehicular, consumer, or some type of designated activity.

In a simple web traffic visual, a map can illustrate cross sections of time and area of a webpage that are receiving high user traffic. This can provide strategists with actionable information to more effectively apply online marketing tactics (e.g., display banners in hot spots on a particular page at a particular time).

Civil engineering can leverage heat maps by incorporating GPS data to investigate hot areas of traffic incidents (congestion, accidents) and optimize new designs to alleviate existing trouble areas and in designing new roadways.

Figure 11.12 provides a standard heat map where "hot colors" depict more intense activity. In this case, the hotter areas depict areas where job vacancies are difficult to fill.

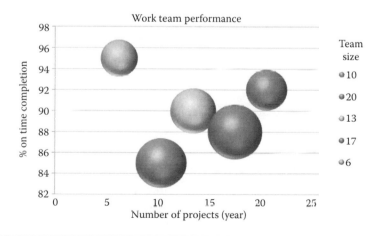

Figure 11.11   (See color insert.) Bubble chart depicting workforce team performance.

Harder-to-fill jobs  Easier-to-fill jobs   Unavailable

Figure 11.12   (See color insert.) Heat map that illustrates areas of hard-to-fill job vacancies. (From Wanted Analytics, http://www.wantedanalytics.com.)

Map visuals are particularly applicable in the big data era, when real-time, high-velocity analytics and voluminous sources are involved. Applications that leverage big data include geovisualization that involves the analysis of geographic specific flows of data and bioinformatics and sensor output in the healthcare spectrum. For example, the healthcare industry is increasingly utilizing streaming sensor data generated by various treatment and diagnostic technologies. For diagnosis (magnetic resonance imaging [MRI]), these data describe the characteristics of a patient. Visual displays of this source are essential to extract information on trouble areas for patients. Chapter 9 (Figure 9.5) provides more detailed information corresponding to this concept. As big data sources emerge, the application of heat maps should become a common visual technique for providing analysts with a mechanism to enhance strategic initiatives. Figure 11.13 depicts a heat map showing percentage likelihood that a primary melanoma site will show lymphatic drainage to axillary lymph-node fields. While Figure 11.14 depicts an example of computerized tomography, three dimensional image of the brain and blood vessels.

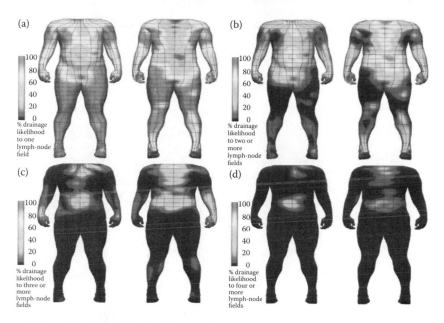

Figure 11.13 (See color insert.) Three-dimensional visualization of lymphatic drainage patterns in patients with cutaneous melanoma. (From Reynolds, H., Dunbar, P., Uren, R., Blackett, S., Thompson, J., and Smith, N. Three-dimensional visualisation of lymphatic drainage patterns in patients with cutaneous melanoma, *Lancet Oncol* 8:806–12, 2007 (Figure 1), http://www.thelancet .com/journals/lanonc/article/PIIS1470-2045%2807%2970176-6/fulltext?rss=yes.)

Value of Data and Analytics

We began this chapter by stressing the importance of analytics as an essential component to deriving value from data, where the era of big data adds intensity to the concept, as it adds new dimensions to the equation. Regardless of the source of data, its value is not realized unless it provides some resource to a strategic endeavor. Rarely does a decision maker reference a data source without first formulating a reason to do so. Once the conceptual need is defined, only then can data provide value.

The conceptual need involves the quest to better understand a process with the goal of enhancing its efficiency or productivity. Simply analyzing random data and coming up with associations between variables may actually generate negative returns because the analytic process requires time and resources, and the result may not add meaningful information.

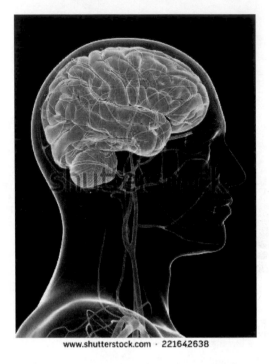

www.shutterstock.com · 221642638

Figure 11.14 **(See color insert.)** Computer tomography image. (From Shutterstock, http://www.shutterstock.com/pic-221642638/stock-photo-medical-illustration-of-the-brain-and-head-arteries.html.)

Consider the growing data resource in the area of sports. More variables (variety) and real-time downloads of various athletic activities at corresponding events (velocity and volume) may seemingly provide great value to understanding various attributes of different athletes and sports teams. However, to truly generate value for decision making, a conceptual model must be created. Consider the quest to better understand what leads a team to achieve a winning record. An analysis of corresponding data could yield the following result: basketball teams with winning records generally score more 3-point shots.

At first glance, this may seem to be very valuable information, but the revelation proves limited at best when looking to make a strategic decision. What does a coach do in leveraging this associative pattern—encourage players to take more shots from the 3-point zone? Does he change practice to intensify skills for increasing 3-point percentages for players? And if so, what happens to the team's performance from the 2-point zone, and does a reduction in 2-point conversions decrease the likelihood of winning a game despite an increase in 3-point shots? In the case at hand, does the variable of number of 3-point shots really add descriptive value to what leads to a team's success? Perhaps more appropriate variables that can provide strategic action could entail

Team practice data (frequency, drills, duration)
Player descriptions (height, speed, position, age)
Type of offensive and defensive tactics

Identifying patterns among these types of variables empowers a coach (decision maker/strategist) to implement strategic initiatives that impact a performance metric or defined objective—winning.

Closing Comments on Efficiency and Productivity

The concept of value also extends to three often cited benchmarks in the realm of commerce: efficiency and productivity. One should note that although the three terms appear synonymous, there are noteworthy differences among them, so when seeking to succeed in strategic endeavors, decision makers must clearly understand the entire initiative from the perspective of these three concepts.

Analytics of all types naturally address the quest for enhancing efficiencies of corresponding processes. Enhancing efficiency naturally leads to cost reduction for the defined process; however, simply increasing efficiency for a particular activity does not necessarily imply an increase in productivity and profitability at the organizational level. Consider a marketing department for a small retailer that depends on more traditional mail order initiatives to generate sales. The department could consistently achieve increased efficiency in the process of creating printed marketing materials, generating addresses, and mailing literature to the market. These efficiencies could be achieved by implementing new printing technologies, data-based endeavors, and so forth. However, productivity as measured by response rate or increased product sales may not necessarily increase. Perhaps traditional mail is no longer the most effective marketing medium for the type of product given the evolution of e-marketing tactics and the adoption of smartphones and electronic communication by consumers, or perhaps the target market has changed its behavior and a different segment is actually more appropriate for the product. What may actually transpire for this endeavor is an efficient process that yields decreased productivity for the organization (deploying resources and achieving decreased returns).

Just as analytics were utilized to better understand what drives wasteful activities for the mail order marketing initiative, so too should they be utilized for such endeavors as better understanding overall marketing effectiveness and target marketing. Simply put, strategic endeavors must incorporate a bigger picture than simple processes.

This idea reigns true in the realm of healthcare. With evolving data resources that provide the building blocks to actionable information, analysts and decision makers need to keep in mind the big picture when implementing new initiatives. Analytics provide insights into achieving efficiencies in treatments, workflows, and so forth where the ultimate goal of achieving a healthier population and higher quality of life while effectively managing costs should not be forgotten.

References

1. Parmanto B, Scotch M, Ah SA. 2005. Framework for designing a healthcare outcome warehouse. *Perspect Health Inf Manage* 2:3.
2. Rajaraman A, Ullman J. 2011. Mining data streams. In *Mining of massive data sets* (pp. 129–132). Cambridge, UK: Cambridge University Press.
3. Pande P, Neuman R. 2000. *The Six Sigma way: How GE, Motorola, and other top companies are honing their performance*. New York: McGraw Hill.
4. Symmetry® Episode Treatment Groups® (Measuring health care with meaningful episodes of care). White Paper. Eden Prairie, MN: OPTUMInsight™.

12

ENHANCING DATA RESOURCES AND BUSINESS INTELLIGENCE IN HEALTHCARE

STEPHAN P. KUDYBA AND MARK RADER

Contents

Introduction

The healthcare industry has been a focal point in the pursuit of enhancing operational efficiency. The complex nature of the industry and its diverse technologies, procedures, medicines, and facilities to diagnose and treat individuals of all demographic and physical make-ups in a setting of ever rising costs add up to a formidable and complex task. A core resource necessary to generating actionable information that can help manage these variables is data. One of the first phases of the recent information technology (IT) transformation in healthcare entailed the process of transforming paper information to digital data while also incorporating such platforms such as computerized physician (or provider) order entry (CPOE) to maintain robust data on an ongoing basis. Management at a New Jersey–based Health System was not dissuaded as they sought to improve their business of providing patients with high-quality treatment and care more efficiently.

Saint Clare's Health System comprises four hospitals and more than 3000 personnel who provide care across a spectrum of patient needs such as behavioral health, cardiovascular, diabetes, and dialysis. Management identified procedures in selected operations, the efficiency of which could be enhanced through the utilization of IT. More specifically, Saint Clare's sought to generate more robust information resources from digitizing activities in certain treatment and care procedures. The organization realized that there was a source of valuable information in existing paper documents, charts, and general treatment activities that could provide enhanced intelligence about the effectiveness of treatment procedures for patients. By transforming paper and procedural activity inputs into data resources, Saint Clare's could enhance efficiency by mitigating lost information, increase productivity of care-providing personnel, better identify areas for improvement of care procedures, and ultimately enhance the quality of care for patients. Areas involving data assets include medical reports, nursing documentation, medical administrative records, radiology information, and pharmacy information.

Secrets to Success

The best technological platform and the most ingenious data-based strategy cannot yield positive results without proper implementation guidelines and organizational buy-in by stakeholders of the system. Essential implementation guidelines on the technology side in this case included an invited request for proposal (RFP) process to system vendors and an open forum of internal hospital users and stakeholders to gain a sense of the corresponding technology's functionality. Once the right platform was selected, formal and extensive training was conducted to ease the system into real-time usage. A true measure of success in increasing efficiency from system implementation does not revolve around technology functionality alone; it arises from continued usage by all hospital stakeholders and adoption of the system as an integral tool supporting everyday treatment activities. To achieve this, the organization launched a cultural change strategy that promoted use of the system to work smarter and more efficiently by leveraging its resources. So far, the results have been a success and the organization has experienced positive outcomes on a number of fronts.

Sources of Efficiency Gains

The IT platform enabled Saint Clare's to enhance efficiency in the short run by mitigating the potential risk of lost information (e.g., paper documents, charts, reports), which often plagues paper-based environments. By storing existing documents and initiating the ongoing input of procedural data, Saint Clare's created a more reliable method to organize, archive, and access information. Other gains include reducing the time for nursing staff to complete required paperwork, document vital treatment information for patients, and access past treatment information. The information download process has been enhanced by a user-friendly input interface, which also promotes a coherent, standardized database of treatment-related activities. Reduction in data access and downloading time from the previous paper report environment has increased the time available for nurses to concentrate on patient care. That is a classic case of increased productivity—accomplishing the same task in less time and increasing available employee time to address other tasks where the level of quality of each is increased.

"Patient Treatment" Intelligence

One of the most promising gains to efficiency lies in the ability to analyze the data that describe the treatment and care processes supported by the system. By transforming existing paper information into digital form and systematizing current and future procedure (treatment) information, Saint Clare's is creating building blocks to perform more advanced analytics of patient care activities. Systematizing data enables users to analyze data elements more effectively in a logical, coherent manner. When compared to reading hundreds of paper reports and charts to formulate trends in patient response to treatments, the system effect provides the capability to identify and view trends over time. This applies to patient treatment outcomes and also to the effectiveness of treatment types across a variety of patients. The accessibility of more descriptive, coherent, and timely reports and graphics gives doctors, nurses, and hospital staff enhanced treatment intelligence.

Positive returns from business intelligence are generally achieved over time as data resources grow and develop and as new software applications augment data analysis. Increased usage of business intelligence enabled by higher quality information can assist treatment providers in better understanding treatment procedures, outcomes, and care for patients. With the establishment of an effective information management system and through the use of digital infrastructure, the implications for long-term efficiency gains through enhanced analytics and business (treatment) intelligence are far reaching.[1]

Introduction to Business Intelligence

In the purest form, business intelligence can be summed up as the methodologies and technologies utilized for collecting, manipulating, analyzing, and presenting information that enables business leaders to both make informed decisions for the actions that will need to be taken and evaluate the effectiveness of actions that have already been executed. The information corresponding to processes that have been created and are continuously utilized by companies represents their current and primary business intelligence. Business intelligence actually originates with the employees of organizations. Workers utilize workflows, policies, and procedures based on best practices that evolve over years of experience, education, and training. There is no limit to the amount of actual business intelligence that is consciously maintained on any given day; however, the truly valuable information may actually lie in the areas that are not analyzed as deeply as they should be. This concept refers to the constant refinement of business intelligence applications, where today's environment calls for data to be recorded and utilized across processes of an organization that are pulled together and taken through evaluative methodologies that produce quick-hitting measures of company operations. This process has been intensified with the introduction of big data. High-volume, real-time data streams (e.g., wireless sensor data) require business intelligence components such as dashboards to provide information assets to users. In healthcare, facilities put their knowledge in the policies and procedures that they have found to be most effective for treating and managing their patients. Medical staff recognize and utilize these same methods, but refer to them as evidence-based medicine. In evidence-based medicine practice is based on what has been proven to be safe and effective in the treatment of any particular condition. Medical publications publish the findings, and standards and practice committees determine if and how the findings should be followed. In much the same way, business intelligence creates actionable items from available data in any environment and can provide the feedback required to determine what is the best methodology, practice, or steps to apply to a given situation.

In the following example we show how data being collected in healthcare can be rapidly evaluated using business intelligence with readily available tools. Figure 12.1 shows a series of Diagnosis-Related Group (DRG) codes of medical diagnosis, for patients admitted to a hospital within a one-month period, who were readmitted to the facility within 14 days of their initial discharge. The new diagnosis at the readmission is deep vein thrombosis (DVT). Immediately, there is a visual understanding that the patients with a DRG code of 6 on their initial admission to the hospital are the most at risk for developing DVT during or after their stay at the facility. This assumption was immediately available because of the application of business intelligence methods to existing data across time periods within an electronic system. Now this report can be generated on demand and with very little effort. Previously, chart reviews would have been needed, which could introduce potential inaccurate numbers. Now it can be

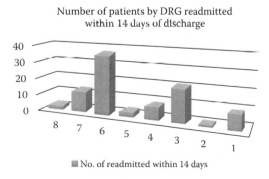

Number of patients by DRG readmitted
within 14 days of discharge

■ No. of readmitted within 14 days

Figure 12.1   Histogram chart to evaluate readmissions.

seen easily where the problem areas are and what patients need to be targeted for specific evaluations while admitted to the facility.

Herein lies the power of business intelligence that was not previously seen by the healthcare industry as a whole. Previously reviews were completed and case studies performed that targeted specific areas of demographics and conditions to produce a final result, but now we can create assumptions and gain direction from a system based on an even larger case mix. However, it must be kept in mind that these numbers are generated from a system that is simply collecting data in the manner in which it was designed. So the results may be indicators but not absolute definitive outcomes. The results of business intelligence are best when utilized as guiding points of information that will bring forward areas of review with a high acuity. This guiding light principle will bring forth new ideas and understanding of just how patients and outcomes are affected by the decisions made during their treatment. Business intelligence is not just a tool or a method, but a way of effectively evaluating the facts that are already known, and by applying knowledge of the business practice, or in this case of healthcare treatments, it is possible to identify areas of improvement and key indicators of best practices.

Business Intelligence in Electronic Medical Records: A Look at Strategy and Six Sigma

The intelligence side of business intelligence is by far the most astounding concept to emphasize when considering what can be produced from a system is not only intellectual property that may not have been previously thought to be possessed by a healthcare organization, but also the information needed to make business or healthcare decisions that may have been previously overlooked. With proper data management principles deployed and an eye on strategic demand of process information, business intelligence and strategic analytic methods can yield valuable results.

Evaluation

When an electronic medical record system is implemented in an organization a process begins with a simple set of facts, and over time, a minimum of six months, a repository of workflow, treatment, and response information is established that, when put through a discriminating analysis, can be used to create a reliable and actionable set of information. This collection of facts will remain part of the database and be used to review charts on an as-needed basis for historical purposes. Data or the collection of facts provides the basis of creating information describing a multitude of activities in healthcare facilities. To accomplish this, a deep understanding of the processes, workflows, data capture, and regulatory requirements must be established. This is where a business strategy or process and performance evaluation methodologies such as Six Sigma come into play. Six Sigma can be viewed as either a business strategy tool that is effective at identifying the areas that require change or a performance evaluation methodology examining the effectiveness of process modification for a company. For an electronic medical record (EMR), it is important to understand how the data that underpin business intelligence and strategic methods such as Six Sigma are collected.

Reviewing a Workflow (Business Intelligence and Six Sigma)

One of the driving forces of customer or patient satisfaction is the effectiveness of a process or workflow in a healthcare organization. Any facility can claim it has policies and procedures that address those factors that lead to a positive patient experience; reality, however, indicates that what is dictated on paper may or may not be consistent with applications. Patients who visit facilities where they are able to navigate smoothly from one point in the process of registration to the next step generally have more positive feedback than those experiencing difficulty finding their way from one end of the building where they register to the other end, where radiology and the laboratory are located. A lack of clear workflow design (e.g., user-friendly directions for patients undergoing a process of events) can no doubt result in a negative patient experience. The application of business intelligence reporting coupled with a Six Sigma DMAIC project methodology review can identify how to improve the existing workflow. Clear directions on moving the patient from one area to the next that incorporate the activities of both patients and healthcare providers are critical to enhancing workflow efficiency and ultimately the patient experience.

The Six Sigma DMAIC project methodology is used for projects aimed at improving an existing business process. Each of the letters in the acronym identifies a phase of the project and was inspired by Deming's plan–do–check–act cycle. The DMAIC project methodology is laid out as follows.

Define high-level project goals and the current process.

Measure key aspects of the current process and collect relevant data.

Analyze the data to verify cause-and-effect relationships. Determine what the relationships are, and attempt to ensure that all factors have been considered.

Improve or optimize the process based on data analysis using techniques such as design of experiments.

Control to ensure that any deviations from the target are corrected before they result in defects. Set up pilot runs to establish process capability, move on to production, set up control mechanisms, and continuously monitor the process.

Given the preestablished processes that exist in the healthcare environment, business intelligence begins at the M phase of the project and continues through the final C phase. Each phase has distinct requirements that need to be accomplished before the process can move to the next phase. With the implementation of business intelligence, those taking part in the project can establish the goal, measure what currently exists, conduct analysis to identify key indicators, and produce information that can be acted on. Improving the process in the I phase is supported by visual representation to those responsible for executing the process, where the final stage of continually monitoring the process is accomplished by the timely updating of data resources and analysis of reports and graphics.

To illustrate the Six Sigma business intelligence approach, let us turn to a hypothetical healthcare application. In this case, an emergency room was honored with a national award for having the highest customer satisfaction rating of all the facilities participating in the survey. Although this is a very prestigious award, this kind of recognition means further scrutiny by those visiting that see the award prominently displayed on the wall of the waiting area. To maintain these performance achievements, analysis of what is currently in place, including time frames from each point in the process, is required, where considering the time it takes to move the patient between each point in the process is essential. A brief review by the project initiators identifies that the average wait time for a patient is more than 45 minutes before he or she has a medical service exam (MSE) by a physician. This identifies the area of workflow improvement that must be addressed. In parallel with the workflow, policy, and procedure evaluation, all current workflow points need to be identified in the system. The ability to extract these points should be available because a typical EMR would have the ability to add tasks, markers, or events in the system to identify when you have reached a point in the workflow or process. Event elements of the workflow process can be analyzed because informatics applications have the ability to time-stamp these events that indicate start and completion times. In an ideal situation the identified points in the workflow would be created and completed automatically by the software as personnel move the patient through the emergency department and complete the tasks or events previously defined. This prevents missing data from personnel overlooking the need to enter any time stamp information. The ultimate result is a data resource that enables decision makers to identify bottlenecks in the workflow, investigate causes of delays, and if feasible, introduce guidelines to address the issues at hand.

Initial review of data includes a column for every step in the process that contains the time to complete that task. In this facility the patient arrives, which is the starting time stamp of the process, and then moves into triage with a nurse, and is assigned and moved into a bed in the emergency department. Nurse evaluation and a medical history review are then conducted and completed. Next, a medical service exam is performed by the physician, which may be followed by testing, procedures, medication administration, and treatment. Disposition of the patient is performed to indicate if the patient is going home after treatment or being admitted. These are just some of the initial steps that can be identified for tracking purposes, and the time frame between each step indicates where potential bottlenecks exist in the process. Identification of the areas between the arrival and the MSE become visible as extended time frames from arrival to the triage occur, and the time from the MSE being requested to when it was completed by the physician may become elevated. The next step is to look at what personnel are involved with moving the patient through the process, or perhaps personnel staffing levels at those times versus the number of patients coming to the facility for treatment. By doing this we complete the M and A phases of the project through measurement and analysis of what is currently in place by business intelligence tools available within the EMR. Further detail and alternate representation of the data would be needed to drive the changes in the I phase of the project. The timing of workflows is imperative to the successful treatment of a patient because the feeling of adequate care can generally be linked to the timeliness of movement of the patient through the emergency room, or any other department in a facility. However, one step that makes the largest impact is that of the physician coming in to see the patient. Of the data that have been collected to this point, the arrival time of the patient is available and it is known when the physician starts the MSE, or first visits the patient in the room, because there is a time stamp associated with the event and the physicians have agreed to log in to the computer and start the event prior to visiting with the patient. This agreement can be easily acquired from the physician since he or she will typically log in to the computer to gather the data that have been collected during triage and initial nurse evaluation. On the completion of the shift the system is left with time stamps and events from every patient and every physician, and the business intelligence system can now run automatically to produce the chart seen in Figure 12.2. What is immediately seen is that some physicians are adequate at arriving to see the patient

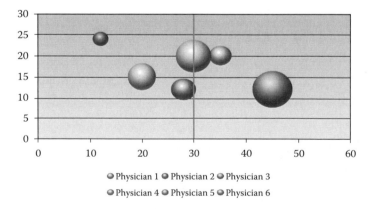

Figure 12.2   Bubble chart to identify physicians with average door to MSE times greater than 30 minutes.

and begin their exam in under 30 minutes, and typically those physicians have a lighter load than others. The physician who stands out is physician 6 because he had one of the lightest loads for the shift but was unable to meet the required 30-minute time frame. Now the administration can delve deeper into why this was occurring and sit down with the physician after reviewing the data to see if there was an outlier that caused the physician to fall outside the acceptable range. Whatever the reason, by simply having the data in place and available for them to see how well they are performing, the physicians will typically strive to meet the goal because they do not want to be the outlier in meeting the needs of both the patients and the facilities. Any administrator would love to be able to create an environment where personnel strive to increase performance and patient satisfaction without any monetary output to the physicians themselves.

Improvement may be needed in the specific areas that have been identified as a source of process delays. This can be accomplished through the analysis of process-related information via reports and graphics that depict excessive lag times for certain procedures beyond normal and acceptable levels. Initiatives such as increasing labor resources (e.g., specific healthcare personnel) to areas where bottlenecks occur, or systematizing procedures that cause undue delays in patient care activity (e.g., administrative) can be implemented. Applications of charts and graphics that report on daily performance metrics involve the C phase, which enables decision makers to quickly view on a daily basis, at a high level, reports indicating trends in process performance rates. Robust business intelligence technology enables users to drill into the low-level reports to see where incidents are causing delays and inhibiting process performance. This allows personnel to address problems as they are occurring to alleviate negative patient experiences in the pipeline. As an example of how you can identify causes in disruption of workflow, a Pareto chart was utilized to determine the potential causes of patients being delayed in movement from the emergency department to the nursing units (see Figure 12.3). Again, we can rapidly identify the areas that need improvement, where it is understood that to make the largest improvement in process, you need to identify the causes of delay that happen 80% of the time. With a review of the chart the three main problems are the areas of the emergency department physician and the admitting physician exchanging

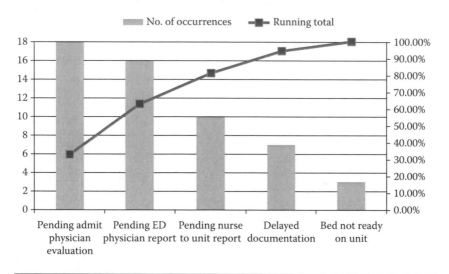

Figure 12.3   Factors for patient delays.

their reports with each other, and the delay in the nursing staff giving a report to the admitting nurse on the unit. The directors of the organization now have a clear path to alleviate patients waiting excessive times before being taken to their beds. A new methodology for handling patient needs to be evaluated is required. Once that methodology is put in place, the same evaluation of data can be run again to see the results of time frames and the causes for delay. With enough data collected over time, trending can then be added to identify points in time and the changes that were put in place at that time to produce the effect on the statistical measures.

Data Mining

The advantage of leveraging data resources with business intelligence is extended through the utilization of data mining applications. These sophisticated analytic applications grounded in quantitative methodologies enable decision makers to identify actionable information in the form of recurring patterns and trends among data variables that describe various healthcare-related processes. These techniques have been utilized to determine likelihoods of patients to be classified as high risk for particular ailments, identify effective clinical and treatment procedures that lead to positive outcomes, uncover fraudulent financial activities, and help better describe performance of general operational processes that underpin various healthcare activities, such as identifying variables that account for excessive lengths of stay and throughput metrics (time for physicians to receive lab results). Data mining models enhance the ability to determine not just what has happened in healthcare performance, but why things are happening and what is likely to happen in the future.

Closing Comments

To accomplish an effective business intelligence platform, stakeholders who are involved in the processes and treatment activities that are incorporated in data, reports, and graphics; stored; and analyzed by the technology should have input into the design of system output. The result of including accurate and relevant data (e.g., those variables that appropriately underpin process activities) in a business intelligence platform that can quickly provide actionable analytic information describing processes and activities is a more efficient organization that better manages costs, produces an enhanced customer experience, and achieves high standards in patient care and outcomes.

This chapter was originally published in *Healthcare Informatics, Improving Efficiency and Productivity*, Taylor & Francis, New York, 2010.

Reference

1. Kudyba S. 2008. Productivity gains at St. Clare's health system. *Information Management Magazine*, March 11, 2008.

13

TAKING ACTION FOR HEALTH PLAN MEMBERS' HEALTH

An Argument for an Expert System's Approach to Optimizing Care Management Utilization and Financial Outcomes

STEPHAN P. KUDYBA, THAD PERRY, AND JOHN AZZOLINI

Contents

"Hot spotting" has practically become the battle cry for managed care organizations since an article of the same name was published in *The New Yorker* in January 2011.[1] In this article a physician, Jeffrey Brenner, realized after attempting to save a shooting victim that it was possible to study healthcare utilization patterns in much the same way assault and crime patterns are tracked. For example, Brenner discovered that across a six-year period, more than 900 people in Camden, New Jersey, accounted for more than $200 million dollars in healthcare expenses. One of these patients had 324 admissions in five years while the care for another patient cost $3.5 million dollars. In addition, he found that *1 percent* of the patients who used Camden's healthcare facilities accounted for *30 percent* of the total costs.

Called the "Top 1%" by the managed care industry, Brenner's observation was important not because it was new information,[2] but because it clearly articulated this situation to the general public. Patients like these, "hot spots," were the ones in need of better quality of care. From his experience as a physician, he knew that those patients with the highest costs are usually the ones who have experienced the worst care. Though hardly a new idea, the concept of identifying and intervening with the most severe or clinically complex patients to lower future healthcare costs has seen resurgence in the managed care arena.

State Medicaid agencies have embraced the "hot spotting" concept, challenging their Medicaid Managed Care Plans (MCPs) to decrease overall healthcare expenditures by increasing the quality of care for their member populations, especially those who are currently a significant cost burden to the program. As early as 2005, the Ohio Commission to Reform Medicaid (OCRM) published a report on Ohio Medicaid making recommendations and outlining action steps focused on (1) long-term care, (2) care management, (3) pharmacy management, (4) member eligibility, (5) financial administration, and (6) overall program structure and management.[3] Recognizing the difficulty of healthcare reform, this report, and subsequent study, underscored the complexity of the relationships between quality, delivery, management, administration, cost, and payment of healthcare.

Clearly, quality of care, and cost of care are on a collision course. Is it possible to develop a system that establishes and supports our nation's need for quality, affordable healthcare, or have decades of fee-for-service payment systems that are independent of quality of care and/or patient outcomes made it impossible to reform health care delivery? Unfortunately, as long as healthcare facilities, providers, and suppliers fail to work together and independently treat patients as profit centers, there appears to be little hope for healthcare reform.

This is one reason that the new healthcare reform law is so controversial. It is widely known that health plan members who receive the right type of care at the appropriate time have better health outcomes, thereby decreasing their cost burden on an already overstressed healthcare economic system. Proponents and critics of healthcare reform do agree on one thing: there are ways to decrease overall healthcare costs through population-based care management programs. Brenner asserted in *The New Yorker* article, "For all the stupid, expensive, predictive-modeling software that the big venders sell, you just ask the doctors, 'Who are your most difficult patients?,' and they can identify them." Though this statement has simplistic appeal, it cannot exist as a management strategy applicable to broad populations. The process of designing and running a population-based program is not as trivial as this statement implies.

To be effective, a data-driven, procedural approach must be taken, which allows for the coordination and collaboration of all constituents in the healthcare delivery process. Moreover, robust data management, data mining, and analytic processes are essential for successful population-based programs because improvements in quality and cost of care can occur only when *the right members receive the right services at the right time.*[4-6] For these data-driven methods to influence clinical and financial outcomes of our healthcare delivery system, the information derived from them must be *actionable.*

Clearly, care management programs already exist to address these issues. However, one must consider the following questions: If there are already programs, protocols, processes in place, why are we not seeing significant improvements in quality and cost of care? Why are health plans, facilities, and provider practices still challenged with improving quality of care while reducing overall costs? Therefore, we are not presenting new concepts in care management, but rather a conceptual framework comprising factors influencing one's overall healthcare experience. This combination of factors allows for the optimization of care management interventions that maximize the ability to target and identify those members whose cost burden will continue to increase in the absence of care management support activities.

To develop actionable care management information, it is necessary to create a framework that takes into account data derived from numerous sources. Expert systems created to support Clinical Decision Support Systems (CDSS) are relatively common in facilities and provider offices. Many of these systems are designed to improve (1) patient safety, (2) quality of care, and (3) efficiency of delivery.[7,8] These expert systems are extremely helpful in clinical settings because they provide *actionable information.* That is, the information derived from these systems is directly applicable to improving the treatment of specific patients. If expert systems are successfully implemented at a provider/facility level, then it is reasonable to expect that expert systems can also be implemented at a health plan/managed care level.

Actionable Information: A Conceptual Framework

We propose developing a care management expert system that combines information from three healthcare cost and utilization domains.

- Current and Predicted Healthcare Costs
- Utilization Impact
- Member Engagement

Using current and predicted healthcare costs, it is possible to identify those health plan members who are currently highest cost and will remain high cost in the absence of healthcare interventions. Because it is known that current high cost does not necessarily predict future high cost,[9] predictive modeling is necessary to determine those individuals with the highest probability of either remaining or becoming high-cost health plan members. Without these analytic methods, it would not be possible to direct care management interventions to the right risk groups to significantly influence the overall cost burden of these health plan members. To simplify the challenge, it is helpful to visualize the relationship between current and future healthcare costs using a resource allocation matrix.[10]

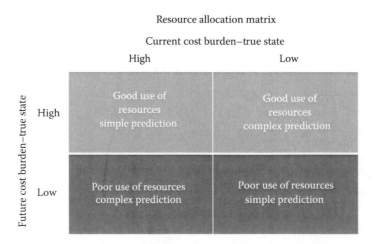

Resource allocation matrix

As shown in the diagram above, the relationship between current and future cost burden is an important factor in determining where to allocate resources. Simple predictions (i.e., those that do not require involved predictive modeling techniques) allow for the classification of members into either "good use" or "poor use." Likewise, complex predictions (i.e., those that require involved predictive modeling techniques) do the same. It is, obviously, more difficult to determine those low-cost members who will become high cost as well as those high-cost members who will become low cost. By identifying those future high-cost members, the correct resources can be allocated to the appropriate interventions needed to help control healthcare costs. As the challenge of this care management strategy is to control future healthcare costs, the first step in creating actionable information is to classify the member population into these three groups.

Knowledge Discovery through Multivariate Analytics

Simple database queries can be utilized to search vast data sources to identify current high-cost patients in a patient population (e.g., those incurring extensive health treatments, as mentioned in *The New Yorker*). This information can be beneficial because resources can be applied to those particular cases to address those factors contributing to continued poor health maintenance. One limitation of this approach, however, is that it requires individuals to become high service utilizers or high cost before resources can be applied to alleviate or mitigate the problem. In other words, the limitation of this more hind-sight or reactive analytic method is that the focus is placed on what has already happened, where little knowledge is generated as to why individuals become high cost.

More effective cost reduction and health enhancement policies can be achieved through proactive analytics that identify likely future "poor health" or high-cost candidates.[11] Advanced analytical methods applied to robust data resources enable decision makers to identify individuals at risk of requiring extensive health treatments or high-cost candidates. Methodologies such as logistic regression help identify noteworthy patterns existing in corresponding data. These patterns can include variables involving patient demographic and behavioral information, symptomatic and diagnostic data, and treatment-related data, to name a few. The resulting models not only identify the segments of a patient population that are likely high-cost candidates but also provide the possible factors that lead patients to be high cost—or the "why" behind the high-cost results.

Advanced analytic methods that incorporate a multivariate approach and the utilization of mathematical and algorithmic processing of data in conjunction with statistical testing techniques are often referred to as "knowledge discovery techniques." The "knowledge" refers to the identification of patterns or relationships between variables in a particular data set that explain "why" things happen, not simply "what" has happened. Perhaps the most important information to extract from data with regard to the complexity of individuals' health status include patterns in dietary behavior, physical attributes, treatment and medication practices, and so forth that can provide insights as to what combination of behavioral and descriptive variables lead to a less healthy, higher cost individual. This information is truly actionable as it empowers healthcare providers to more accurately apply available resources to mitigate costs and maintain a healthier population by implementing preemptive or proactive treatment for high-risk candidates, thus mitigating costs before they incur. The result is not only reduced cost for providers but also a healthier population.

The next step in the conceptual model involves determining the opportunity to impact a member's healthcare utilization level. This step is multifaceted and requires the integration of both a member's health status as well as his or her use of healthcare services. Health status refers to the current standing of an individual's clinical, physical, and mental health.[12] Health status is commonly determined through general health assessments (GHAs), health risk assessments (HRAs), clinical severity estimators (e.g., Adjusted Clinical Groups [ACGs]), as well as other sources of member-specific healthcare information (e.g., provider records, treatment notes, etc.). This type of information allows care managers to better understand if they can impact these members' utilization behaviors, given their current health statuses. If a member suffers from a disease or condition that cannot be impacted by care management interventions, then decisions must be made as to the level and type of services and support he or she receives.

Similarly, a member's utilization history must be analyzed to determine the opportunity to modify his or her behavior. For example, it has been well documented that care management interventions can influence health plan members' emergency department and hospital admission rates.[13] With the current market focus on emergency department diversion (EDD), readmission rates, and prescription drug rates, it is becoming increasingly important to integrate these sources of information. The development of enterprise data warehouses (EDW) at health plans is a direct result of the need to collect and use these data sources to track their members' utilization behaviors. As described earlier from the "hot spots" article, when a health plan member has 324 admissions in a five-year period, one has to ask if this level of utilization was necessary. Consequently, the second step of this process involves an assessment of health status and utilization history, which further filters the membership population by taking those members who are predicted to be future high cost and identifying those who can be impacted by care management interventions.

Understanding and measuring member engagement is the final step in this conceptual model. Engagement can mean many different things, but in this context it refers to a member's willingness to transmit, receive, and act on customized communications. Engagement is emotional in nature; it often describes one's connection with healthcare providers and predicts how actively a member participates in the management of his or her own healthcare.[14] In other words, engagement involves a member's management of his or her own healthcare services to meet his or her healthcare needs. When members are engaged, they are actively involved and focused on their healthcare behaviors, resulting in better choices, better provider communications, and, ultimately, better outcomes.[15]

Patient adherence to treatment regimens is a good example of why engagement is important in this conceptual model. For example, glycemic control is essential for individuals suffering from either type 1 or type 2 diabetes. This condition requires a high level of self-management; in other words, highly engaged individuals with diabetes have much better outcomes that those who are not engaged. Engaged individuals will most likely adhere to the treatments prescribed by their providers.[16,17] Therefore, when members are defined by their future high cost, impact of care management interventions, and engagement in healthcare, the resulting actionable information increases the opportunity provide *the right members, the right services, at the right time* (see following figure for a description of the process).

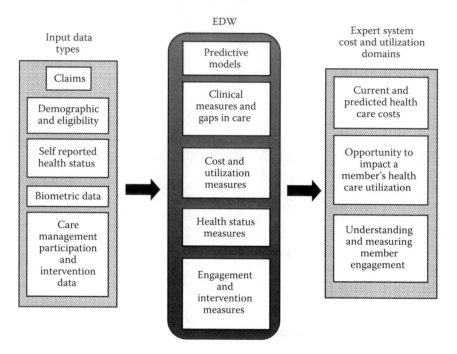

Conclusions

There is no mistaking that population-based care management programs are difficult to develop, implement, and manage. The following are a few of the more pervasive issues.

- Healthcare data sources are seldom standardized, often full of errors, and difficult to aggregate.
- Privacy and security regulations add additional complexity to data management efforts.
- Administrative claims data are collected on multiple systems and have varying file formats and record layouts.
- Health plan membership constantly changes, with members entering and exiting the program based on employment and eligibility status.
- Provider enrollment is extremely variable based on the provider's participation status, physical location, and professional specialty.

- The prevalence of chronic conditions continues to rise at an alarming rate.
- Treatment and drug regimens continually evolve as well as practice guidelines, evidence-based medicine, and medical technology.
- Healthcare reform brings new concepts such as Health Homes, Accountable Care Organizations, and Health Insurance Exchanges.

The preceding list only scratches the surface. However, as one contemplates current healthcare delivery challenges, a common theme surfaces. All of these issues have a singular dependency—*actionable information.*

The following figure represents a very elementary formulation of the conceptual framework proposed in this chapter. The input to this model (Multiple Data Sources) continues to be an important topic by itself. Data management, data aggregation, and data warehousing of the multitude of disparate healthcare data sources must occur before any other activity can take place. The scope and magnitude of this effort cannot be overemphasized. To manage health plan members effectively at a population level, administrative claims data sources (e.g., medical claims, pharmacy claims, durable medical equipment and supply claims, laboratory claims, behavioral health claims, dental claims, home health claims, skilled nursing and nursing home claims, etc.), health and risk assessment data sources (e.g., general health assessments, health risk assessments, disease specific surveys, etc.), risk and grouping data sources (e.g., Episode Treatment Groups®, Diagnosis-Related Groups, adjusted clinical groups, etc.), as well as many other healthcare data sources must be combined in an understandable, functional way. Health plans and business intelligence vendors are working on this challenge, with varying degrees of success as they work toward building enterprise data warehouses (EDWs). This is the healthcare industry's biggest challenge because without clean, robust data, it is not possible to implement data-driven care management programs, not to mention all of the new processes and programs created by the Affordable Care Act (ACA).

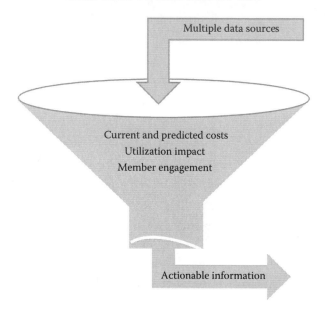

Once data are entered into the system, the process of identifying the best candidates for care management programs begins. Following the proposed framework, each of the three categories acts as a population filter. Once the target population is identified (e.g., members with asthma), current and predicted cost burden is calculated for each individual member. The result of this analysis is a ranking of all members with asthma (continuing with this example) from highest to lowest predicted cost. The next step involves assessing the estimated utilization impact of the care management program's interventions on these members with asthma. Those members who are determined to be most "impacted" by the care management program are ranked higher than those who are not. These two sources of information (predicted cost burden and utilization impact) are then combined to produce a new risk ranking; this ranking takes into account those members with the highest predicted cost burden who also have the highest probability of utilization impact by the care management program.

Combining these two sources of information gives care managers the ability to identify not only those members with the highest predicted costs but also those members they will have the best opportunity to impact. Consequently, a member with high predicted cost with low utilization impact would be ranked lower than a member with a moderately high predicted cost with a high utilization impact. Using this methodology, the entire population of members with asthma can be ranked from highest to lowest risk based on predicted costs and utilization impact. As described previously, this actionable information allows care managers to make appropriate resource allocation decisions. Because it would be a poor use of resources to concentrate efforts on high-cost members with low to no probability of utilization impact, this information would be very valuable for program management.

Nevertheless, this proposed framework has one final filter: member engagement. Once the member population is identified and risk ranked by predicted cost and utilization impact, member engagement is assessed. It does not matter how high someone's financial risk might be or how impacted he or she could be by care management interventions if the member is not engaged in the process. If a member is not emotionally invested in the program, there is little chance that he or she will benefit from the care management interventions. Without engagement, care management does not work. Consequently, at a population level, using engagement as the last filter will further refine the information derived from the model, thereby increasing the chances that care managers are expending efforts on those members who will be high future cost, have high utilization impact opportunities, and are engaged in the care management process. This framework, comprising three information filters, will identify those members who, if left unattended, will present the highest cost and utilization risk and are able to engage successfully in the program. This information is essential at a population management level because only limited care management resources are available and correct resource allocation is paramount to program success.

Clearly, population management programs rely on data-driven methods to target populations, identify high-risk members, allocate limited resources, and assess program outcomes. To increase quality of care while decreasing healthcare costs, care management programs must focus their efforts on intervening with the right members, with the right services, at the right time. Once data are transformed into actionable information, program successes are possible, resulting in positive care management utilization and financial outcomes. Possessing data is not enough—actionable information must be created and used by health plans to meet current and future challenges.

The conceptual model proposed in this chapter is one example of how the thoughtful consolidation of information can assist in the correct allocation of resources in a population-based care management program.

To be effective, a data-driven, procedural approach must be taken, which allows for the coordination and collaboration of all constituents in the healthcare delivery process.

Acknowledgment

This chapter was first published by the International Institute of Analytics, *Using Advanced Analytics To Take Action For Health Plan Members' Health*, January 2012.

References

1. Gawande A. 2011. The hot spotters: Can we lower medical costs by giving the neediest patients better care? *The New Yorker* January 24.
2. Stanton M, Rutherford M. 2005. The high concentration of U.S. health care expenditures. *Research in action*, Issue 19. AHRQ Pub. No. 06-0060. Rockville, MD: Agency for Healthcare Research and Quality.
3. *Revisiting Medicaid reform: A project of The Center for Community Solutions and the Center for Health Outcomes, Policy, and Evaluation Studies (HOPES) of Ohio State University.* 2009. A status report on recommendations from the Ohio Commission to Reform Medicaid four years later: January 2005–January 2009.
4. Cousins M, Shickle L, Bander J. 2002. An introduction to predictive modeling for disease management risk stratification. *Dis Manage* 5:157–67.
5. Perry T, Tucker T, Hudson L, Gandy W, Neftzger A, and Hamar G. 2004. The application of data mining techniques in health plan population management. *IT solutions series: Managing data mining.* Hershey, PA: Idea Group Publishing.
6. Perry T, Kudyba S, Lawrence K. 2007. Identification and prediction of chronic conditions for health plan members using data mining techniques. In *Data mining methods and applications* (pp. 175–82). New York: Taylor & Francis.
7. Coiera E. 2003. *The guide to health informatics*, 2nd ed. London: Arnold.
8. Raghupathi W. 2007. Designing clinical decision support systems in health care: A systematic approach. *IJHISI* 2(1):44–53.
9. Ridinger M, Rice J. 2000. Predictive modeling points way to future risk status. *Health Manage Technol* 21:10–12.

10. Donaldson C, Currier G, Mitton C. 2002. Cost effectiveness analysis in health care: Contraindications. *BMJ* 325:891.
11. Kudyba S, Hamar B, Gandy W. 2005. Enhancing efficiency in the health care industry. *Commun ACM*, pp. 107–10, December.
12. Kudyba S, Perry T, Rice J. 2008. Informatics application challenges for managed care organizations: The three faces of population segmentation and a proposed classification system. *IJHISI* 3(2):21–31.
13. Brandon W. 2011. Reducing emergency department visits among high-using patients. *J Fam Pract* FindArticles.com. November 15, 2011.
14. Arnold S. 2007. Improving quality health care: The role of consumer engagement. *Robert Wood Johnson Foundation Issue Brief* October 2007.
15. Protheroe J, Roger A, Kennedy A, MacDonald W, Lee V. 2008. Promoting patient engagement with self-management support information: A qualitative meta-synthesis of processes influencing uptake. *Implement Sci* 3:44.
16. Delamater A. 2006. Improving patient adherence. *Clin Diabet* 24(2):71–77.
17. Milano C. 2011. Can self-management programs ease chronic conditions? *Managed Care*, pp. 28–31, January.

14

AN INTRODUCTION TO DATA AND TEXT MINING IN HEALTHCARE

A Focus on Building Alerting Systems for Decision Support

BILLIE ANDERSON, CALI M. DAVIS, AND J. MICHAEL HARDIN

Contents

Introduction to Healthcare Alerting Systems

Alerting systems for healthcare have been in existence since the 1950s in the United States and focused initially on the development of diagnostic systems.[1] One of the earliest examples of a successfully implemented healthcare alerting system was in an emergency department in the United Kingdom between 1969 and 1974 that diagnosed the cause of a patient's abdominal pain.[2]

More recently, researchers have used advances in data mining to enhance healthcare alerting systems. Perhaps the most notable recent development in data mining alerting systems is the Washington-based company Veratect, which used data mining techniques to predict the swine flu 18 days before the World Health Organization (WHO). Eighteen days before WHO issued the alert about the possible swine flu pandemic, Veratect reported a strange outbreak of respiratory disease in La Gloria, Mexico, noting that local residents thought the flu outbreak was related to contamination from pig breeding from nearby farms. Veratect uses a mining technique to automatically search tens of thousands of websites daily for early signs of medical problems. When items of interest are found, the results are turned over to analysts who post the results on the company's website.[3]

Data mining alerting systems are algorithms that require training a set of solutions to a problem and can make decisions on new problems with incomplete facts. They are commonly used in biomedical pattern recognition. These types of alerting systems are the main focus of this chapter. The three main algorithms that are emphasized are logistic regression, decision trees, and artificial neural networks (ANNs). Before these algorithms are described, an overview of data mining for healthcare alerting systems is presented.

An Overview of Data Mining for Healthcare Alerting Systems

Over the last decade there has been widespread use of medical information systems and an explosive growth of medical databases. These stockpiles of data mainly contain patient data. But the data's hidden value, the power to predict certain trends, has largely gone untapped. Unless the data are used properly, it is a waste of resources to collect and store them. The data gathered in medical databases require specialized tools for storing and accessing data, data analysis, and effective use of the data. In particular, the increase in data causes great difficulties in extracting useful information for decision support.

To counter the difficulty of trying to analyze large amounts of data, the medical community has turned to data mining techniques. Data mining is the analysis of data sets to find unsuspected relationships and to summarize the data in novel ways that are both understandable and useful to the data owner.[4] Data mining, in general, can help extract regularities hidden in the data and formulate knowledge in the form of patterns and rules.

Published reviews of using data mining alerting systems in the healthcare industry have concluded that the most promising systems are for drug dosing and preventive care.[5,6] These studies serve to alert against adverse effects from prescription drugs, or to promote greater compliance with practice guidelines in health maintenance activities such as vaccinations and mammography. One review paper noted that computer-aided evaluation of mammograms already helps to cut the number of missed lesions by half without increasing the false-positive rate.[7]

Data mining has been used to automatically identify new, unexpected, and potentially interesting patterns in hospital infection control at the University of Alabama Hospital.[8] A decision support system was implemented that used association rules to represent outcomes and monitor changes in the incidence of those outcomes over time. The hospital was able to demonstrate that the data mining decision support system developed proved to be effective and efficient in identifying potentially interesting and previously unknown patterns.

Specific data mining algorithms such as decision trees and logistic regression have been used in many published studies to develop alerting systems in healthcare. In particular, readmissions to hospitals prove very costly, and are usually a sign of patients not understanding how to appropriately obtain the necessary follow-up care after leaving the hospital. Traditionally, decision trees and logistic regression have been used as the primary decision support tools, primarily because of time constraints.[9] A recent study compared logistic regression to decision tree models, along with other complex models, to determine which was more effective in terms of predicting hospital readmissions within 45 days of discharge.[10] The researchers specifically examined patients suffering from pulmonary-type diseases and asthma. The results of the study found that the logistic regression and decision trees predicted a comparable accuracy rate of hospital readmission as compared to the more complex statistical models. Given that the models have produced excellent predictive accuracies, this could be a valuable decision support tool for healthcare managers and policymakers for informed decision making in the management of diseases, which ultimately contributes to improved measures for hospital performance management.

Delen et al. reported a research study in which they developed several prediction models for breast cancer.[11] Specifically, they used three popular data mining methods: decision trees, ANNs, and logistic regression. They acquired a large database of breast cancer patient information: 433,272 patients with 72 predictor variables. The purpose of the models was to predict survival five years from the date of diagnosis. The results of the study indicated that the decision tree performed the best among the three models examined. The decision tree helped identify certain important predictor variables that clinicians could look for when examining new patients.

Medical researchers have begun to examine the methodology of particular data mining algorithms such as ANNs to develop alerting systems. Shukla et al. provide a comprehensive literature review detailing how ANNs are being used in the medical community as alerting systems.[12] The published literature suggests that ANN models have been shown to be valuable tools in reducing the workload on clinicians by detecting patterns and providing decision support.[13,14]

Big Data in Healthcare Today

An overview of data mining in healthcare would not be complete without a discussion of big data. The impact of big data on data analytics in the healthcare field is enormous, with the potential to improve patient outcomes, save lives, change healthcare policy, reduce costs, and more efficiently manage resources. Bates et al. give several examples of using big data to showcase how the resource is providing opportunity to change the healthcare landscape, ranging from treatment optimization to reducing the number or readmissions to hospitals.[9]

One example concerns chronic conditions that encompass multiple organ systems; these are among the costliest conditions to treat.[9] The authors illustrate the use of clinical data analytics that allow the organ path of the disease to be detected. Being able to detect which organ the disease will attack next allows the healthcare workers to target the organ proactively with specific treatments. Tailoring a treatment to a specific patient has the ability to save patient lives and enhance treatment regimens for patients.

At the core of big data analytics is the healthcare organization's ability to analyze a wide range of big data. From within and outside its four walls, the organization can determine what is happening in real time with regard to patients. For example, a recent study reported that healthcare providers were using smartphones to allow patients in rural areas to take pictures of their eyes, send those images to the healthcare provider, employ an ANN to detect retinal disease within a matter of minutes, and provide the patient with a real-time diagnosis, thus allowing the patient to receive any follow-up care in a more efficient manner. The system provided an 87% accuracy diagnosis and is currently being tested to detect skin cancer.[15]

As the healthcare industry faces a rapidly changing data environment, it is vital that healthcare organizations become data driven. They must treat data as a strategic asset and put processes and systems in place that allow them to access and analyze data in many different formats and forms, to inform decision-making processes and drive actionable results. The case study in the next section illustrates how data can be used to support clinical decision making.

Case Study of Decision Support Systems

The objective of this case study is to use SAS® Enterprise Miner™ 6.1 to build a decision tree, logistic regression, and ANN to predict five-year survival of colorectal cancer (CRC) patients. First, a description of the data set is given. Then, the three data mining models used are summarized. Finally, we show how to use SAS Enterprise Miner 6.1 to build a valid analytical process flow for these data mining methods. In the demonstration, it is assumed that the user knows how to import data into Enterprise Miner and produce an analytical workflow. The results of the modeling nodes will not be shown or discussed. The purpose of this demonstration is to collect the appropriate diagnostic statistics from Enterprise Miner and do a comparison to see which predictive model performs the best.

Description of Data

The target variable for the predictive models is a binary variable indicating survival (or death) five years postsurgery for patients with CRC.

The input variables used to build the predictive models consisted of age, race, and different types of variables that described tumor state, tumor differentiation, and the location of the tumor. Two CRC biomarker variables were also available. There were 500 observations and 107 input variables.

Using all the described variables, a logistic regression, decision tree, and ANN will be built using SAS Enterprise Miner 6.1. The following is a brief description of each model type.

Data Mining Models

Logistic Regression   A logistic regression model was built to model the probability of survival (or not) five years postsurgery for CRC. Logistic regression is used to model data when the target variable is binary (e.g., survive—yes/no; recurrence—yes/no). The probability of an outcome is related to a set of predictor variables by an equation of the form

$$\log[p/(1-p)] = \beta_0 + \beta_2 X_1 + \ldots + \beta_k X_k$$

where p is the probability of survival five years postsurgery for CRC, β_0 is an intercept term, $\beta_1, \ldots, \beta_k$ are the coefficients associated with each variable, $X_1, \ldots, X_k$ are the values of the predictor variables, and k is a unique subscript denoting each variable. The standard assumption is that the predictor variables are related in a linear fashion to the log odds $\{\log[p/(1-p)]\}$ of the outcome of interest.

Decision Trees   The type of decision tree used in this analysis was a classification and regression tree (CART).[16] The settings in SAS Enterprise Miner can be adjusted to create such a tree. CART is an algorithm that is used to split the data into smaller segments called nodes that are homogeneous with respect to the outcome variable. At each node the algorithm examines all values of the predictor variables with respect to determining the best predictor variable and a value of that predictor variable that will best separate the data into more homogeneous subgroups with respect to the outcome variable. In other words, each node is a classification question, and the branches of the tree are partitions of the data set into different classes (those patients who will survive/not survive five years postsurgery). This process repeats itself in a recursive, iterative manner until no further separation of the data is feasible. Therefore, the terminal nodes at the end of the branches of the decision tree represent the different classes.

The second part of the algorithm is known as *pruning*. Pruning is applied to the decision tree to ensure that the algorithm does not overfit the training data. At each subsequent node, smaller amounts of observations are available. Toward the end of the splitting algorithm, idiosyncrasies of the training observations at a particular node can display a pattern that is specific only to those observations that can become meaningless and detrimental for prediction when applied to larger populations. Pruning removes smaller branches that failed to generalize using the validation data set.

Artificial Neural Networks   The original development of the neural network was inspired by the way the brain recognizes patterns.[17] The goal of an ANN is the same as in logistic regression, predicting an outcome based on the values of predictor variables; however, the approach used in developing the neural network model is quite different from that for logistic regression.

ANNs have the ability to "learn" mathematical relationships between a series of input (predictor) variables and the corresponding output (outcome) variables. This is achieved by "training" the network with a training data set that consists of the predictor variables and a known outcome variable. Once the ANN has been trained, the model can be used for classification on a validation data set.

Figure 14.1 illustrates an ANN that has been trained to predict the probability of a patient dying of CRC five years postsurgery based on only two predictor variables: age and race. ANNs are often represented in diagrams such as the one in Figure 14.1. The circles in the diagram are known as *nodes*. A typical neural network consists of three layers of nodes: input, hidden, and output nodes. The values of the predictor variables reside in the input node. The output node contains the predicted output of the network. The hidden nodes in the diagram contain a function known as the *activation function* that allows the network to model complex nonlinear associations between the predictor variables and the outcome.

Each input node is connected to each hidden node, and each hidden node is connected to the output node. In this example, there are

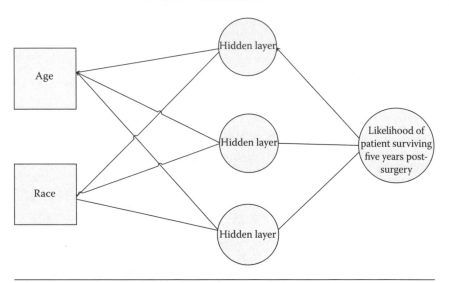

Figure 14.1 Diagram of neural network trained to predict the probability of a CRC patient's survival five years postsurgery on the basis of age (X_1) and race (X_2).

two input nodes where the values of age (X_1) and race (X_2) are input into the network along with a bias weight, which is the equivalent to an intercept term found in a regression model.

The input nodes are connected to the hidden nodes by a *connection weight* (the connection weights are the lines in Figure 14.1 connecting the input and hidden nodes). The connection weights can be thought of as the neural network equivalent of the β coefficients in a logistic regression model. At each hidden node the connection weights are passed to an activation function, most commonly the sigmoid function. The activation function uses the connection weights to model any nonlinear relationship among the predictor variables and the outcome variable. Another set of connection weights is then passed from the hidden node to the output node to obtain the output of the network. This output of the network corresponds to the predicted probability of the outcome variable.

In the ANN analysis performed there were as many input nodes as predictor variables: three hidden nodes (the default setting in SAS Enterprise Miner) and one output node (probability of survival five years postsurgery for patients with CRC).

Each box represents an input node in which the predictor variables are input into the network. Each line represents a connection weight. Each circle in the middle of the diagram represents the hidden layers where the relationship between the predictor variables and the outcome is modeled. The last circle at the end of the diagram is where the probability of survival is output from the network.

Assessment of Data Mining Models

Kolmogorov–Smirnov Statistic   The Kolmogorov–Smirnov (KS) statistic was used as the measure to evaluate model performance. The KS statistic measures the difference between two distributions, where the actual KS statistic is the maximum difference between two different distributions. In this case, the two distributions of interest are the estimated probabilities of belonging to the survival or nonsurvival groups produced by the models. If the two distributions are the same, this implies the model did not effectively separate between survivors and nonsurvivors (implying a small KS statistic). On the other hand, significantly different distributions suggest good separation between the two groups (implying a larger KS statistic). The KS statistic has a known theoretical probability distribution, so a p-value was computed to determine if the two distributions are significantly different.

The predictive models were built on the training data set, and the validation data set was used to obtain the KS statistics and the corresponding p-value.

Area under the Receiver Operating Characteristic Curve   Another common predictive model diagnostic is the area under the receiver operating characteristic curve (AUC). For every given probability cutoff, the confusion matrix in Table 14.1 is computed.

The receiver operating characteristic (ROC) curve is a plot of the false positive rate (x-axis) and true positive rate (y-axis) for every single probability cutoff. The ROC curve gives an indication of how well the models are separating between those patients who died and

Table 14.1   Example of a Confusion Matrix

	TRUTH	
PREDICTED	GOOD	BAD
Good	True positive	False positive
Bad	False negative	True negative

those who survived. A good predictive model will go up fairly steep and then start to level off. There is a 45° diagonal reference line on the ROC plot, as shown in Figure 14.2. The diagonal line represents where the false-positive and true positive rates are the same. If the ROC curve falls below this diagonal line, the model is no better than randomly assigning patients as dead or alive five years postsurgery. A model that has an ROC curve above this line is considered to be a good predictive model. Hence, the higher the AUC value, the better is the predictive model.

ROC curves have been shown to be valuable tests in evaluating the detection of certain types of cancer.[18] With the appropriate use of ROC curves, investigators of cancer detection tests can improve their research. In many cases, ROC curves help the medical community focus on classification rules with low false-positive rates, which are most important for the detection of cancer. However, these ROC curves should always be put in perspective, because a good classification rule for the detection of cancer does not guarantee that cancer screening will reduce cancer mortality.

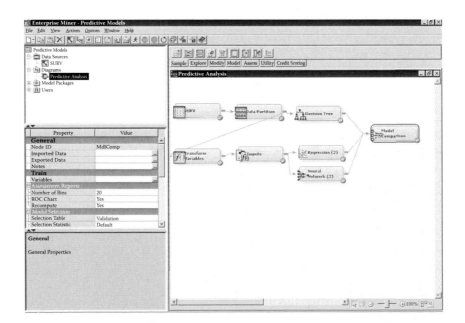

Figure 14.2   ROC plots for the three predictive models.

Three Data Mining Models for Colorectal Cancer

Figure 14.3 displays the analytical process flow used in SAS Enterprise Miner 6.1.

Once the data are brought into Enterprise Miner, the first issue that needs to be addressed is splitting the modeling data set into training and validation data sets.

A critical step in prediction is choosing among competing models. Given a set of training data, you can easily generate models that very accurately predict a target value from a set of input predictor variables. Unfortunately, these predictions might be accurate only for the training data themselves. Attempts to generalize the predictions from the training data to an independent but similarly distributed sample can result in substantial reductions in accuracy.

To avoid this pitfall, SAS Enterprise Miner is designed to use a validation data set as a means of independently gauging model performance. Typically, the validation data set is created by partitioning the raw analysis data. Observations selected for training are used to build

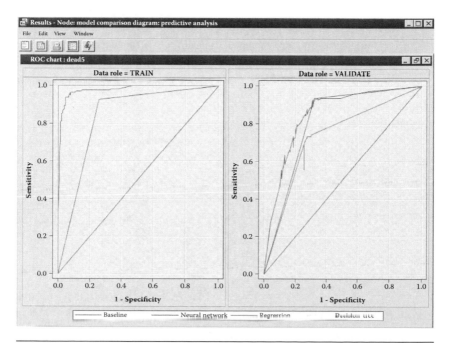

Figure 14.3   Analysis flow for the three predictive models in SAS® Enterprise Miner™ 6.1.

the model, and observations selected for validation are used to tune and compare models. For this modeling exercise 60% of the data were allocated to the training data set and 40% to the validation data set.

The first analysis built was the decision tree. Decision tree models are advantageous because they are conceptually easy to understand, yet they readily accommodate nonlinear associations between input variables and one or more target variables. They also handle missing values without the need for imputation. CART was the specific decision tree used in this study. Enterprise Miner help files discuss how to set up the decision tree node as a CART.

The next node used in the analysis was the transform node. Sometimes, input data are more informative on a scale other than that on which they were originally collected. For example, variable transformations can be used to stabilize variance, remove nonlinearity, improve additivity, and counter nonnormality. Therefore, for many models, transformations of the input data (either dependent or independent variables) can lead to a better model fit. These transformations can be functions of either a single variable or of more than one variable. For this analysis, many of the input variables were highly skewed. Several different transformations were examined. The best transformation, in terms of making the input variables more symmetric, was the log.

After the transform node was used, the imputation node was used for the logistic and ANN models. In SAS Enterprise Miner, however, models such as regressions and neural networks ignore observations altogether that contain missing values, which reduces the size of the training data set. Less training data can substantially weaken the predictive power of these models. To overcome this obstacle of missing data, imputation of the missing values can be performed before the models are fit. For this analysis, the imputation technique chosen was the mean.

After the models are run, the model comparison node allows the user to obtain diagnostic statistics such as KS and AUC.

Figure 14.3 displays the ROC curves for each of the three models. Based on the AUC values in Table 14.2, the ANN is outperforming the other two models. In terms of which model is best at separating those patients who will and will not die five years postsurgery, the ANN is also superior based on the KS statistics displayed in Table 14.3. Also note the p-value reported for each of the KS statistics; all indicate that there is a significant difference between the distribution of the survival

Table 14.2   AUC for ANN, CART, and Logistic Regression Models

MODEL	AUC
ANN	0.85
CART	0.80
Logistic regression	0.73

Table 14.3   KS Statistic for ANN, CART, and Logistic Regression Models

MODEL	KS (*P*-VALUE)
ANN	1.42 (<0.0001)
CART	0.98 (<0.0001)
Logistic regression	0.72 (<0.0001)

and nonsurvival populations. This result indicates that all the models are doing a good job of separating these two populations. Overall, the ANN is the champion model for this particular data set.

Text Mining Healthcare Alerting Examples

Text mining is a data mining methodology intended to extract meaningful information from unstructured textual data. Text and data mining have much in common; underlying each is the assumption that knowledge lies buried in a large mass of data. Data mining primarily relies on statistical methods to uncover trends in structured data, whereas text-mining techniques seek to make sense of information that is unstructured, such as a doctor's notes on a patient's chart or discharge record. Other forms of unstructured data include text files, HTML files, chat messages, emails, images, or handwritten notes. One recent study reported that an estimated 80% of a healthcare organization's information is contained in an unstructured textual format.[19] Text mining converts the unstructured data into a structured resource that can be used for analysis purposes.

In many cases, unstructured text remains the best option for healthcare providers to capture the depth of detail required, for example, in a clinical setting, or to preserve productivity by incorporating dicta-tion and transcription into the workflow. Unstructured text records contain valuable narratives about a patient's health and the reasoning behind healthcare decisions.

Several recently published studies illustrate the use of text mining in the healthcare field to alert healthcare professionals to potential epidemics, hospital readmissions, and drug safety. Some examples are given in the text that follows.

Data gathered from social media websites such as Facebook or Twitter fit into the "V" for Volume of the big data definition. Although data from Facebook or Twitter posts are unstructured, they contain a wealth of information useful in alerting healthcare professionals to potential health epidemics. One recent study described how to uti-lize Twitter post data to effectively track an epidemic in real time.[20] The authors discuss how Twitter posts from October 1, 2009 through May 20, 2010 were searched using text mining techniques; the fre-quency of words such as *h1n1*, *flu*, *swine*, and *influenza* was counted. The information derived from the frequency of the words was incor-porated into a predictive model that assisted the researchers in pre-dicting on a weekly basis whether an influenza epidemic was present or not in the United States.[20]

It is well known that billions of dollars are spent annually in the United States when patients return to the hospital because of a lack of appropriate follow-up care.[21] A hospital readmission is defined as an admission to a hospital or a healthcare setting within a certain time frame, following an original hospital stay. A readmission can occur at either the same hospital or a different hospital, and may involve planned or unplanned surgical or medical treatments. One recent change to the U.S. Healthcare Affordable Care Act is that healthcare providers will be subject to a financial penalty if their readmission rates are too high. Many providers are looking to healthcare text ana-lytics to help address this challenge.

One way would be to analyze a hospital's discharge instructions. Discharge planning is the development of an individualized dis-charge plan for the patient before he or she leaves the hospital, to ensure that patients are discharged at an appropriate time and with provision of adequate postdischarge services. The discharge planning process seeks to determine the appropriate level of services required by the patient, and then matches the patient to an appropriate site of care.

Five investigators from the Mayo Clinic presented a unique research project that used automated text mining to determine whether a hospital discharge summary contained a follow-up clinic appointment.[21] A dataset consisting of discharge records was manually reviewed to determine whether the records contained follow-up appointment instructions. The same dataset was evaluated for the same criteria using SAS Text Miner software. The two assessments were compared to determine the accuracy of text mining.

Of the 6,481 discharge records reviewed, 3,576 (55.2%) were identified as containing all criteria for follow-up appointment instructions through manual review, 113 (3.2%) of which were missed through text mining. Text mining incorrectly identified 107 (3.7%) follow-up appointments that were not considered valid through manual review. Therefore, the text mining analysis concurred with the manual review in 96.6% of the appointment findings.

The Mayo Clinic researchers concluded that text mining of medical records can accurately detect whether elements of follow-up appointment instructions are documented in hospital discharge notes. The results also suggest that text mining software can be used to identify specific appointment criteria in a large number of textual medical records, thus saving considerable resources required for manual evaluation in quality-related research and performance assessment.

The results of this research project provide a platform for the Mayo Clinic to automatically track its clinic appointment follow-up after hospitalization, develop new strategies for improvement, and reduce its hospital readmission rate.

Today, most automated electronic medical records contain a substantial amount of information that is stored as text. Data mining provides a powerful tool to now use this data for operations improvements; in particular, it may be used to ensure drug safety.

Adverse drug events result in more than 100,000 deaths per year and are the fourth leading cause of death, ranking ahead of pulmonary disease, diabetes, AIDS, pneumonia, accidents, and automobile deaths.[22] When a new drug is brought to market, it is tested for adverse reactions. However, given the infinite number of ways that drugs can interact, it is not practical to test every possible drug interaction. Iyer et al. reported on how text mining has been used to alert healthcare professionals to patient drug safety. The study[23] analyzed more than 50 million clinician notes that are part of the electronic health record (EHR) using text mining techniques as well as the structured component of the EHR. The study included 1,165 drugs and 14 adverse events. The researchers developed a predictive model, using both structured and unstructured data, to determine if a patient was likely to have an adverse reaction. This information would assist the clinical decision support team by allowing the healthcare workers to intervene in the patient's care if an adverse drug affect was predicted. The study demonstrated that by incorporating unstructured data, patient care can be improved and lives saved by implementing this type of warning system.

Conclusion

In conclusion, this chapter demonstrates the usefulness of data and text mining analytic methods in the healthcare industry. When considering CRC, predictive models and their ability to separate between survival and nonsurvival for CRC patients five years postsurgery is a promising approach for developing a diagnostic evaluation. This initial case study reveals the strong potential for data mining methods for CRC. Particularly, this study has shown the promise of using ANNs for decision support among researchers and clinicians in the CRC community.

In this case study, the ANN outperformed the more well-known and understood models, such as the decision tree and logistic regression. In particular, ANNs have been shown to be very powerful and superior over decision trees and logistic regression in predicting a clinical outcome in patients with CRC.[24–26]

As described in the preceding text, a series of recent reports in the literature have shown that data mining techniques such as ANN provide higher predictive accuracy than familiar, traditional models such as logistic regression.[27–30] ANNs and other data mining tools are often called "black box" techniques because the logic used to determine the final model is not transparent. This lack of transparency is the greatest disadvantage that medical researchers find when they use ANNs for decision support. Yet, for this one disadvantage, there are many advantages for the medical community to use ANNs for clinical decision support. Claimed advantages of ANNs include:

1. Ease of optimization with the advancement of easy-to-use software such as SAS Enterprise Miner
2. Accuracy for predictive inference, with potential support for clinical decision making

As shown in this chapter, data mining models, especially ANNs, can be developed that accurately predict the outcome of a medical condition. These predictive models can be valuable tools in medicine. They can be used to assist in determining successful treatments, prognosis, or interventions. However, there are areas of concern in the development of ANNs as data mining models for use as alerting systems in the medical community. The U.S. Food and Drug Administration (FDA) has issued a guidance document for software for medical support. The document has a section on using ANNs. Some of the points highlighted by this document are that ANNs can behave in a nondeterministic way. The medical researchers must be able to justify and explain the choices made for the ANN model and the topology. The researchers must also be able to describe how overfitting is avoided (e.g., using training and validation data sets). The document specifies additional data sets to be processed through the ANN to ensure that performance remains as expected.

Although data mining can provide useful information and support to the medical community by identifying patterns that may not be readily apparent, there are limitations to what data mining can do. Not all patterns found are interesting. For a pattern to be interesting, it should be logical and actionable. Data mining requires human intervention to exploit the extracted knowledge. For example, data mining can provide assistance in making the diagnosis or prescribing the treatment, but it still cannot replace the physician's intuition and interpretive skills.[6]

Data and text mining methods used as alerting systems in healthcare are capable of identifying patterns and discovering relationships in large medical databases, but without cooperation and feedback from the medical community, the results are useless. The patterns found via data mining methods should be evaluated by medical professionals with many years of experience in the problem domain to decide whether the patterns are logical, actionable, and novel enough to be directed in new clinical research directions. Data mining should not aim to replace medical professionals and researchers, but to complement their invaluable efforts to save more human lives by appropriate intervention using some of the healthcare alerting systems described in this chapter. Intervention and decision support can be found more quickly with data and text mining techniques.

References

1. Miller RA. 1994. Medical diagnostic decision support systems—Past, present, and future: A threaded bibliography and brief commentary. *J Am Med Inform Assoc* 1:8–27.
2. Beaver K. 2003. *Healthcare information systems*, 2nd ed. New York: Auerbach Publications.
3. Linder B. Data mining predicted swine flu 18 days before WHO. http:// infopackets.com/news/technology/it.
4. Cios KJ, Moore GW. 2002. Uniqueness of medical data mining. *Artif Intell Med* 26:1–24.
5. Hunt DL, Haynes RB, Hanna SE, Smith K. 1998. Effects of computer-based clinical decision support systems on physician performance and patient outcomes. *JAMA* 280:1339–346.
6. Richards G, Rayward-Smith VJ, Sonksen PH, Carey S, Weng C. 2001. Data mining for indicators of early mortality in a database of clinical records. *Artif Intell Med* 22:215–31.
7. Weiner MG, Pifer E. 2000. Computerized decision support and the quality of care. *Managed Care* 9:41–51.
8. Brossette SE, Sprague AP, Hardin JM, Waites KB, Jones WT, Moser SA. 1998. Association rules and data mining in hospital infection control and public health surveillance. *J Am Med Inform Assoc* 5: 373–81.
9. Bates DW, Saria S, Ohno-Machado L, Shah A, Escobar G. 2014. Big data in healthcare: Using analytics to identify and manage high-risk patients. *Health Affair* 33:1123–131.
10. Demir E. 2014. A decision support tool for predicting patients at risk of readmission: A comparison of classification trees, logistic regression, generalized additive models, and multivariate adaptive regression splines. *Decision Sci* 45:849–80.
11. Delen D, Walker G, Kadam A. 2005. Predicting breast cancer survivability: A comparison of three data mining methods. *Artif Intell Med* 34:113–27.
12. Shukla DP, Patel SB, Sen AK. 2014. A literature review in health informatics using data mining techniques. *IJSHRE* 2:123–29.

13. Dey M, Rautaray SS. 2014. Study and analysis of data mining algorithms for healthcare decision support systems. *IJCSIT* 5:470–77.
14. Emanet N, Oz HR, Bayram N, Delen D. 2014. A comparative analysis of machine learning methods for classification type decision problems in healthcare. *Decis Analyt* 1:1–20.
15. Bourouis A, Feham M, Hossain M, Zhang L. 2014. An intelligent mobile based decision support system for retinal disease diagnosis. *Decis Support Syst* 59:341–50.
16. Brieman FJ, Olson RA, Stone CJ. 1984. *Classification and regression trees.* Monterrey: Wadsworth & Brooks & Cole.
17. White H. 1989. Learning in artificial neural networks. *Neural Comput* 1:425–26.
18. Baker SG. 2003. The central role of receiver operating characteristic (ROC) curves in evaluating tests for the early detection of cancer. *J. Natl. Cancer Instit* 95:511–15.
19. Herland M, Khoshgoftaar TM, Wald R. 2014. A review of big data in health informatics. *J Big Data* 1:1–35.
20. Jencks S, Williams MV, Coleman EA. 2009. Rehospitalizations among patients in the Medicare fee-for-service program. *N Engl J Med* 360:1418–428.
21. Rudd KL, Johnson MG, Liesinger JT, Graft CA, Naessens JM. 2010. Automated detection of the follow-up appointments using text mining of discharge records. *Int J Qual Health C* 22:229–35.
22. U.S. Food and Drug Administration. Preventable adverse drug reactions: A focus on drug interactions. http://www.fda.gov/Drugs/DevelopmentApprovalProcess/DevelopmentResources/DrugInteractionsLabeling/ucm110632.htm.
23. Iyer SI, Harpaz R, LePendu P, Bauer-Hehren A, Shah NH. 2014. Mining clinical texts for signals of adverse drug interactions. *J Am Med Inform Assoc* 21:353–62.
24. Snow P, Kerr K, Brandt J, Rodvold D. 2001. Neural network and regression predictions of 5-year survival after colon carcinoma treatment. *Cancer* (Suppl.) 91:1673–678.
25. Grumett S, Snow P, Kerr D. 2003. Neural network and regression predictions of 5-year survival after colon carcinoma treatment. *Clin Colorectal Cancer* 4:239–44.
26. Anand SS, Smith AE, Hamilton PW, Anand JS, Hughes JG, Bartels PH. 1999. An evaluation of intelligent prognostic systems for colorectal cancer. *Artif Intell Med* 15:193–214.
27. Finne P, Finne R, Auvinen A, Juusela H, Aro J, Maattanen L. 2000. Predicting the outcome of prostate biopsy in screen-positive men by a multilayer perceptron network. *Urology* 56:418–22.
28. Matsui Y, Egawa S, Tsukayama C, Terai A, Kuwao S, Bab S. 2002. Artificial neural network analysis for predicting pathological state of clinically localized prostate cancer in the Japanese population. *Jpn J Clin Oncol* 32:530–35.

29. Remzi M, Anagnostou T, Ravery V, Zlotta A, Stephan C, Marberger M. 2003. An artificial neural network to predict the outcome of repeat prostate biopsies. *Urology* 62:456–60.
30. Song JH, Venkatesh SS, Conant EA, Arger PH, Sehgal CH. 2005. Comparative analysis of logistic regression and artificial neural network for computer-aided diagnosis of breast masses. *Acad Radiol* 12:487–95.

15

DATA MINING IN HEALTHCARE

WULLIANALLUR RAGHUPATHI

Contents

Overview

With the development and maintenance of large health data repositories of structured and unstructured data, health organizations are increasingly using data analytics, including data mining, to analyze and utilize the patterns and relationships found in the data to make improved clinical and other health-related decisions. This chapter discusses the potential of data mining in healthcare and describes the various applications of data mining methods and techniques. A brief review of examples of data mining in healthcare is also offered. An ongoing project in the mining of the unstructured information in cancer blogs is also described. Conclusions are then offered.

Introduction

Health data, including general patient profiles, clinical data, insurance data, and other medical data, are being created for various purposes, including regulatory compliance, public health policy analysis and research, and diagnosis and treatment.[1] The data include both structured data (e.g., patient histories as records in a database) and unstructured data[2] (e.g., audio/video clips, textual information such as in blogs or physician's notes). Data mining methods can be applied to search and analyze these large repositories to shed light on a wide range of health issues, including drug reactions, side effects, and other issues. For example, data mining techniques revealed the association between Vioxx, the arthritis drug, and increased risk of heart attack and stroke. The drug was withdrawn from the market (http://www.informationweek.com/news/business_intelligence/mining/showArticle.jhtml?articleID=207300005).

In another example, IBM has been working with the Mayo Clinic for mining the data of millions of patient records to "analyze the information, look for similarities from one patient and another, and identify patterns" (http://www.healthcareitnews.com/news/data-mining-key-phase-2-ibm-mayo-partnership).

Healthcare organizations, including hospitals, HMOs, and government entities such as the Centers for Disease Control and Prevention (CDC), are establishing numerous health data repositories. These are typically large, relational databases that store different types of clinical and administrative data from primary electronic health sources such as hospital admission records. These repositories collect comprehensive data on large patient groups in longitudinal fashion, thereby permitting the examination and analysis of patterns and trends over time.[1] Tasks include utilization statistics and outcomes. The data can be used for quality assurance and clinical management queries.[3,4] Although the breadth and depth of the repositories include a variety of health and medical data, including genetic data, biomedical data, and data for general health issues such as quality control (e.g., medical error patterns), data mining applications are relatively new.[5–8] Additionally, challenges are also foreseen. For example, large repositories may lead to a combinatorial explosion of alternatives. On the other hand, the multiple dimensions of the data for very complex relationships are typically rarely available because the relationships are spread thinly across the several dimensions.[1] Fortunately, the developing large medical and health repositories can alleviate these challenges to an extent. These are providing integrated views of the patient encounters. Data mining of these quantitative and qualitative data has great potential for improving the quality of healthcare and reducing the costs of healthcare delivery.

In this chapter we discuss the potential of data mining in healthcare. An outline and discussion of the steps involved is also provided. Our ongoing research in the data mining of health-related blogs using the Unstructured Information Management Architecture is then described. Finally, conclusions are offered.

Data Mining in Healthcare

The Value of Data Mining

Data mining is defined as "the nontrivial extraction of implicit previously unknown and potentially useful information from data."[9] The value for healthcare delivery is enhanced when the data mining has specific purposes and health/medical questions to answer. Typically, the healthcare process being data rich, many potential patterns can be discovered by the use of different types of algorithms. However, the patterns have value for enhancing the quality of the healthcare delivery process only when specifically addressing a particular issue or question. For example, using a data mining method involving clustering, a user can automatically discover distinct patient sets classified by one or more variables. It is not necessary to hypothesize a solution or delve into the details of the clustering. An application with a well-defined user interface has the potential to make the mining process transparent and seamless.[10] The application with the underlying algorithm works on the data repository to enable the user to find solutions (e.g., categorizing patients, grouping patients by drug reactions, profile of emergency visit patients) in the most promising way. The data themselves become an active part of the solution. To this end, data mining is data driven. As Mullins et al. suggest, it is pertinent as a strategy to "discover" patterns already known to be true in the preliminary stages of the health data mining task. It is important to confirm the tool, build confidence in the approach, and often, seren-dipitously, revelations may occur.[1]

In healthcare, therefore, pattern-discovering algorithms in the data mining process can transform raw data into useful decision-making information with minimal intervention by the user, be it a physician or a hospital administrator. The data repositories created by health delivery organizations and health insurance companies are not in vain as the role of the data is enhanced. These organizations can tap into the discovery role of data mining, just as the financial services industry has done, and provide higher-quality healthcare as participants in the healthcare delivery process are empowered with useful information.

In the healthcare domain encompassing bioinformatics, medical informatics, and health informatics, data mining offers many new opportunities for practitioners and researchers. Some of the more significant ones the following:[10]

- Discovery of previously unknown facts (e.g., correlation between a drug and side effect). In this situation the application learns associations and flags the user, or the application facilitates the health data to identify value (e.g., potential drug discovery).
- Organization of large repositories of health and medical data for very complex problems (e.g., pandemic patterns and clusters). In this regard, the application can provide real-time alerts as to particular situations that require immediate attention, as well as provide insight into what might occur next.
- Prediction of the future in various situations and scenarios (e.g., what-if analysis in clinical trials, consequences of certain actions on public health policy). Data mining can help forecast trends (as in epidemics) and threats as well as opportunities, thereby enabling the organization, be it for profit or nonprofit, to deal with the future effectively with knowledge.[10]

Data Mining as a Process in Healthcare

The typical types of healthcare questions that are solvable by data mining techniques can be divided into two main categories: those that are solved by discovery techniques and those solved by predictive techniques.[10] If the healthcare problem requires the researcher to find useful patterns and relationships in the data (e.g., relationship between a particular diet and blood pressure), that problem will lead the researcher to a discovery method. On the other hand, if the healthcare problem requires the researcher to predict some type of value (e.g., the radiation dosage for a particular profile of cancer patients), that problem would obviously lead the researcher to a predictive method. In the pharmaceutical industry, for example, a range of methods, including associations, sequences, and predictive methods for clinical disease management, associations and prediction for cost/quality management, and segmentation and clustering for patient groupings in clinical trials, have tremendous potential.

Typical questions include the following:

- What do my patients look like?
- What is the drug dosage–patient profile association?
- With which other drugs does the new drug interact negatively?
- What effect does use of a particular drug for a disease have on other conditions?
- Does the drug cause side effects, and if so, what?

Many of the typical problems and questions can be resolved by one of a few data mining techniques.[10] They include three discovery techniques (clustering, associations, and sequences) and two predictive techniques (classification and regression).[10]

Discovery Techniques The data mining techniques based on this method find health or medical patterns that preexist in the data, but with no a priori knowledge of what those patterns may be. One could think of these patterns as serendipitously discovered, although the goals are inherently present in the data themselves. Three of the popular discovery techniques include the following:

1. The *clustering technique* groups health/medical records into segments by how similar they are based on the characteristics under study. Clustering could be used, for example, to find distinct symptoms of diseases with similar characteristics to create a disease/patient segmentation model.

2. *Association* is a type of relationship analysis that finds relationships or associations among the health/medical records of single transactions. A potential use of the association method is for health group analysis, that is, to find out what diseases tend together to form a group, such as viral or bacterial (or patient groups), which is quite useful in epidemic/pandemic surveillance and identifying cause-treatment protocols for particular diseases.

3. The *sequential* pattern discovers associations among health/medical records, but across sequential transactions. A hospital could use sequential patterns (longitudinal studies) to analyze admissions over time, and to provide customized patient care.[10]

Predictive Techniques   The predictive techniques of classification and regression are data mining techniques that can help forecast some type of categorical or numerical value (e.g., optimal dosage of a drug, drug pricing).

1. The technique of *classification* can be used to forecast the value that would fall into predefined grouping or categories. For example, it can predict whether a particular treatment will cure, harm, or have no effect on a particular patient.

2. On the other hand, the technique of *regression* is used to predict a numerical value on a continuous scale, for example, predicting the expected number of admissions each hospital will make in a year. In contrast, if the range of values is between 0 and 1, then this becomes a probability of an event occurring, such as the likelihood of a patient dying (repeat visits) or getting well, for example.[10]

In many instances a combination of data mining techniques is necessary (e.g., first perform patient segmentation using the clustering technique to identify a target group of patients); this is followed by a grouping analysis using the associations technique with the transactions (data) only for the target group to find drug affinities on which to base treatments.[10]

Mining and Scoring The five mining techniques outlined in the preceding text are used against current health/medical data to create a data mining model. The process of applying an existing mining model against new data is called scoring.[10] Each of the five techniques has an associated scoring method that is used to apply against new data. Cluster scoring can be used, for example, to assign a new patient to the appropriate clinical trial based on the existing cluster model (or a drug for treatment).

To select the initial mining technique, one may develop a short list of typical health questions that the most common mining method or combination of methods may help answer. For example:

1. What do my patients look like? Clustering
2. Which patients should be targeted for drug (treatment) promotion (trial)? Clustering
3. Which drugs should I use for the trial (treatment)? Association or sequential patterns
4. Which drugs should I replenish in anticipation of an epidemic? Associations
5. Which of my patients are most likely to get well (based on a protocol)? Classification or regression
6. How can I identify high-risk patients? Clustering
7. When one drug fails, which others are most likely to fail too? Sequential patterns
8. Who is most likely to have another heart attack? Classification or Regression
9. How can I improve quality of care (or patient satisfaction)? Clustering plus associations

Build and Deploy Data Mining Application

The process of building and deploying a data mining application is highly iterative.[10] This process may include three specific steps:

1. Health/medical data preparation
2. Creation and verification of the particular mining model
3. Deployment of the model in some way

The process of data preparation involves finding and organizing the health/medical data for the chosen mining technique. Once the data are ready for use, the mining technique can be involved in the development of the mining model, which is then confirmed by the developer. It is possible that the process goes through several iterations until one obtains a refined data model. After confirmation, the model is ready to be deployed for use. Generally speaking, the data preparation step comprises the identification of the specific data requirements, the appropriate location of the data, and the extraction and transformation of the data into the appropriate format for the chosen mining technique.[10]

The data mining model is created once the data are transformed and ready for use. The particular application/tool is used on the data set after choosing the technique and providing the parameters. Multiple algorithms may be used with the input parameters. In predictive techniques additional steps may be involved, including a training phase and a testing phase. The resulting model can be stored and possibly viewed using an appropriate visualization tool in the application.[10] The visualization process plays a critical role in presenting information about model quality, specific results such as associations, rules, or clusters, and other information about the data and results pertinent to the particular model. This information enables the data mining analyst to evaluate the model quality and determine whether the model fulfills its healthcare purpose. If need be, improvements to the input data, model parameters, and modeling technique can then be made to obtain a good model that reflects the healthcare objective.[10] In the final step, the data mining results are deployed in the healthcare organization as part of a business intelligence (data analytics) solution. Data mining results can be deployed by several means.

1. Ad hoc decision support: Use data mining on an ad hoc basis to address a specific nonrecurring question. For example, a pharmaceutical researcher may use data mining techniques to discover a relationship between gene counts and disease state for a cancer research project.
2. Interactive decision support: Incorporate data mining into a larger health intelligence application for ongoing interactive analysis.

3. Scoring: Apply a data mining model to generate some sort of prediction for each health/medical record, depending on model type. For example, for a clustering model, the score is the best-fit cluster for each patient. For the association model, the score is the highest-affinity item (variable), given other items (variables). For a sequence model, the score is the most likely action to occur next. For a typical predictive model, the score is the predicted value or response.[10]

Examples

Mullins et al.[1] report on the application of Health Miner to a large group of 667,000 inpatient and outpatient digital records from an academic medical system. They used three unsupervised methods: Clici mines, predictive analysis, and pattern discovery. The initial results from their study suggested that these approaches had the potential to expand research capabilities through identification of potentially novel clinical disease associations. In other examples, the prior analyses using large clinical data sets have typically focused on specific treatment or disease objects.[1] Most have examined specific treatment procedures, for example, cesarean delivery rate,[11] coronary artery bypass graft (CABG) surgery volume,[12] routine chemistry panel testing,[13] patient care, cancer risk for nonaspirin NSAIDs (nonsteroidal/anti-inflammatory drugs) users,[14] preoperative beta-blocker use and mortality and morbidity following CABG surgery,[15] and incidence and mortality rate of acute (adult) respiratory distress syndrome (ARDS),[16] to name a few. These studies have several factors in common: large sample size, clinical information source, and they support or build on preestablished hypotheses or defined research paradigms that use specific procedures or disease data. Clinical outcome algorithms have also been applied to harness large health information databases to generate models directly applicable to clinical treatment. These models have been used successfully to create mortality risk assessments for adults[17–19] and pediatric intensive care units.[20]

In other studies, Uramoto et al. describe the application of IBM TAKMI (Text Analysis and Knowledge Mining) for biomedical documents to facilitate knowledge discovery from the very large text databases characteristic of life science and healthcare applications. MedTAKMI dynamically and interactively mines a collection of documents to obtain characteristic features within them.[21] By using multifaceted mining of these documents together with biomedically motivated categories for term extraction and a series of drilldown queries, users can obtain knowledge about a specific topic after seeing only a few key documents.

Inokuchi et al. describe MedTAKMI-CDI, an online analytical processing system that enables the interactive discovery of knowledge for clinical decision intelligence (CDI). CDI supports decision making by providing in-depth analysis of clinical data from multiple sources.[22,23] These and other examples indicate the potential and promise of data mining in healthcare.

Mining of Cancer Blogs with the Unstructured Information Management Architecture

In this section we describe our ongoing research project in the use of the Unstructured Information Management Architecture (UIMA) in mining textual information in cancer blogs. Health organizations and individuals such as patients are using information in blogs for various purposes. Medical blogs are rich in information for decision making. Current software such as Web crawlers and blog analysis are good at generating statistics about the number of blogs, top 10, etc., but they are not advanced/useful computationally to help with analysis and understanding of the social networks that form in healthcare and medical blogs, the process of diffusion of ideas (e.g., the commonality of symptoms and disease management), and the sharing of ideas and feelings (support and treatment options, what worked). Therefore, there is a critical need for sophisticated tools to fill this gap. Furthermore, there are hardly any studies or applications in the content analysis of blogs.

There has been an exponential increase in the number of blogs in the healthcare area, as patients find them useful in disease management and developing support groups. Alternatively, healthcare providers such as physicians have started to use blogs to communicate and discuss medical information. Examples of useful information include alternative medicine and treatment, health condition management, diagnosis–treatment information, and support group resources. This rapid proliferation in health- and medical-related blogs has resulted in huge amounts of unstructured yet potentially valuable information being available for analysis and use.[2] Statistics indicate health-related bloggers are very consistent at posting to blogs.

The analysis and interpretation of health-related blogs are not trivial tasks. Unlike many of the blogs in various corporate domains, health blogs are far more complex and unstructured. The postings reflect two important facets of the bloggers: the feeling and the mind of the patient (e.g., an individual suffering from breast cancer but managing it). How does one parse and extract the deep semantic meanings in this environment? Mere syntactic analysis would not do.

The UIMA defines a framework for implementing systems for the analysis of unstructured data.[2, 24–26] In contrast to structured information, whose meaning is expressed by the structure or the format of the data, the meaning of unstructured information cannot be so inferred.[2] Examples of data that carry unstructured information include natural language text and data from audio or video sources. More specifically, an audio stream has a well-defined syntax and semantics for rendering the stream on an audio device, but its music score is not directly represented.[27] The UIMA is sufficiently advanced and sophisticated computationally to aid in the analysis and understanding of the content of the health-related blogs. At the individual level (document-level analysis) one can perform analysis and gain insight into the patient in longitudinal studies. At the group level (collection-level analysis) one can gain insight into the patterns of the groups (network behavior, e.g., assessing the influence within the social group), for example, in a particular disease group, the community of participants in an HMO or hospital setting, or even in the global community of patients (ethnic stratification). The results of these analyses can be generalized. While the blogs enable the formation of social networks of patients and providers, the uniqueness of the health/medical terminology comingled with the subjective vocabulary of the patient compounds the challenge of interpretation. Taking the discussion to a more general level, while blogs have emerged as contemporary modes of communication within a social network context, hardly any research or insight exists in the content analysis of blogs. The blog world is characterized by a lack of particular rules on format, how to post, and the structure of the content itself. Questions arise: How do we make sense of the aggregate content? How does one interpret and generalize? In health blogs in particular, what patterns of diagnosis, treatment, management, and support might emerge from a meta-analysis of a large pool of blog postings? The overall goal, then, is to enhance the quality of health by reducing errors and assisting in clinical decision making. Additionally, one can reduce the cost of healthcare delivery by the use of these types of advanced health information technology.

Therefore, the *objectives* of our project include the following:

1. To use UIMA to mine a set of cancer blog postings from http://www.thecancerblog.com
2. To develop a parsing algorithm and clustering technique for the analysis of cancer blogs
3. To develop a vocabulary and taxonomy of keywords (based on existing medical nomenclature)
4. To build a prototype interface with Eclipse (based on our existing work in the use of Eclipse in the development of an electronic health record system)
5. To contribute to social networks in the semantic Web by generalizing the models from cancer blogs

The following levels of development are envisaged.

First level: Patterns of symptoms, management (diagnosis/ treatment)

Second level: Glean insight into disease management at individual/ group levels

Third level: Clinical decision support (e.g., generalization of patterns, syntactic to semantic)

Typically, the unstructured information in blogs comprises:

Blog topic (posting)—What issue or question does the blogger (and comments) discuss?

Disease and treatment (not limited to)—What cancer type and treatment (other issues) are identified and discussed?

Other information—What other related topics are discussed? What links are provided?

What Can We Learn from Blog Postings?

Unstructured information related to blog postings (bloggers), including responses/comments, can provide insight into "diseases" (cancer), "treatment" (e.g., alternative medicine, therapy), support links, etc.

1. What are the most common issues patients have (bloggers/ responses)?
2. What are the cancer types (conditions) most discussed? Why?
3. What therapies and treatments are being discussed? What medical and nonmedical information is provided?
4. Which blogs and bloggers are doing a good job of providing relevant and correct information?
5. What are the major motivations for the postings (comments)? Profession (e.g., doctor) or patient?
6. What are the emerging trends in disease (symptoms), treatment and therapy (e.g., alternative medicine), support systems, and information sources (links, clinical trials)?

What Are the Phases and Milestones?

This project envisions the use of UIMA and supporting plug-ins to develop an application tool to analyze health-related blogs. The project is scoped to content analysis of the domain of cancer blogs at http://www.thecancerblog.com. Additional open-source plug-ins and an Eclipse development environment with Java/XML plug-ins, limited AJAX capability, and a social network analysis tool such as Apache Agora would provide the desired capabilities. In a typical scenario, the cancer blogs can be stored in an open-source Derby database application.

Phase 1 involved the collection of blog postings from http://www.thecancerblog.com into a Derby application.

Phase 2 consisted of the development and configuration of the architecture—keywords, correlations, clustering, and taxonomy.

Phase 3 entailed the analysis and integration of extracted information in the cancer blogs; preliminary results of initial analysis (e.g., patterns that are identified).

Phase 4 involved the development of taxonomy.

Phase 5 proposes to test the mining model and develop the user interface for deployment.

We propose to develop a comprehensive text mining system that integrates several mining techniques, including association and clustering, to organize the blog information effectively and provide decision support in terms of search by keywords.

Conclusions

The development and application of large repositories of patient-specific clinical, medical, and health data generated during patient encounters in the routine delivery of healthcare was, until recently, limited to static uses of utilization management, quality assurance, and cost management.[1] However, with the focus on reducing medical errors through evidence-based health management, these repositories are being subjected to more sophisticated analyses using data mining techniques. These techniques offer numerous opportunities to perform in-depth analysis of the data to gain new insights into the healthcare process with the resultant decision support for a range of tasks. In the future, we will see not only an increased use of data mining techniques in healthcare but also their integration with health intelligence and health organization strategy. The overall goals include the delivery of quality care with a simultaneous decrease in costs.

This chapter was originally published in *Healthcare Informatics, Improving Efficiency and Productivity*, Taylor & Francis, New York, 2010.

References

1. Mullins, IM, Siadaty, MS, Lyman, J, Scully, K, Garrett, CT, Miller, WG, Muller, R et al. 2006. Data mining and clinical data repositories: Insights from a 667,000 patient data set. *Comput BiolMed* 36:1351–377.
2. Spangler S, Kreulen J. 2008. *Mining the talk—Unlocking the business value in unstructured information*. Upper Saddle River, NJ: IBM Press.
3. Einbinder JS, Scully K. 2002. Using a clinical data repository to estimate the frequency and costs of adverse drug events. *J Am Med Inform Assoc* Suppl. S:S34–38.

4. Scully KW, Pates RD, Desper GS, Connors AF, Harrell FE, Pieper KS, Hannan RL, Reynolds RE. 1997. Development of an enterprise-wide clinical repository: Merging multiple legacy databases. *J Am Med Inform Assoc* Suppl. S:32–36.

5. Brosette SE, Sprague AP, Hardin JM, Jones WT, Moser SA. 1998. Association rules and data mining in hospital infection control and public health surveillance. *J Am Med Inform Assoc* 5:373–81.

6. Downs SM, Wallace MY. 2000. Mining association rules from a pediatric primary care decision support system. In *Proceedings of the AMIA Symposium* 2000 (pp. 200–4).

7. Holmes JH, Durbin DR, Winston FK. 2000. Discovery of predictive models in an injury surveillance database: An application of data mining in clinical research. In *Proceedings of the AMIA Symposium* 2000 (pp. 359–63).

8. Prather JC, Lobach DF, Goodwin LK, Hales JW, Hage ML, Hammond WE. 1997. Medical data mining: Knowledge discovery in a clinical data warehouse. *Proceedings of the AMIA Symposium* 1997 (pp. 101–5).

9. Frawley W, Piatetsky-Shapiro G, Mathews C. 1992. Knowledge discovery in databases: An overview. *AI Magazine*, pp. 213–28.

10. Ballard C, Rollins J, Ramos J, Perkins A, Hale R, Dorneich A, Milner EC, Chodagam J. 2007. *Dynamic warehousing: Data mining made easy.* IBM Redbook (www.redbooks.ibm.com).

11. Lin H-C, Xirasagar S. 2004. Institutional factors in cesarean delivery rates: Policy and research implications. *Obstet Gynecol* 103:128–36.

12. Peterson ED, Coombs LP, DeLong ER, Haan CK, Ferguson TB. 2004. Procedural volume as a market of quality for CABG surgery. *JAMA* 291: 195–201.

13. Bock BJ, Dolan CT, Miller GC, Fitter WF, Hartsell, BD, Crowson AN, Sheehan WW, Williams JD. 2003. The data warehouse as a foundation for population-based reference intervals. *Am J Clin Pathol* 120:662–70.

14. Sorensen HT, Friis S, Norgard B, Mellemkjaer W J, Blot JK, McLaughlin A, Ekbom JAB. 2003. Risk of cancer in a large cohort of nonaspirin NSAID users: A population-based study. *Br J Cancer* 88:1687–92.

15. Ferguson TB Jr, Coombs LP, Peterson ED. 2002. Preoperative beta-blocker use and mortality and morbidity following CABG surgery in North America. *JAMA* 287:2221–27.

16. Reynolds HN, McCunn M, Borg U, Habashi C, Cottingham C, Bar-Lavi Y. 1998. Acute respiratory distress syndrome: Estimated incidence and mortality rate in a 5 million-person population base. *Critical Care* (London) 2:29–34.

17. Knaus WA, Wagner DP, Lynn J. 1991. Short-term mortality predictions for critically ill hospitalized adults: Science and ethics. *Science* 18:389–94.

18. LeGall JR, Lemeshow S, Saulnier F. 1993. A new Simplified Acute Physiology Score (SAPS II) based on a European/North American multicenter study. *JAMA* 270:2957–63.

19. Lemeshow S, Teres D, Klar JS, Avrunin SH, Gehlbach JR. 1993. Mortality probability models based on an international cohort of intensive care unit patients. *JAMA* 270:2478–86.
20. Pollack MM, Patel KM, Ruttimann UE. 1996. PRISM III: An updated pediatric risk of mortality score. *Crit Care Med* 24:743–52.
21. Uramoto N, Matsuzawa H, Nagano T, Murakami A, Takeuchi H, Takeda K. 2004. A text-mining system for knowledge discovery from biomedical documents. *IBM Syst J* 43:516–33.
22. Inokuchi A, Takeda K, Inaoka N, Wakao F. 2007. MedTAKMI-CDI: Interactive knowledge discovery for clinical decision intelligence. *IBM Syst J* 46:115–33.
23. Wang XS. Nayda L, Dettinger R. 2007. Infrastructure for a clinical-decision-intelligence system. *IBM Syst J* 46:151–69.
24. Ferrucci D, Lally A. 2004. Building an example application with the Unstructured Information Management Architecture. *IBM Syst J* 43:455–75.
25. Mack R, Mukherjea S, Soffer A, Uramoto N, Brown E, Coden A, Cooper J, Inokuchi A, Iyer B, Mass Y, Matsuzawa H, Subramaniam LV. 2004. Text analytics for life science using the Unstructured Information Management Architecture. *IBM Syst J* 43:490–515.
26. Nasukawa T, Nagano T. 2001. Text analysis and knowledge system mining. *IBM Syst J* 40:967–84.
27. Gotz T, Suhre O. 2004. Design and implementation of the UIMA common analysis system. *IBM Syst J* 43:476–89.

Index

Page numbers followed by f and t indicate figures and tables, respectively.